Dropping In

Dropping In

WHAT SKATEBOARDERS
CAN TEACH US ABOUT LEARNING,
SCHOOLING, AND YOUTH
DEVELOPMENT

ROBERT PETRONE

University of Massachusetts Press

Amherst and Boston

ISBN 978-1-62534-715-2 (paper); 716-9 (hardcover)

Designed by Sally Nichols
Set in Scala Pro
Printed and bound by Books International, Inc.
Cover design by adam b. bohannon
Cover photo by Nicolas Picard, *Skatepark*, 2017, unsplash.com.

Library of Congress Cataloging-in-Publication Data

Names: Petrone, Robert, 1974– author.
Title: Dropping in : what skateboarders can teach us about learning,
schooling, and youth development / Robert Petrone.
Description: Amherst : University of Massachusetts Press, [2023] | Includes
bibliographical references and index.
Identifiers: LCCN 2022051940 (print) | LCCN 2022051941 (ebook) | ISBN
9781625347152 (paperback) | ISBN 9781625347169 (hardcover) | ISBN
9781685750145 (ebook)
Subjects: LCSH: Underachievers—Education—United States—Case studies. |
Students with social disabilities—Education—United States. | School
failure—United States. | Motivation in education—United States. |
Effective teaching—United States. | Youth development—United States. |
Skateboarders—United States—Interviews. | Skateboarding—Social
aspects—United States.
Classification: LCC LC4691 .P48 2023 (print) | LCC LC4691 (ebook) | DDC
370.15/4—dc23/eng/20230127
LC record available at https://lccn.loc.gov/2022051940
LC ebook record available at https://lccn.loc.gov/2022051941

British Library Cataloguing-in-Publication Data
A catalog record for this book is available from the British Library.

Small portions of Chapters 3, 5, and 7 were originally published in Petrone, R. (2010.) "You
have to get hit a couple of times": The role of conflict in learning how to "be" a skateboarder.
Teaching and Teacher Education, 26, 119–127. Copyright © 2009 Elsevier.

Contents

List of Illustrations vii

"In Your Own Words": Some Heartfelt Acknowledgments ix

PART ONE: ENTERING THE BOWL

CHAPTER ONE
"What Else Would We Have?"
Introducing Dropping In

3

CHAPTER TWO
Learning by Observing and Pitching In as a Theoretical Framework to
Understand "Purposive Learning" at Franklin Skatepark

27

CHAPTER THREE
Behind the Bowl
A Discussion of Research Methodology

48

CHAPTER FOUR
Entering the Bowl
An Introduction to Finley, Franklin Skatepark, and Its Diehard Locals

78

PART TWO: CARVING THE BOWL

CHAPTER FIVE
Participation Structures and Spatial Production of/at Franklin Skatepark

103

CHAPTER SIX
"It All Goes Together, You Know?"
Processes of Learning How to Skateboard at Franklin Skatepark
123

CHAPTER SEVEN
"Whatta Ya Gotta Be a 'Scene Kid'?"
Examining Discursive Practices to Explore Power and Learning at Franklin Skatepark
154

CHAPTER EIGHT
Cultural Theorists on Wheels
The Role of Literacy in Learning How to Skateboard and Be a Skateboarder
182

CHAPTER NINE
Learning to Contribute, Contributing to Learn(ing)
Why Learning Happens at Franklin Skatepark
207

PART THREE: BEYOND THE BOWL

CHAPTER TEN
Beyond the Bowl
Reimagining Possibilities for Learning, Schooling, and Youth
231

References 249
Index 265

List of Illustrations

FIGURES

FIGURE 1. The facets of Learning by Observing and Pitching In (LOPI). 36

FIGURE 2. Bird's-eye view of Franklin Skatepark. 105

FIGURE 3. Field view of Franklin Skatepark. 105

TABLES

TABLE 1. Overview of Participants. 85

"In Your Own Words"

SOME HEARTFELT ACKNOWLEDGMENTS

I'M THE FOURTH of five children, and I grew up, along with my siblings, as I discuss in Chapter 3, amid parental disability, a circumstance that thrust my family down several pegs in the socioeconomic ladder. Growing up, money was tight, and ideas of doing something with my life beyond laboring in rich folks' backyards on Long Island existed for so long as the stuff of movies, not my real life. I am the only person in my family with a Ph.D., and before going to college as an undergrad, I never knew anyone who had one—and if I'm honest, I don't think I'd ever even heard of a "doctorate."

Getting a Ph.D. has changed me. In so many ways, it shifted me away from my family, my forever primary discourse, and I feel this the most when I write up my research, casually dropping in words like *positionality, habitus,* and *ontological.* I often feel a fraud through my writing—not only the usual grip of imposter syndrome but more so as I think of that glazed look in my siblings' eyes when they ask me to tell them what it is I do as a researcher. I hate that my research writing so often leaves them feeling alienated from my work—and me from them.

In recent years, I've begun to hold my sister, Veronica—who is a sensitive, smart, and skillful trauma therapist who works with children in NYC—as my imagined reader. I want my writing to, if not matter for her, at least make sense to her, and I often conjure her saying to me, as she typically does after reading one of my articles, "Robert, why don't you tell me what *hegemony* means, *in your own words.*" More than anyone, Veronica forces me to figure out what sense I actually do make of such ideas as hegemony and how to communicate those ideas in my own way. Of course, in writing, we have particular audiences in mind, but, for me, Veronica has become my first audience. I want her and the rest of my family to always be able to read what I've written and to know it, to *feel* it.

For this, I acknowledge my siblings—Tammie Ann, Veronica, Michael, Joann—my forever first audience. Thank you four for keeping me grounded in who I am and who and where I come from.

And, of course, none of my siblings would be around if not for the prime movers of our family, my parents, Gloria and Thomas Petrone. Thank you, mom and dad.

On the heels of my family, the guys highlighted in this book—the "diehard locals" of Franklin Skatepark—have been instrumental in my growth not only as a scholar but also as a person. Their generosity and openness, their vulnerability, and, with each passing year it took me to write this book, their abiding patience, changed me, too. Among so many other things, these young men taught me the value of "failing" over and over—and then getting up and doing it again.

To these young men—especially Crazy K, Derrick, Matt, Luis, TS, Hollywood, Santana, and Houston—I offer this book to you as a small token of my deep gratitude. In writing this book, I am most accountable to you. My hope is that *Dropping In* does justice to your experiences of Franklin Skatepark, and that, like my family, when you read this book, you can know and *feel* it, too.

I'd be remiss—and likely scolded—if I didn't also thank Santana's mom, who, with every interaction, always asks, "When am I going to be holding a copy of the book?" Thank you, Angela, for your support, communication, and encouraging spirit throughout this entire process!

Thank you, too, to Sandra, who first introduced me to Franklin Skatepark, and her husband, Crazy K. Without Sandra, I never would have even considered skateboarding as a topic for research.

I'm grateful to Matt Becker at UMASS Press for seeing promise in this book and me, and for being so great to work with. I appreciate, in particular, his patience. Related, I want to give a shout-out to Wendy Williams, author of *Listen to the Poet*. After reading a draft of her book for UMASS, I thought the press might be interested in my work with the skateboarders, and so I reached out to her and asked for her assistance with the process of procuring a contract with the press. Thank you, Wendy.

One of my best friends, Paul Goldsmith, is one of the most beautiful writers I've ever read, and, at times, I enlisted his help with the actual writing of this book; another of my best friends, Matt Helm, is a spiritual guru, and, at times, I enlisted his help to stay sane while doing the writing! Another close friend, Roberto Amada-Cattaneo III, who is a phenomenal photographer, provided technical support for some images. Thank you three for supporting in your ways.

I thank Ernest Morrell, a mentor of mine when I was a doctoral student, who, among many other things, nurtured my identity as a writer. I also thank Jabari Mahiri, one of Ernest's mentors from when he was a doctoral student, for meeting me over coffee one morning in Bozeman, Montana, to talk through some ideas in this book.

Since starting my career in a small classroom at North High School in Denver, Colorado, I've been graced by the presence of so many brilliant colleagues, scholars, and students—near and far—and I'm truly grateful for their perspectives, critiques, humor, and writing—all of which has shaped my own thinking, writing, and living. Related, the "References" section of this book is nearly 20 pages long, and I feel I could give shout-outs to just about everyone represented there. I'm in awe of just how smart so many people are, and I'm so grateful to be standing on the shoulders of so many giants.

A special thank you to Barbara Rogoff, for being in communication about LOPI, and to two of the trailblazing scholars in skateboarding, Becky Beal and Iain Borden, for reading and providing feedback on earlier drafts of this book. Y'all are rockstars in my book!

As thinking partners and research assistants, Aaron Padgett and Monica Kleekamp provided phenomenal assistance with literature reviews, theoretical development, and pragmatic issues. Thank you two for your brilliance and attention to detail. Thank you to my colleagues at Mizzou, Angie Zapata and Mike Metz, for being so encouraging and making our work environment such a fun and caring space, and to Claire Syler and Chuck Munter for talking LOPI and communities of practice over drinks on the back porch.

To my writing group (Deb Bieler, Nadia Behizadeh, Noah Golden, and Amy Vetter): your "warms" always connected to the emotional core of this book and made me feel so seen as a scholar and writer. I'm lucky to be in such beautiful dialogue with you all.

Finally, I love my "little family": Melissa, Miss Maupin, Norm, and, of course, Koy Marie. In the end, your love and support made it possible for me to write this book—not to mention, Melissa, your brilliant insights, depth of knowledge of social theory, and intellectual pushing of me and my ideas. Thank you, chosen family.

Dropping
In

PART ONE
ENTERING THE BOWL

CHAPTER ONE

"What Else Would We Have?"

INTRODUCING *DROPPING IN*

There's a lot of people in this world that have a common misconception about skateboarders and punk rockers. A lot of people just think that we're just a bunch of loser, drop-out drug users that have nothing better to do with their time than to raise hell and skateboard. That's not the case. A lot of skateboarders are really cultured people, especially kids in the punk rock scene, too. I mean, they may not be intelligent in the ways of traditional teachings, things like that, but as far as music goes, there's a lot to be learned from kids like me.

—Luis, a 20-year-old skateboarder, punk rock drummer, and welder; self-identifies as "blue-collar" and "Hispanic"; graduated from high school after five years with a 1.4 GPA[1]

As the cloak of humidity so typical for a summer afternoon in the Midwest gradually gives way to an evening breeze, three young men take turns skateboarding in the deepest bowl at Franklin Skatepark. Houston, who identifies as white, and, at 13, is the youngest of the three, drops into the bowl and rolls across the concrete to the top of the other side, where he turns 180 degrees and then glides back down into the bowl to return to where he initially started his run. He exits the bowl, kicking his board into his hands, and stands next to Kevin, who also identifies as white and, at 20, is the oldest of the three skaters.

As the two stand on the edge of the bowl, Hollywood, 17, who identifies as Filipino and Native Hawaiian, drops in. When he gets to the top of the opposite side of the bowl, he rests the front half of his skateboard on the cement lip (known as "coping"), "rocks" on the board from one side to the other, and then releases his board and rolls back to where he started—a skateboarding trick known as a "rock to fakie."

---

1   All names of people and locations throughout the book are pseudonyms.

At the moment Hollywood's board rests on the coping, Kevin, without shifting his eyes from Hollywood, asks Houston, "Do you know how to do a rock to fakie yet?"

"No, not yet," Houston replies, also keeping his eyes fixed on Hollywood.

"I'll talk through it when I go next," Kevin responds as he slaps the tail of his board on the ground to congratulate Hollywood on his run.

Kevin enters the bowl next, and, as promised, briefly explains what he is doing as he moves in and out of a rock to fakie. After observing, Houston follows him, attempting the trick unsuccessfully a few times while Hollywood and Kevin watch and shout instructions and encouragement despite his consistent "failure."

After taking a few more turns in the bowl, Hollywood skates near me to grab a drink of water. I am sitting on one of the "ledges" in the skatepark, which is an area that enables me to observe the action in the bowl without being in the way. Familiar with each other from my many previous visits to the park, Hollywood and I start talking, and within a few minutes, Houston and Kevin join us. Kevin takes a seat next to me on the ledge, and Houston squats on his skateboard, slowly rolling it back and forth. Sweat drips profusely from their bodies as they pass around a gallon jug of water.

When the conversation comes to a lull, I ask them to tell me about Franklin Skatepark. Without hesitation, Kevin starts:

> This is honestly our getaway. This is *our* getaway. This is *our* paradise. If we didn't have this, what else would we have? Finley [the town where they live] doesn't have a lot to offer. This is one of the only places Finley has for kids, for teens to hang out.

Curious about his use of *getaway* and *paradise*, I say, "Tell me more about what you mean by *paradise*." He continues,

> Well, for some of these kids, it's a second home. It's a place to get away from the problems that you have, you know, that you have in your life. This is my way to get away from everything, from my home stress, work stress. I get out of work, I come up here every night, meet up with my friends, and skateboard a little.

At this point Hollywood jumps into the conversation: "If I didn't have this skatepark, I'd be in jail. I would." As I shift my gaze from Kevin to Hollywood, I ask, "Why do you say that?" He explains,

I didn't start skating til this skatepark opened here. Before that I was in and out of detention at school, I was doing drugs, doing stupid shit—going into stores and stealing shit. Since then I've been skating a lot. Plus, I wouldn't have the friends I do.

Just as Hollywood finishes speaking, Kevin jumps back in:

But, the thing is, you're accepted when you come up here. I mean it doesn't matter if you're bad or you're good [at skateboarding]. If you show respect, you're accepted. And that's a good feeling to have. I mean there's nowhere in town you can go to get that level of respect. You know, people will come up and show you how to do things, all that, and you learn from it. It's like you are building your own character, like through these kids.

Pointing to Houston, Hollywood says, "Like, he's what—you're 13? Sixth grade. Five foot . . . *zero*."

Houston interjects, "Four foot—"

"Four foot, what *two*?" Hollywood interrupts. "I mean, shit, where else is he going to fit in? Especially with his smart-ass mouth?"

At this point, everyone, including Houston, laughs.

As the laughter dies down, Kevin clears his throat, pauses, and, looking at me, says, "This is our freedom. This is where we go to open up."

And with that final statement, Kevin grabs his skateboard and rolls away with Houston and Hollywood close behind him.

WHAT ELSE *DO* THEY HAVE?
WHY *DROPPING IN*

I was probably one of the smartest kids in my class . . . , but you would have never known it. [*Laughs.*] You would have never known it . . . because where my intelligence lay was not able to be tapped within that particular system, and I didn't know how to do it myself until music came along and opened me up not just to the world of music but to the world period—to the events of the day, to the connection between culture and society. And those were things that riveted me, engaged me in life, gave me a sense of purpose . . .

—Bruce Springsteen, interview excerpt from *60 Minutes*, July 27, 2008

As I sat on the ledge, watching these three young men skate with each other, the images and words of so many of the other young men I had gotten to know up to that point in my multiyear research at Franklin Skatepark entered my mind. I thought, for instance, about the time I sat across from Luis, whose words open this chapter, in his living room as he told me what the park meant to him: "I mean, that place is as big a part of my life, possibly, as my *family*. It's like my second home. And I have so much respect for that place." I thought about driving in my car with Matt, who also identifies as "Hispanic," as he explained how he feels like the skatepark "raised" him and many of the other young men who regularly hang out there.

I also considered how virtually all the young men I had gotten to know throughout my research would talk to me about their experiences of Franklin Skatepark not only in terms of "home" and "family" but also in relation to school, doing so to provide a contrasting experience to illuminate what the park meant to them. As they explained their sense of belonging at Franklin Skatepark, they often expressed, unprompted by me, their feelings of alienation from school, including their contentious relationships with who they referred to as "jocks" and "preps"; their lack of connection to many of the teachers and extracurricular outlets offered through school; and the deficit ways they were labeled in school by being put in certain remedial classes (the "stupid classes," as several of them said) or sent to the alternative high school.

I thought specifically of Derrick, another young man you will get to know better throughout this book, who, like Matt and Luis, identifies as "Hispanic." As an eighth grader at the time I began my research, Derrick was adamant about staying in school and earning his high school diploma, yet, by the time he barely finished ninth grade, he was quickly on his way to being pushed out—something that did eventually occur. When I asked him explicitly about school during one of our many talks, he immediately began sharing about skateboarding. He told me that as a skateboarder he "can still make up new tricks," and he feels like he "belongs there [at the park]" because he has "got something to say," and he's "trying to get his word out." He contrasted this with his experiences at school by saying that "you can't say nothing back to the teachers. You can't . . . you can't teach *them*. They just try to teach you. You try to teach them, they'll just kick you out. As far as teachers, they don't care what you've got to say."

As I felt the frustration in Derrick's words and thought of him slipping away from the achievement ideology he espoused so adamantly when I first met him, I thought about how he and the rest of the young men highlighted in this book—all of whom, across their racial affiliations, come from and identify with working-class, or, as they say, "blue-collar," backgrounds and lifestyles—are, according to mainstream narratives of youth labeled "at-risk," typical statistics, playing their parts in the system of social reproduction (Bourdieu & Passeron, 1990). They unequivocally underachieve in school, many of them carrying GPAs below a 2.0; frequently get in trouble with school authorities; and eventually drop out, get kicked or pushed out, or finish high school on the five-year plan. If at all, they sporadically attend community colleges (never four-year colleges), and, in general, they do not ascribe or aspire to the types of lifestyles, careers, and/or next steps for which schools typically prepare young people.

Having spent the past 20-plus years in and around public schools—as a reading and English teacher, a basketball coach, a literacy teacher educator, and a youth and educational researcher—I have becoming increasingly interested in learning more about youth who, similar to Derrick and the other young men of Franklin Skatepark, do not find or see a place for themselves in schools, and, in fact, often experience schooling to be confining, useless, hostile, harmful, or otherwise alienating. As an educator, I had grown accustomed to popular and even scholarly discourses of deficit surrounding youth in general (Lesko, 2012; Lewis & Petrone, 2010; Petrone & Lewis, 2012) and specifically involving young men of color and/or lower socioeconomic status who were too often labeled "at-risk," "failing," "underachieving," "illiterate," and the like (Kirkland, 2013; Mahiri, 2004). From early in my career as a high school reading teacher in Denver, where the vast majority of my Latinx students were from low-socioeconomic backgrounds, I quickly came to know what was "wrong" with male youth who were failing and dropping out of school (as framed by mainstream discourses): they weren't motivated; they were disrespectful, resistant, and/or aloof; they couldn't read or write; they came from "bad homes and communities"; and so on, ad infinitum.

Unsatisfied with such depictions, particularly given how my lived experiences with my students were so contrary, over time, I came to understand how these young people's "failures" connected to and were often produced by systemic marginalization and oppression of some youth by structures of schooling that both reflect and facilitate inequities, particularly linked to class, dis/ability, language, place, race, gender, and sexuality (e.g., Connor, Valle, & Hale, 2015; Cookson, 2013; Davis, 2017; Eckert, 1989; Heath, 1983; Kirkland, 2013; Kozol, 2005; MacLeod, 1995; Miller & Gilligan, 2014; Morrell, 2004a, 2008; Patel, 2012; Paris, 2011; Petrone & Wynhoff Olsen, 2021; Vasudevan & Campano, 2009).

As a way to contribute to scholarly inquiry designed to illuminate and reform such systemic barriers, I set out in this research to find out what was *right* and *working* in such young men's lives. In particular, I deliberately set out to see a group of so-called failing young men on different terms than those by which they are normally judged. I wanted to observe and interact with them in spaces when and where they were engaged and motivated, were actively consuming and producing culture, and were not framed as "resistant" or "oppositional" to or by schooling. In large part, this focus was motivated by prior experiences working with youth, during which if there is one thing I have learned in my career, it is this: to best meet the needs of youth, particularly those who are marginalized by structures of schooling and/or labeled "at-risk," it is as essential to understand how, why, and where they *are* engaged meaningfully in their lives as it is to understand how, when, and why they are *not* engaged in their lives—which is the typical starting point for interventions focused on youth labeled "at-risk." This lesson learned is a central assumption underlying this book.

Given that schools serve as one—if not the *most*—important socially sanctioned and supported space for youth development in contemporary U.S. society, I have long wondered where youth for whom schools do *not* work—and often actually work *against* them—go and what they do in order to meet their intellectual, learning, and literacy needs—to develop their creativity, to imagine their future selves, and to become engaged in the world. In other words, to borrow from Kevin in the opening vignette of this chapter, I wonder, What else do they have?

This book explores "what else" one group of such young people has created to meet their social and educational needs. Specifically, *Dropping In* explains how Luis, Matt, Derrick, and a small group of other working-class, racially diverse young men make meaning and find purpose in their lives through their engagement in skateboarding and related cultural communities. For these young men, these cultural communities function as a central means whereby they meet their intellectual, literate, and learning needs; cultivate meaningful and supportive relationships;

develop a larger understanding of their place in the world; and, much as Bruce Springsteen explains regarding his own discovery of playing music, find themselves "engaged" and "riveted" in life.

The core of this book is an attempt to explain *how* and *why* these cultural communities work, with particular emphasis on *learning*. Moreover, in taking a lead from Luis's belief articulated at the beginning of this chapter that "much can be learned from kids like me," this book is also an attempt to explore how and why these young men's involvement in these communities matters for the field of education, particularly those committed to rethinking schooling structures and practices to provide equitable education for all students. As educational sociologist Patel (2019) argues, "Educators have much to learn about learning itself and that much of learning must come beyond brick and mortar schools" (p. 256).

Perhaps the central tenets of *Dropping In* are best understood through its title. On one level, "dropping in," as a skateboarding term, honors and centers the language and practices of the participants of this study, *in their own words*, as a way to demonstrate a valuing of what they value. On another level, I purposefully conjure the similarities between dropping *in* and dropping *out* to draw attention to the ways the young men in this book are often understood and labeled—nearly all of them do not meet the expectations set for them by schools, and, so, to many, these young men are "dropping out." However, in this book, they are not framed as dropping *out* but rather as dropping *in* . . . to learning, literacy, and engagement. In this way, the framing is not one of deficit or negation (who they are not or what they are not doing) but rather one of agency and intentionality, a proactive movement *toward* something.

And, finally, on a third level—and perhaps most importantly—the title addresses not the skateboarders or even systems of schooling but rather the audiences for this book; my goal, with this book, is for us to "drop into" the world of the locals of Franklin Skatepark so we can look around, listen, and get to know them and their worlds with the hope that doing so might help us imagine new possibilities for working alongside youth like them. As educational scholar Django Paris (2013) writes, "Any understanding of change begins with listening to youth about the changes they care about, participate in, and live" (p. 135). In this way, the heart of *Dropping In* is an attempt to inspire those who have an interest in youth development—in other words, all of us—to learn from youth who are known as "failing" so we may best help meet their needs for all forms of "success."

INTENDED AUDIENCES AND
RELATED SCHOLARSHIP

My favorite part is you go to these, you know, I go to these heavy shows. I'll go see Marilyn Manson or Slayer, or you know, just with my buddies. And people, you know, the rest of society they hear about that or they see my tattoos they're like they're like, "Oh my God! What a waste of the youth." But if you actually take the time to go to these concerts and to meet these people that go to these tattoo conventions and stuff—the coolest freakin' people you're ever going to meet. They're so happy, so loving and caring you know. Just . . . it's completely backwards.

—Larry, 20-year-old skateboarder, musician, poet; dropped out of high school because he was bored; earned a perfect score on the verbal portion of GED; identifies as white and "blue-collar"

Over the course of several summers, and intermittently for several years afterward, I immersed myself in the lives of the young men known as the "diehard locals," as one of them says, of Franklin Skatepark. Though my time with them involved hanging out in tattoo parlors, city streets, church basements, movie theaters, pizza shops, and their homes (among other locations), the vast majority of our time together took place at the skatepark, which serves as the main setting for this book. As mentioned, Franklin Skatepark functioned as a "second home" for many of these young men as well as the primary physical hub for the more extensive networks they developed and participated in through their engagement in a range of cultural practices.

Analytically, I focused my attention on *learning* and *literacy*. In a broad sense, I was interested in understanding how learning occurred among the skaters at the park: How did they learn to skateboard and become skateboarders? How did Franklin Skatepark function as a learning environment? I was interested, too, in understanding the roles literacy played in these young men's lives, particularly how texts and textual activities mediated their participation in this community and broader cultural practices. Which texts did they consume, produce, and distribute? What functions did these texts serve? Over time, I became interested in the *whys* of these young men's participation. Why were these cultural practices so integral to them and their lives? What functions were these practices serving for them?

By decoupling learning and literacy from schooling, *Dropping In* renders visible and challenges many taken-for-granted underlying assumptions and structures that govern much of how learning and teaching are organized in schools. Therefore, while this book is about understanding "what else" this group of young men create to meet their intellectual and creative needs—and how learning occurs there—it is also designed to help stimulate thinking about how schools might reform to become more hospitable and engaging places for all youth, but especially those for whom schools currently are not such places. In a basic sense, this book is a plea for schools to be run on better theories of learning and social organization, as well as more expansive and complicated conceptions of youth and adolescence/ts. As Nasir et al. (2021) explain, "How we theorize the nature of learning has direct implications for the ways we teach, how we arrange classrooms and other learning settings, and how we organize schools and institutions of learning" (p. 557).

Thus situated, *Dropping In* is written primarily for educators: practicing and future classroom teachers, teacher educators, educational researchers, and those who work and ally with youth in other capacities. I also hope that others beyond this primary audience, particularly scholars of Critical Youth Studies, sociologists who focus on youth, researchers who study skateboarding, and skateboarders themselves, will find value in *Dropping In*.

Before highlighting my hopes for each of these audiences, I hover here to tease out some complexities and challenges, especially from my vantage as a writer, in having these multiple audiences in mind.

First, I want to be very clear that while I make significant critiques of schooling throughout this book, I am not attempting to vilify, essentialize, be reductive about schools (and certainly not educators), or set schools up as a straw man of sorts. I recognize that schools are variable, complex institutions with myriad factors that contribute to what does and does not occur there—everything from parents to students to systemic racism to externally imposed assessments to corporate-sponsored curricula to caring educators to socioeconomics to . . . this list could go on and on.

I also do not want to dichotomize schools and skateparks or any other non-school spaces of learning for youth. My view is not that schools are "bad" and out-of-school spaces for youth are "good"—or that either is unilaterally any one way. Similarly, I'm not saying that learning at Franklin Skatepark is some type of idealized utopia. Rather, through contrast, I aim to show how the skatepark is organized and structured—what values and principles undergird it—and how these work for the participants, and, by contrast, how the values and principles of learning that undergird schools do not work for these young men. In this sense, I am hoping to point to *structural reasons* for both these young men's successes at the park as well as their failures at school. Thus, the inquiries and critiques about schooling I offer throughout this book are meant to be levied not at individual teachers but rather at broader structures, values, principles, and systems of schooling that most of us in the United States have been so powerfully apprenticed into from the time we first entered schools.

Related, throughout the book I offer contrasts between schooling and the skatepark, toggling, at times, from one to the other. I move back and forth between the two to make visible those aspects of schooling that have become so naturalized as not to be even noticed. In this sense, I'm trying to make, as the saying goes, the "familiar strange" or the "invisible visible"—with the familiar and invisible here being how learning and participation are often structured in schools. In other words, I want those of us in education, as we read about Franklin Skatepark, to notice things that may be "invisible" to us about how learning is organized in schools and wonder why and how they are the way they are—and how they might be different. For instance, why are children and youth segregated by age in schools? How does this social arrangement constrain possibilities for learning? How else might we imagine possibilities for designing learning environments within schools that might draw on cross-age groupings?

I am also deliberate throughout the book in using terms typically ascribed to school settings (e.g., curriculum, assessment) to explain learning and teaching at Franklin Skatepark; in doing so, I want to create some modicum of cognitive dissonance to help reconsider not just the terms themselves but the concepts they point to as well. How is it that one skateboarder watching another and giving them pointers is a type of formative assessment? In what ways might the participants, who are typically understood as "at-risk" or "struggling," be reframed as "gifted and talented" and "expert" when it comes to learning?

I also note that by constantly bringing schools back to the conversation about the skatepark I run the risk of diminishing the learning that is occurring at the park on its own terms, as well as continuing to recenter schooling, which I'm explicitly trying to *decenter*. In fact, this tension was brought to light by one of the reviewers of this book, who asked, "Is this a study about schooling or about skateboarding?" After consideration, my response to this question is that it is both. The study's empirical emphasis is, obviously, on skateboarding, and, if I was writing this book primarily for learning scientists or scholars of skateboarding, I would further delve into how the guys at Franklin Skatepark can help deepen understandings of learning theories, as well as skateboarding and skateparks as cultural phenomena. It's not that I am not interested in these things or think they are not important; rather, a primary aim in writing this book is to provide an in-depth example of learning in an out-of-school context that can be leveraged both as a way to illuminate normative structures of schooling and as rationale for design recommendations in schooling, teacher education, and other domains involving youth.

Given such a sense of audience and purpose, one of my most difficult challenges as a writer was grappling with the inevitable choices that need to be made at every turn in constructing this text: what to keep and emphasize and what to cut or limit. In some ways, there's more that lives in me as an author that isn't said than what is. For instance, there were times when I curtailed my diving into theoretical nuance or limited links to skateboarding scholarship to maintain a focus on the primary audience of educators and the purpose of drawing attention to and opening up possibilities for redesigning structures of schooling. While I imagine some of these choices might prove disappointing to some readers primarily interested in innovations in learning theory or skateboarding, I anticipate that the story of Franklin Skatepark, particularly given its fine-grain ethnographic detail, will offer new provocations for these audiences.

(Teacher) Educators, Educational Researchers, and Youth-Focused Workers and Allies

From the beginning of this project through the writing of this book, I have always kept close to me—anticipating the inquiries the (future) teachers with whom I work would make when I explained my research to them—the questions *So what?* and *Why and how (and for whom) does this matter?* I have always wanted to connect what I was discovering in my research with implications and applications for schooling, teacher education, and youth allies working with and on behalf of young people. Therefore, the central audience for this book is educators and educational researchers who work within or around normative schooling structures and are interested in disrupting deficit narratives of failure and promoting expansive possibilities for learning.

I encourage this audience to read *Dropping In* through a lens of educational reform: How might Franklin Skatepark help draw attention to and reimagine possibilities for social arrangements and participation structures that shape learning within schools? How might their experiences help reframe the terms by which youth labeled "at-risk" are understood and measured? More specifically, as you read, I invite you to pay particular attention to the following:

- expansive views of youth, particularly young men labeled "at-risk";
- how and why engagement and excitement for learning exists for these young men;
- various ways the social organization, configurations, and values at the skatepark promote ways of being and learning (e.g., age heterogeneity, expectations, and opportunities to contribute);
- particular learning practices that take into consideration improvisation, self-direction, embodiment, and talking;
- the multimodal nature of textuality and critical media literacy; and
- potential "funds of knowledge" (Moll et al., 1992) that could hold interdisciplinary links with literacy, history, media studies, science (think of all the physics going on in skateboarding), and, of course, physical education, among other disciplines.

I offer these specific considerations to stimulate connections to be made while reading this book, even if I do not make them explicitly; in fact, in many places I resist making too many direct linkages myself so as not to constrain thinking of possibilities.

For an education audience, I situate *Dropping In* most centrally within a robust line of inquiry that examines the interplay between youth learning, language, and literacy practices as they occur across a range of contexts (e.g., Caraballo & Lyiscott, 2020; de los Ríos, 2020, 2021; Gustavson, 2007; Kinloch, 2009, 2011; Kirkland, 2013; Mahiri, 2004; Mirra, Garcia, & Morrell, 2016; Moje, 2000, 2008; Morrell, 2008; Paris, 2011; Patel, 2012; Watson & Beymer, 2019; Williams, 2018; Winn, 2011). By locating myriad ways youth, particularly those from historically marginalized populations, engage cultural practices, this scholarship has pushed empirical and theoretical horizons regarding youth learning, language, and literacy, and in doing so, reveals youth as capable, innovative intellectuals who draw on and use a range of cultural practices and resources to help them engage deeply in contemporary society. These renderings contrast the dominant—often deficit, diminished—understandings of youth that tend to circulate unproblematically within educational discourses (Petrone & Lewis, 2012; Lesko, 2012).

Furthermore, this scholarship has put forth a range of pedagogical innovations designed to facilitate more equitable educational opportunities for youth, including "culturally sustaining pedagogies" (Paris, 2012), "pedagogical third spaces" (Kirkland, 2008), "permeable" curricula (Dyson, 2003), "restorative justice" (Winn, 2013), and "critical literacy pedagogies" (Morrell, 2008). Overall, these innovations have opened a range of ways educators can develop curricula and instructional approaches that value and build on the linguistic and literacy resources students bring with them into classrooms—and transform official school curricula in the process. In this way, this work encourages educators to adopt an ethnographic stance to attune themselves to their students' rich literate and cultural lives (Petrone, 2013).

Situated within these pedagogical innovations, one of the most significant insights to emerge from the young men's experiences of Franklin Skatepark is just how integral their sense of being a *contributor* to the overall community is for their own participation (as will specifically be discussed in Chapter 9). As expressed by Derrick earlier in the chapter, at the park these young men experience a sense that their know-how and perspectives matter and that they can affect the people and culture at the park. From this important lesson, as will be explored in the final chapter of this book, I explore what I refer to as a "repositioning pedagogy" (Petrone & Rink, with Speicher, 2020; Petrone & Sarigianides, 2017). In short, a "repositioning pedagogy" is an approach to working with youth that overtly positions them as capable and able and places them in roles whereby they have opportunities to contribute to the learning of others.

Critical Youth Studies and Sociology of Youth

As an interdisciplinary field of study, Critical Youth Studies (CYS) draws on a range of theoretical and methodological approaches to interrogate normative, dominant ideas of adolescence and youth as a natural experience grounded in biological and psychological developmental paradigms (Ali & McCarty, 2020; Austin & Willard, 1998; Best, 2007; Lesko & Talburt, 2012; Ibrahim & Steinburg, 2014). More specifically, CYS argues that what has become known as the natural life stage of adolescence is a social and historically situated *construct*, or, as Vadeboncoeur (2005) suggests, a "fiction"—"a function of political, economic, educational and governmental discourses," or "a story made universal, and as such, a time and space that adults impose on and negotiate with young people" (p. 6).

From this general perspective, CYS takes as one of its central aims the location and disruption of the ways these naturalized discourses of adolescence and youth circulate in contemporary society to make more readily available multiple understandings of and material practices involving young people. For instance, Patel (2012) demonstrates how the "single story" of adolescence as one of "raging hormones, rebelliousness, and defiance of authority" (p. 36) renders "flat" and constrains understandings of and possibilities for many immigrant youth in the United States. Through her ethnographic research, she demonstrates how examining the lived realities of immigrant youth demonstrates a much different "story" that highlights how the social, political, and economic contextual factors contribute to the identity development, decision making, and life chances for youth—all of which engender a different set of "interventions" adults might implement on their behalf.

Given that CYS demonstrates how youth can be understood in society beyond the terms of schooling and developmental paradigms, I situate *Dropping In* within this tradition to not only destabilize some of the formidable ways of knowing "failing" young men but also help make available more comprehensive understandings of and for both youth and the adults with whom they collaborate. Similar to Kirkland's (2013) account of the lives of a group of young Black men typically understood as "undeveloped," a central aim of *Dropping In* is to have the stories of the young men highlighted in this book shared with a wider audience. Given that their stories—and by proxy, the stories of so many other young people who similarly fall or are pushed by the wayside of traditional means of success—are so frequently rendered invisible, or worse, as mere statistics that capitulate their labels of failure, it feels imperative that fuller versions of these young men's stories be disseminated.

Therefore, I urge pursuit of the following questions: How might the ways in which the participants of Franklin Skatepark take up responsibility for the welfare of the park and other participants help reimagine possible ways of knowing "youth" or "adolescence" as a category of representation that currently exists in our cultural imagination as diminished and deficit (Elman, 2014; Lesko, 2012)? How might this exploration of Franklin Skatepark as a context of learning inform the design of other "informal" learning environments or programs? In what ways might these findings complicate normative notions of "adolescent development" and "adolescence"?

In thinking with these questions and situated within a CYS perspective, one of the most significant insights to emerge from the young men's experiences in *Dropping In* is just how quickly the normative assumptions of the socially constructed categories of "adolescence" and "teenagers" break down, particularly in relation to working-class, racially diverse young men. From this, I have developed, along with colleagues, what we refer to as a "Youth Lens," which is an analytic approach to examining representations and discourses of age, adolescence/ts, and teenagehood in texts, talk, and institutions (Petrone, Sarigianides, & Lewis, 2015; Sarigianides, Petrone, & Lewis, 2017). As I discuss in the final chapter, a Youth Lens both draws attention to ways dominant systems of reasoning and contexts marginalize youth and advances the proliferation of more comprehensive, accurate representations of young people and social systems to support them.

It is important to note, however, that at the same time that I am interested in reframing many of the dominant ways these young men are named and known, I am not at all interested in romanticizing, sensationalizing, uncritically celebrating, or otherwise fetishizing them or their cultural practices and communities—concerns that some CYS scholars have rightly raised about research focused on youth and youth cultures (Best, 2007; Ibrahim & Steinburg, 2014; Moje, 2008). Nor am I attempting to demonize, minimize, or neglect schools, academic literacy, or any of the seemingly startling statistics of violence, drug and alcohol use, and mental health issues among young men. In this way, I do not shy away from some of the more problematic aspects of these cultural practices and communities (e.g., the homophobic language use explored in Chapter 7). Hence, I hope to offer an honest and realistic account of the young men of Franklin Skatepark's learning lives and the possibilities they hold for rethinking schooling and youth advocacy.

Scholars of Skateboarding

In recent years, skateboarding has become an international phenomenon that is a virtual mainstream thread in the fabric of today's worldwide popular culture: it recently premiered as an Olympic event, has been integrated into some physical education curricula in schools, and can be found in one form or another on the backs and feet of thousands of people who have never even touched foot to grip tape. Alongside its growing public popularity, academic scholarship related to skateboarding has also increased, including a recently developed academic conference in the United Kingdom focused exclusively on skateboarding scholarship titled "Pushing Boarders" (https://www.pushingboarders.com).

From my position as an academic, skateboarding studies, as an ever-growing field, has been one of the most exciting I've encountered. The field is wildly interdisciplinary, engaging scholars from architectural studies (e.g., Borden, 2001, 2019), urban planning (e.g., Howell, 2008), education (e.g., Sagor, 2002; Shaver, 2020), media studies (e.g., Thorpe, 2017; Wheaton & Beal, 2003; Yochim, 2010), learning sciences (e.g., Ma & Munter, 2014), sociology (e.g., Dupont, 2014), psychology (e.g., Seifert & Hedderson, 2010), sociology of sport (e.g., Beal, 1995, 1996, 1998; Beal & Weidman, 2003; Beal & Wilson, 2004; Howe, 2003), and youth development (Sorsdahl et al., 2021), among others. In these ways, the field affords opportunities to study the body and senses (e.g., Bäckström, 2014; Fors, Bäckström, & Pink, 2013); spatial production and spatial politics (e.g., Hollet & Vivoni, 2021; Karsten & Pel, 2000; Németh, 2006); notions of (sub)cultural capital and "authenticity" (e.g., Beal & Weidman, 2003; Dupont, 2020); various categories of social representation, including gender, race, and age (e.g., Carr, 2017; O'Connor, 2018; Willing et al., 2019); issues of surveillance, governmentality, and neoliberalism (Howell, 2008; Tsikalas & Jones, 2018); and, among many other topics, mental and emotional health (Sorsdahl et al., 2021).

This type of collective and varied sense making aligns quite poetically with the ethos of skateboarding and skateboarders—a joint and distributed approach to problem solving, a valuing of differentiated expertise, and a joining of individual and communal facets of engagement. Moreover, this interdisciplinary spirit also links with the fact that there is so much debate about what skateboarding even is: is it a sport, an action or extreme sport, a "totalizing lifestyle" (Borden, 2019, p. 45), a hobby, a culture, an art form, or, as Ian MacKaye argues, "a way of learning how to redefine the world around you" (quoted in Borden, 2019, p. 24)?

Furthermore, skateboarding studies enables and brings together deep theorization with pragmatic outreach and activism, including, for instance, social/global initiatives such as the Skatepark Project (formerly the Tony Hawk Foundation); the nonprofit organization Skateistan, which has developed skateparks in several urban areas around the world (Jordan, South Africa, Cambodia) with the specific purpose of facilitating youth (especially female youth) empowerment and leadership (https://www.skateistan.org); and the Apache Passion Project, which aims to support the development of skateparks for Native American youth living on reservations (Lerner, 2021).

Related, various educational programs linked with skateboarding have been developed and implemented around the world. For instance, Bryggeriets Gymnasium in Malmö, Sweden, is a nonprofit high school that is literally built around a skatepark and centers skateboarding in its curriculum (Nielsen, n.d.). Similarly, the newly developed FAR Academy, which is organized through the nonprofit FAR Skate Foundation (https://www.farskate.co.uk) in the United Kingdom, is an alternative school setting that supports, through skateboarding and the business aspects of skateboarding, youth who have been identified as struggling with their social, emotional, and mental health and wellness. I also draw attention to the work of Mark Rivard, a skateboarder, artist, and educator located in Minneapolis, Minnesota, in the United States. As founder of the nonprofit Do Rad Things (https://www.doradthings.net), Mark has developed a series of educational skateboard arts programs that draw on the values and lessons learned through the creative and physical process of being a skateboarder and artist.

In recent years, scholarship has given particular attention to how significantly skateboarding has changed since its origins, not just in the nature of the activity itself but also in relation to commercialization, the proliferation of skateparks, and the increasing assemblage of stakeholders involved in governing skateboarding. Atencio et al. (2018), based on their research of four newly developed skateparks in the Bay Area, explain that "the current state of skateboarding is not only being influenced by parental support, but also by corporate, government, and nonprofit bodies that are spreading their particular visions of urban and youth development"

(p. 6). In this sense, skateboarding has become increasingly imbued with symbolic meanings regarding notions of progress and development—not only at the level of the individual or broader demographic of youth but also related to ideas of parenting, social ordering, and economics. As Atencio et al. (2018) argue, "Skateparks have added new dimensions to skateboarding, with these spaces becoming vehicles for modern parenting, youth development, and community renewal" (p. 25).

Research on skateparks has proliferated in recent years, as have the parks themselves. Some of this research reveals that these parks provide a space for youth to engage in leisure activities while also cultivating peer friendships and gaining social acceptance (Shannon & Werner, 2008; Taylor & Khan, 2011), as well as function as a health resource (Dumas & Laforest, 2009) and a space for "prosocial behavior" (Bradley, 2010; Dumas & Laforest, 2009; Wood, Carter, & Martin, 2014). Certainly, the research reported in this book supports many of these previous findings, even if not termed in the same ways as these studies. In fact, my work adds to this scholarship the idea that Franklin Skatepark operated as an important form of "sponsorship" (Brandt, 1998) for social, intellectual, economic, and emotional opportunities for the participants, including job networking, emotional connectivity, literacy development, and geographic exploration. In these ways, the skatepark nurtured the well-being of these young men much more so than schools.

Another line of inquiry related to skateparks examines how parks may unwittingly reinforce (or in the case of DIY parks, disrupt) neoliberal agendas (Hollett & Vivoni, 2021; Howell, 2005, 2008; Glenney & O'Connor, 2019; Vivoni, 2009). For instance, Howell (2008) explains how urban officials view the building and maintenance of skateparks as ways to foster entrepreneurship among young people, reduce the liability cases for injuries, assist in bolstering monetary values of low-income communities, and aid in self-policing practices. Howell (2005) also argues that these parks function whereby skateboarders often enter spaces that were abandoned or filled with other "undesirables" (e.g., homeless, drug users). They reclaim spaces and bring activity to the area while pushing these people out. In these ways, skateboarders add to the social capital of a cityscape (Jenson, Swords, & Jeffries, 2012) and often engage in public-private partnerships to clean up areas of the city through the funding of skateparks (Vivoni, 2009).

As skateparks continue to proliferate, they are increasingly becoming complex sites of spatial politics involving various stakeholders—corporations, nonprofits, municipalities, skateboarders—and interests, including neoliberalism, youth development, parental desires (Atencio et al., 2018; Borden, 2019; Hollett & Vivoni, 2021). For example, in his research on the opening of a skatepark in Hong Kong, O'Connor (2016) explores how a mandatory helmet rule at the park revealed ideological divides between the skateboarders, who viewed the issue as one of participant control, and the government, which understood this as an issue of accountability. Ultimately, this example demonstrates issues of control and negotiation of terms of participation, particularly given the increasing reach and regulation of these parks by non-skateboard entities.

At the same time, recent scholarship also notes how more regulated skateparks may open opportunities for female participation (Atencio et al., 2018), which is significant given how male-dominated skateboarding has been and largely continues to be (Carr, 2017), which is the case with Franklin Skatepark (addressed in Chapter 4). Moreover, as increased regulation in skateparks occurs, so, too, do official programming and practices, including formalized periods of instruction (e.g., lessons) by trained/certified instructors. Often, these types of activities are on a cost basis (as in entrance to some parks), though sometimes these costs are defrayed by another entity (e.g., corporate sponsor).

Given these complexities, in offering the findings of my research, I carry a tension within me, particularly when it comes to thinking of significance, implications, and advocacy. On the one hand, I see the value of many of these initiatives, and, in many ways, support them, especially in relation to imagining unique opportunities for building intergenerational, place-based connections within rural communities. However, on the other hand, I worry that such research as reported in this book could be co-opted as part of neoliberal agendas for so-called youth or community development, particularly given how many such initiatives emerge from and reify perspectives of "child(hood)," "adolescence/ts," "learning," and "appropriate" social behavior rooted in whiteness, coloniality, and capitalism (Howell, 2008; Lesko, 2012).

Franklin Skatepark, likely due, in part, to its rural location, has not been as embroiled in such broader entanglements. What I find interesting to consider is that if Franklin Skatepark were to be taken up in the rise of increased "adult regulatory practices" (Atencio et al., 2018, p. 246) and commercial interests of skateparks, my sense is that the participants featured in this book would likely not have participated as much or at all in the cultural community there. What they valued so intensely about Franklin Skatepark was that, as Kevin and others say, it was *their* place—and one which, unlike other official youth-sanctioned places, they were able to shape and meaningfully contribute to. In other words, Franklin Skatepark functioned as the type of space it did for these participants due to the seeming *lack* of adult, corporate, and government involvement, and, if it were to resemble more regulated parks, these guys might actually feel alienated from it.

This perspective on Franklin Skatepark resonates with other research on "unorganized" lifestyle sport contexts whereby positive development occurred "not in spite of, but because of the lack of strict rules, formal leaders or a priori performance goals" (Säfvenbom, Wheaton, & Agans, 2018, p. 1990). In this way, I see this book as offering a type of counternarrative to the seeming dominant renderings of contemporary skateparks. My hope is that Franklin Skatepark might offer a "bottom-up" (Atencio et al., 2018, p. 263) approach to thinking about and developing the roles and practices of skateparks—those that prioritize the perspectives of skateboarders.

While this broad swath of research has been informative to my own, some of which will appear throughout this book to help elucidate my findings, I mostly draw on skateboarding scholarship that examines learning (e.g., Ellmer & Rynne, 2016; Enright & Gard, 2016; Hollet, 2019; Jones, 2011; Ma & Munter, 2014). One of the most exciting aspects of this scholarship focuses on the role of digital media within learning to skateboard (Dupont, 2020; Ellmer & Rynne, 2016; Enright & Gard, 2016; Hollet, 2019; Jones, 2011; Thorpe, 2017). In general, this inquiry examines how skateboarders use digital media to not only learn how to skateboard but also build relationships with one another. Another exciting area of inquiry focuses on the sensory and kinesthetic dimensions of learning to skateboard. Specifically, Bäckström (2014) and Fors, Bäckström, and Pink (2013) explore what they call a "multisensory emplaced" conceptualization of learning, which moves beyond embodied notions of learning to consider body within place.

By sharing the stories of the diehard locals of Franklin Skatepark, I hope to contribute to this growing body of scholarship in several ways. First, this research focuses on an understudied demographic of skateboarders: working-class, Latino and white male skateboarders within a rural context. Because of the more remote, smaller nature of the community and park in this research, this study provides in-depth understandings of how social, cultural, and ideological issues commingle with learning practices at a skatepark.

Also, in addition to learning, this project focuses on the participants themselves, including their stories and the underlying social, cultural, political, and emotional aspects of their participation. In this way, this project is as much about a particular group of skateboarders as it is about skateboarding. Thus, this research is meant to humanize these skateboarders and examine the role that skateboarding plays in their lives as racially diverse, working-class young men.

Related, *Dropping In*, as a book-length ethnography, weaves together various aspects of learning and participation to offer a robust, comprehensive portrait of how learning happens within this cultural community and to explore sociocultural aspects of learning in skateboarding, including connections across discrete concepts thus far explored in the scholarship. (The downside, of course, to the broad scope is that it tends to err on the side of breadth rather than depth, and as such, I recognize that at nearly every turn, more can be done to further develop analysis of particular facets of learning.)

The Franklin Skatepark Locals and Skateboarders in General

I should add, too, that in addition to scholars of skateboarding, I hope this book appeals to skateboarders themselves. Of course, this distinction between skateboarders and scholars of skateboarding is a construct, as I see skateboarders—at least the ones I've met along the way—as scholars of skateboarding in their own right, though not necessarily authorized as such by institutions such as universities or socially sanctioned mechanisms such as college degrees. I wrote *Dropping In*—or at least I attempted to do so—in a manner whereby skateboarders who have not been trained as academic researchers could see and feel themselves in this book. As I wrote, I imagined Luis, TS, Crazy K, Matt, and the rest of the diehard locals of Franklin Skatepark flipping through the pages of this book, reading its words, and nodding their heads, saying, "Yeah, that's right, that's what it's like." In many respects, they are my primary audience, for without their stamp of approval—their sense of its "authenticity," so to speak—this book means little.

OUTLINE OF DROPPING IN

Dropping In is organized into three parts: "Entering the Bowl," "Carving the Bowl," and "Beyond the Bowl."

Part One: Entering the Bowl

Part One (which includes this chapter and the subsequent three chapters) overviews the educational issues this book addresses, the central theoretical orientations that frame the research, and salient methodological processes, and introduces the central participants and context.

The next chapter, Chapter 2, explores the guiding theoretical framework for this project, Learning by Observing and Pitching In (LOPI) as developed by Barbara Rogoff and colleagues (Rogoff et al., 2015). Situated within the broader umbrella of sociocultural perspectives of learning, LOPI provides a way to understand intersections of learning and participation within a cultural community. To elucidate the framework, I draw on examples from Franklin Skatepark and contrasting examples of "assembly-line instruction," which is a central approach to learning and teaching in schools. In addition, this chapter critiques the nomenclature of "informal" and "formal" learning since these terms reify power hierarchies regarding knowledge (production); to further this critique, the chapter promotes the language of "purposive" and "non-purposive" learning.

Chapter 3 offers a frank discussion regarding some of the methodological decisions and issues that shaped how and why I designed and carried out this project. Specifically, this chapter explores critical ethnography as an approach, gaining access to Franklin Skatepark, methods of data generation and analysis, and, importantly, the ways I understand how my positionality as a white, heteronormative, cisgender, able-bodied, urban-born and -raised, working-class turned middle-class university professor, informed—and limited—this project.

Chapter 4 uses the annual skate contest at Franklin Skatepark as a narrative frame to introduce the park, the community in which it is situated, and the focal participants. Theoretically, this chapter establishes Franklin Skatepark as a "cultural community" (Rogoff, 2003).

Part Two: Carving the Bowl
Part Two, Chapters 5 through 9, examines how participation and learning occur at Franklin Skatepark. From a learning perspective, this section is the heart of the book.

Chapter 5 explores how participation is structured at Franklin Skatepark. Specifically, it explains the main forms of skating and non-skating participation (e.g., skating with others in sessions, hanging out at the picnic tables), as well as the practice of "snaking," which is a way participants learn and teach spatial relations at the park. Because it provides a broad overview of participation, this chapter functions as an important foundation for subsequent chapters.

Chapter 6 is a robust chapter that examines particular learning practices and processes. Specifically, this chapter highlights (a) "doing it," which emphasizes the importance of individualized, self-selected, and self-directed learner initiative; (b) "skating with others," which demonstrates how more proximal, "side-by-side" (Paradise & Rogoff, 2009) social relations function in learning processes; and (c) "watching others," which focuses on active observation of other skateboarders. Across these practices, this chapter illuminates how learning at Franklin Skatepark is inherently tied to identity, participation, and context.

Chapter 7 examines how power—particularly manifested through performances of class, gender, sexuality, race, and age—interplays with participation at Franklin Skatepark. Specifically, this chapter focuses on how discursive practices—namely "heckling"—illuminate ideological underpinnings and tensions within the community and how these enable and/or constrain participation and learning. Theoretically, this chapter attends to recent calls in the learning sciences for more attention to ways macro-level social ordering (e.g., race, gender) inform micro-level learning activities.

Chapter 8 explores how participation in this cultural community "sponsors" (Brandt, 1998) the participants' consumption, production, and distribution of a wide array of texts and literacy practices (e.g., reading magazines and books, viewing and creating skate videos, social media use, designing tattoos). Framed by sociocultural and critical perspectives,

which understand literacy not as a discrete set of universal, decontextualized mental skills but rather practices that occur in and are shaped by
sociocultural and ideological contexts, this chapter illustrates how the
expectation that all participants eventually become active contributors
to the cultural community facilitates their literacy activities, particularly
as they move from "consumers" of industry texts to being creators and
"producers" of their own texts.

Chapter 9 explores the question of why the participants engage at
Franklin Skatepark by examining the notion of *contribution* as a foundational principle of social organization and motivation at Franklin
Skatepark. Specifically, this chapter looks across three dimensions of
contribution: (1) *style*, which refers to how an individual skateboarder
renders himself and his way of skateboarding; (2) opportunities to *simultaneously mentor and be mentored* by other participants, which engender
emotional bonds to each other and the cultural community; and (3) contributions to the welfare of others through *textual and cultural production
and distribution*. This chapter is significant for several reasons, including
its emphasis on the affective dimensions of learning and participation.

Part Three: Beyond the Bowl

Part Three, which consists of Chapter 10, offers several implications for
schooling and youth development. Specifically, the chapter explores: (1)
theoretical reconceptualizations of adolescence, including the development of the "Youth Lens" (Petrone, Sarigianides, & Lewis, 2015), which
is an analytical approach to denaturalize adolescence in texts and discourses; (2) a "repositioning pedagogy" (Petrone & Rink, with Speicher,
2020), which offers an approach to situating marginalized youth as educational experts and consultants to teach others, especially future teachers; and (3) age-heterogeneous approaches to redesign literacy learning
for secondary "struggling readers" whereby they are positioned as reading tutors for elementary-aged students. Thus, this chapter connects
back to the introduction and title of this book, arguing that an essential
aspect of educational reform efforts targeting marginalized youth must
involve recognizing them as capable and placing them in positions where
they have opportunities for genuine contribution—in other words, situations in which they can be learned *from*.

CHAPTER TWO

Learning by Observing and Pitching In as a Theoretical Framework to Understand "Purposive Learning" at Franklin Skatepark

> For millennia, children have learned the skills, life ways, and philosophies of their communities informally, through their engagement in everyday family and community settings. . . . Learning occurs almost "by osmosis" (Azuma, 1994) in a purposeful incidental fashion while children are engaged with others in accomplishing a shared activity. This form of learning is ubiquitous, though often overlooked, including in societies with extensive Western schooling. (Rogoff et al., 2016, p. 362)

T
O MAKE SENSE of Franklin Skatepark as a context for learning, I draw on the theoretical framework Learning by Observing and Pitching In (LOPI).[1] Initially emerging from ethnographic fieldwork in Indigenous communities in Guatemala, Rogoff and colleagues have developed LOPI over the course of many years as an approach to understand how learning occurs within "cultural communities," which are settings where learners are integrated into the activities of families and communities and have opportunities to contribute to the endeavors occurring therein.

The purpose of this chapter is to elucidate LOPI as a framework and explain how and why I operationalized it for this project. Toward this aim, I weave into my explanation concrete examples both from Franklin Skatepark and from schools. Because LOPI is situated within broader sociocultural theoretical perspectives on learning, and more specifically within scholarship focused on what is known as "informal learning," I contextualize LOPI and this study within these two intellectual traditions,

---

1 Developed over many years by Dr. Barbara Rogoff and various colleagues, the nomenclature of "Learning by Observing and Pitching In" has undergone changes; initially it was referred to as "Intent Participation" and "Intent Community Participation" before being referred to as "Learning by Observing and Pitching In" or "LOPI." Therefore, when I refer to LOPI, I am drawing on a collection of research developed by Rogoff and different colleagues, though some of those publications may not have named the approach LOPI.

drawing particular attention to how research on informal learning helps, in part, render schools visible as contexts for learning, as well as offering insights into understanding processes of learning and imagining possibilities for designing learning environments in and outside of schools.

SOCIOCULTURAL CONCEPTIONS OF LEARNING

The acts, attitudes, and orientations of learning, as well as the social and physical contexts in which it takes place, are interdependently related aspects, not a collection of separable behaviors or factors. (Paradise & Rogoff, 2009, p. 105)

While there are several distinct strands of sociocultural perspectives on learning—including, for example, activity theory/systems (Engeström, 1999), cultural historical psychology (Cole, 1999), and situated learning (Lave & Wenger, 1991)—all of them share several foundational, orienting concepts (Esmonde & Booker, 2017; Lewis, Enciso, & Moje, 2007). In particular, sociocultural theory presumes all learning—whether it be learning to read, cook, or skateboard—is inextricably linked to engagement with others; participation in broader cultural, historical, and social activities; mediation by and through cultural artifacts; and a sense of identity. In other words, learning is less about the acquisition of discrete, decontextualized *knowledge* or *skills* as much as it is about *participation* in a set of practices that are connected to being a certain kind of person within a certain context (Cole, 1999; Esmonde & Booker, 2017; Lave & Wenger, 1991; Lee & Smagorinsky, 2000; Rogoff, 2003).

Within sociocultural perspectives, then, knowledge and skills are learned *as part of the process* of engaging in social practices. This focus on practices enables researchers interested in learning processes to examine how learning is situated in specific contexts, shaped by social interactions, and linked to values, beliefs, ideologies, and culturally patterned ways of knowing, being, and doing. Importantly, then, a sociocultural perspective foregrounds how different configurations of learning in particular groups or contexts are enmeshed with social, cultural, historical, ideological, and political relationships. In this way, sociocultural theory recasts learning from an isolated, universalized cognitive endeavor to a recognition that learning, context, and identity are inextricably linked and constitutive (Esmonde, 2017; Nasir & Cooks, 2009).

For example, learning how to skateboard at Franklin Skatepark is, in many ways, predicated on understanding the terms of cultural participation and how to be a skateboarder within this context, which includes, for example, knowing how to use the physical space of the park; how and when to acceptably "fail"; how and when to congratulate and/or ridicule each other; how to deal with physical pain; who, how, and when to ask for and/or give assistance; and how to perform particular types of raced, classed, and gendered ways of being. In this way, learning the knowledge and skills to skateboard and how to be a skateboarder within this context cannot be understood as separate from one another.

A key facet of sociocultural perspectives on learning, then, is attention to *context*. Any learning that happens always does so in a particular time and place, and these factors shape and are shaped by *how* learning does or does not happen therein. In sociocultural theory, though, context is much more than a physical arrangement or where learning takes place. As Sefton-Green (2012) argues, while physical geography remains critical in thinking about places of learning, "context encompasses the set of relationships—visible, invisible, inherited, and assumed—in which the social interactions of the learning take place," and that "the expectations of a setting and especially the orientation and behaviors of other participants are vital to a full appreciation of context" (p. 20).

Sociocultural scholars also note how spatial and temporal relations trouble traditional renderings of context (e.g., Compton-Lilly & Halverson, 2014; Leander, Phillips, & Taylor, 2010; Ma & Munter, 2014). For instance, Ma & Munter (2014) demonstrate that while spaces in skateparks already exist, the skaters constantly (re)produce the way learning happens in those spaces by shaping the activities they do around them (e.g., using spaces that are less crowded or smaller to practice tricks more quickly). Digital technologies have also reshaped ideas of context by transcending physical place entirely in some instances and/or complexifying learning relations to physical spaces (Coiro et al., 2008; Stornaiuolo, Smith, & Phillips, 2017).

In thinking of context, then, as a complex set of constitutive relationships between physical place, space, people, practices, temporalities, and ideologies, I draw on Rogoff's notion of "cultural communities," which she defines as "groups of people who have some common and continuing organization, values, understanding, history, and practices" (Rogoff 2003, p. 80). She goes on to explain how a cultural community "involves people trying to accomplish some things together, with some stability of involvement and attention to the ways they relate to each other" (p. 80). Rogoff also notes that cultural communities develop practices and traditions that are not beholden to particular individuals as new generations of participants replace previous ones. Furthermore, she explains how the relations among participants in a community "are varied and multifaceted," that "different participants have different roles and responsibilities," and the relations among participants "may be comfortable or conflictual or oppressive" (p. 80).

More recently, Rogoff and Mejía-Arauz (2022) explain how the values and practices of cultural communities "do not exist separately from the people who embody them, resist them, modify them" but rather are "mutually constituting in a dynamic process of change and continuities" (p. 501). In these ways, the conceptualization of Franklin Skatepark as a cultural community enabled me to explore it as a physical context where learning happens with particular focus on the "web of social relationships" and how "contexts are constituted by participants' actions, physical and verbal, as well as where and when they are acting" (Vadeboncoeur, 2006, p. 248). Moreover, as I discuss, particularly in Chapters 4 through 9, I take into consideration the constitutive nature of the physical place and materiality of Franklin Park, the people who participate there, the social and discursive practices they use, broader systems of power, and their literacy practices that relate to but physically occur away from the park. Linguistically, to signal Franklin Skatepark as both a social space and a physical place, throughout the book, I often include "of/at" when referring to the park as a cultural community (e.g., "the cultural community of/at Franklin Skatepark)."

FROM "INFORMAL" TO "PURPOSIVE" LEARNING: RENDERING SKATEPARKS AND SCHOOLS VISIBLE AS CONTEXTS FOR LEARNING

It should be acknowledged that there is nothing in principle that differentiates the use of context in learning in non-formal learning from that taking place in schools. However, studies of learning in non-formal domains almost always draw attention to the specificities of context because it is so crucial in helping us understand the different ways that learners are absorbing information or being socialized, in learning to behave, to imitate, and to be initiated into practice. It is striking how

> learning is so often *not* considered in these ways in the literature about school and schooling because we tend to take the practice, the everyday of schooling, for granted rather than see it as a singularity among others in ways that the not-school tradition allows us to do. (Sefton-Green, 2012, p. 22; emphasis added)

In this section, I briefly situate both LOPI and *Dropping In* within the intellectual tradition of what is often known as "informal learning" (Rogoff et al., 2016). Primarily focused on learning environments beyond schools and/or normative school practices (e.g., after-school clubs), this scholarship has opened up many theoretical advances in understanding learning, especially regarding the intersections of context, learning, and identity (Kirschner & Kaplan, 2017). Though not necessarily the aim, much of this research, whether through explicit comparison or just by virtue of examining learning, often enables possibilities to see and think anew about—or take a "fresh look at" (Lave & Wenger, 1991)—schooling as one such context for learning.

Specifically, this research often exposes both the taken-for-granted learning practices in schools and the underlying "grammar" of learning and social arrangements that structure these practices. For instance, Callanan, Cervantes, and Loomis (2011), based on research in non-school science centers, argue that "what distinguishes informal (out of schools) from formal learning (in schools) is that it is non didactic, highly collaborative, embedded in meaningful activity, and initiated by the learner's interest or choice (rather than resulting from external demands or requirements) and does not involve assessment external to the activity" (Rogoff et al., 2016, p. 389).

This type of comparative work between learning in schools and learning beyond schools is particularly crucial given how, as many sociocultural scholars note, educators and/or schools rarely explicitly address the structures of schooling as contexts for learning when imagining possibilities for pedagogy and school reform. In this way, schools—and their underlying social arrangements and participation structures—are so naturalized as a context for learning that they are taken for granted and become "invisible" or normative. As Rogoff et al. (2015) argue, "For the most part, traditions of learning are unreflectively used by practitioners, based on their own familiarity with particular traditions and practices" (p. 508). This lack of reflexivity about schools as contexts for learning is one way in which the "apprenticeship of observation" (Lortie, 1975) helps reproduce schooling systems.

Given how integral context is to learning, this ironic rendering of schools as invisible as a context limits possibilities for thinking of how learning might be differently organized and facilitated in schools. Thus, one of the most generative aspects of informal learning research has been how it often decouples learning from schooling (and teaching), and, in doing so, helps reclaim notions of learning from schooling. In this way, this line of inquiry has made visible and reminded us that learning occurs in many spaces and places, and looks quite different depending on myriad factors, and that schools do not have a monopoly on (understanding) learning—or even teaching.

Moreover, this type of juxtaposition renders more visible ways students' participation in schools may, in fact, be constrained by how learning is organized in schools. Rogoff et al. (2015) argue, "Attention to the social organization of routine events will reveal reasons for certain children's ease or confusion or even resistance when they enter new settings that are organized in ways that may relate to, differ from, or even conflict with those with which they have experience" (p. 493). In this way, analysis of learning structures makes possible a different way to locate students' academic (dis)engagement as it moves away from personal, individual "failures" and toward systemic issues (e.g., the means and structures of learning) that help produce failures for particular students (Golden, 2017; Golden & Petrone, 2021; Petrone & Stanton, 2021; Vasudevan & Campano, 2009). As Nasir et al. (2021) argue, "We cannot create schools with more equitable learning outcomes without learning theory that supports us in understanding why existing approaches to teaching and learning are not working to move toward equity" (p. 557).

Inspired by the informal learning scholarly tradition, I often refer to my approach in *Dropping In* as an "implied comparative study." What I mean is a study that relies on its readers' ability to hold the research reported herein in comparison to dominant and taken-for-granted ideas and assumptions regarding learning and teaching in schools. The purpose in doing this is to provide a contrast from which, as Mead (1928/2001) writes in her account of Samoan youth, "we may be able to turn, made newly and vividly self-conscious and self-critical, to judge anew and perhaps fashion differently the education we give our children" (p. 11).

A Note on the Nomenclature of "Informal" Learning

As someone interested in the relationships between language and meaning, I want to say something about how I am using the terms "informal learning" and "formal learning." It is customary to contrast "formal" learning as it takes place in schools with "informal" learning as it takes place outside of schools. In this way, the term "informal," particularly its prefix *in-*, which means "not," suggests a non-normative or a residual category. In this case, "formal" functions as the norm by which informal is determined. In other words, informal learning is construed as "not formal learning." Linguistically, this is also often framed as the distinction between learning that happens in schools (formal) and "out-of-school" learning (informal), which similarly maintains school as the norm.

Given how this nomenclature establishes a hierarchical, normative–non normative relationship, in this book, I resist using these particular signifiers unless quoting scholarship. Instead, I reverse this power dynamic and replace the terms with "purposive" (which means "having, serving, or done with a purpose") to refer to what currently counts as "informal," and "non-purposive" (which means not purposive, or *not* having, serving, or done with a purpose) to refer to what currently constitutes "formal." In this way, I view the learning that occurs at Franklin Skatepark as "purposive" and the learning that occurs in schools, for these participants, as "non-purposive."

My use of these terms is meant, to a large extent, to be agitational, particularly given that one of my central purposes with this book is to disrupt deeply ingrained, socialized ways of understanding learning, teaching, and youth that dominate our current schooling paradigm. As discussed in the previous chapter, my aim is not to vilify or essentialize schools or set them up as a straw man: of course, I recognize that not all learning in schools is non-purposive for some students. As a former high school English teacher and current teacher educator, I am cognizant that possibilities for learning that matters to youth can and at times does happen in schools—often by teachers and students who are willing to circumvent the limits of learning placed on them by schools and broader policies (Mahiri, 2000/2001; Watson & Petrone, 2020). In this way, my critique here is not about individual teachers—many of whom, from my experiences, are working tirelessly under severe constraints—but rather broader normative structures of schooling that largely engender non-purposive experiences for many youth (Becker, 1972).

Additionally, I use the labels "non-purposive" and "purposive" for two other reasons. The first is because these descriptors aptly fit with the experiences of the participants of this study—for them, school learning is largely non-purposive, whereas learning at the park is primarily purposive. In this sense, the "non-purposive" and "purposive" labels function as categories emergent from data analysis. Second, I want to draw attention to how school learning is often privileged, despite the fact that it exists as a socially constructed enterprise that many youth, particularly youth who come from historically marginalized communities, do not find purpose in, at best, and at worst find racism, colonialism, and erasure (e.g., Brayboy & Lomawaima, 2018)—and, for some, the other end of the school-to-prison pipeline. In other words, I am arguing that maintaining this hierarchical relationship between formal/school learning and informal/out-of-school learning helps reify and perpetuate systems, ideas, and practices that have damaging material effects for some youth. (I recognize that reversing the ordering of "informal" and "formal" through my replacement, respectively, with "purposive" and "non-purposive," does not actually flatten this hierarchy but rather flips the order of it. In this sense, my goal, at this stage, is to draw attention to the hierarchy and its implications.)

Moreover, the moniker "informal" focuses attention on *where* learning occurs, which, in this case, is not in schools, suggesting that all learning that occurs not in schools is informal. What this type of framing obfuscates is a recognition that distinctions between "informal" and "formal" conceptions of learning actually differ in *how* (not necessarily where) learning is organized and structured across these two conceptions, which often have quite distinct—and often antithetical—aims, purposes, means, and social and discursive practices. Therefore, the ways in which terms such as "informal" and "formal" signal locations of learning constrain understandings of and possibilities for how different conceptions of learning might work in and across different contexts or locations (e.g., "informal" types of learning structures in schools, "formal" types of learning structures in out-of-school spaces). In other words, I see the linguistic terms and uses of "formal" and "informal" as potentially limiting our thinking about learning across multiple contexts, especially schools.

LEARNING BY OBSERVING AND PITCHING IN

Whereas school lessons tend to treat learning as a goal in itself, relatively removed from productive or valued endeavors of importance for which such lessons are preparation, learning by observing and pitching in is solidly embedded in these endeavors and is closely associated with accomplishing goals that are clearly relevant to the family and community. In learning by observing and pitching in, learners assume a major responsibility for learning, in which they may find their own approaches to learning, rather than following a predetermined lockstep ordering of information separate from involvement in the overall process. (Paradise & Rogoff, 2009, p. 107)

Within a LOPI framework, learning is conceptualized as an active process that happens through participants' keen paying attention (and "listening in") to cultural activities occurring around them and participating in and contributing to these ongoing activities. As Paradise and Rogoff (2009) explain, "Children learn by watching, listening, and attending, often with great concentration, by taking purposeful initiative, and by contributing and collaborating" (p. 102). In essence, Learning by Observing and Pitching In is a framework for understanding both the discreteness and interrelatedness of the following facets of learning: goals/aims of learning (why); the content/substance of learning (what); the processes whereby learning occurs (how); and, importantly, the various ways broader cultural and social arrangements and structures, values, identities, and beliefs inform learning (where, when, who, and with whom).

To attend to these various aspects to learning, Rogoff and colleagues (Rogoff et al., 2015) lay out seven distinct domains of this framework (visually represented as prisms—see Figure 1), which are interrelated, multidimensional, and "form a coherent set of features to be considered as a whole" (p. 478). In this way, the presence of particular facets or features of LOPI in a learning environment does not necessarily indicate the presence of a LOPI framework as well. Analytically, all facets of LOPI "need to be present for what is going on to fit the whole pattern comprising this learning tradition" (p. 478). Moreover, Rogoff and colleagues explain that the delineated facets of LOPI "represent 'pure forms' that define the pattern of features" (478), but these forms, in reality, vary in specific characteristics when instantiated within a particular community or institution" (p. 478).

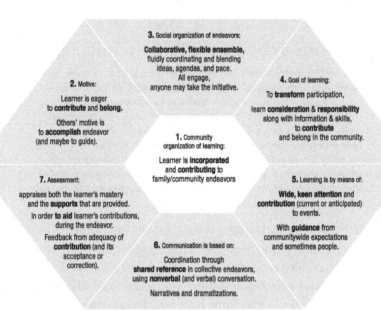

3. Social organization of endeavors:

Collaborative, flexible ensemble, fluidly coordinating and blending ideas, agendas, and pace. All engage, anyone may take the initiative.

2. Motive:

Learner is eager to **contribute and belong.**

Others' motive is to **accomplish** endeavor (and maybe to guide).

4. Goal of learning:

To **transform** participation, learn **consideration & responsibility** along with information & skills, to **contribute** and belong in the community.

1. Community organization of learning:

Learner is **incorporated** and **contributing** to family/community endeavors

7. Assessment:

appraises both the learner's mastery and the **supports** that are provided. In order **to aid** learner's contributions, during the endeavor. Feedback from adequacy of **contribution** (and its acceptance or correction).

5. Learning is by means of:

Wide, keen attention and **contribution** (current or anticipated) to events.

With **guidance** from communitywide expectations and sometimes people.

6. Communication is based on:

Coordination through **shared reference** in collective endeavors, using **nonverbal** (and verbal) conversation. Narratives and dramatizations.

FIGURE 1. The facets of Learning by Observing and Pitching In (LOPI). Reprinted with permission from Barbara Rogoff.

To both illuminate aspects of LOPI and draw attention to how learning is structured in schools, Rogoff and colleagues often contrast LOPI with the "assembly-line instruction" (ALI) framework, which they argue dominates the organization of public schooling in the United States. A primary distinction between these is that, in LOPI, learning—and not instruction—is central. Or, put another way, learning is not principally mediated by instruction, whereas the opposite is typically the case with assembly-line instruction. In fact, a hallmark of ALI, they argue, is that it "aims to control learner's attention, motivation, and behavior in settings isolated from productive contributions to the [broader] community" (p. 75). Given the rhetorical context of this book, and especially an education audience, I similarly explain the LOPI framework, in part, by contrasting it with ALI; the purpose in doing so is not to create a dichotomy of "LOPI good, ALI bad" but rather to use the familiarity of ALI to illuminate the contours of LOPI. In addition, I offer brief explanations of how each facet of LOPI connects to learning and participation at Franklin Skatepark to situate the theory in this study.

In my exploration, I organize the seven facets of LOPI into the following three broad categories as a way to connect them to the particular aims of this research:

- "structuring learning": attends to issues of context, social arrangements, and *where, when,* and *with whom* learning happens;
- "goals and motivations for learning": attends to questions of *why* learning occurs; and
- "the means of learning": attends to issues of *how* learning happens.

It is also important to note that I modify the order of the facets from how Rogoff and colleagues typically present them (though they note the facets are not meant to be in a particular order). Specifically, I place "social organization of immediate face-to-face groups" as the second facet instead of the third. I do so because I have observed that it and the first facet work synergistically to illuminate aspects of context and social arrangements that inform learning.

Structuring Learning: Where, When, and with Whom Learning Happens
FACET I: COMMUNITY ORGANIZATION OF LEARNING. In LOPI, learning happens within "cultural communities," which include a wide range of people (including children and adults) who are engaging in the endeavors of a family and/or community. This type of organizing of learning contrasts with assembly-line instruction, which segregates children—from adults, children of other ages, and their communities—in a "bureaucratically controlled setting" where they are instructed and prepared for *later* participation in the community. In this way, learning within ALI is decontextualized from contexts and people where it matters, whereas learning within LOPI learning is contextualized in a place where it matters and among people with whom it matters.

This facet of LOPI—that all learning is situated within meaningful cultural practice—is perhaps the most foundational underlying structuring of participation at Franklin Skatepark. Learning at the park happens in real time and place and among a wide array of participants, all of whom are, more or less, working together toward common goals. In this way, there is little to no separation between learning and participating in the cultural community. Moreover, skateboarders from different age groups and skill levels are all simultaneously participating, albeit at/with different skills and interests, which allows participants to have access to the full range of mature activities and endeavors at the park and enables them varying entry points into these activities; thus, participants are able to be meaningfully incorporated into the life of the community regardless of their skill or knowledge level. From this research, I would argue that, whereas Rogoff discusses these prisms as equally interrelated, this particular facet of LOPI is foundational and almost a priori to and for the other facets.

FACET 2: SOCIAL ORGANIZATION OF IMMEDIATE FACE-TO-FACE GROUPS. Whereas the previous aspect of LOPI addressed broad cultural and community patterns of organization and values, this facet attends to the organization of immediate face-to-face groups within a learning environment. Within assembly-line instruction, for instance, social organization of face-to-face interactions is "unilateral—the expert controls the learner's pace, attention, and motivation in the attempt to 'transmit' information; the expert divides the labor and does not collaborate with learners in the assigned tasks" (Rogoff et al., 2016, p. 372). In contrast, groups in LOPI "engage collaboratively as an ensemble, with flexible leadership and fluid coordination among people" (p. 372). In this social organization, learners may—and are expected to—take initiative for their learning and participation.

At Franklin Skatepark, for instance, participants have access to and engage with fellow participants across a spectrum of ages, and this age heterogeneity proved an important feature of the context that shaped learning, in particular, by providing opportunities for most participants to simultaneously mentor and be mentored by other participants, which had enduring emotional, as well as learning, effects on participants. (See Chapter 9 for more on this topic.) In other words, face-to-face interactions were multilateral in that different participants could take on different roles and positions in relationship to other participants at different times.

This is not to say that any participant could take up any role at any time but rather that there were times when opportunities presented themselves for varying participation, collaborating in multiple ways, and coordinating efforts. For example, when someone at the park could land a trick that others could not, he was able to take on a teacher role; alternatively, in some instances, he could take on a learner role, even in relation to the participant he was just teaching. In this way, there were opportunities for participants to share and build on each other's ideas and skills, as well as take initiative for their own and others' learning. As explored in Facets 5 through 7, this social organization engendered particular learning practices, communication, and assessments.

Goals and Motivations for Learning: Why Learning Happens

FACET 3: MOTIVATION FOR LEARNING. From a LOPI perspective, because participants in a cultural community are involved in the ongoing activities of that community—in real time and place—and with others in that community, motivation is characterized by a desire to be a valued part of the group, to contribute to the group, and/or to accomplish something deemed important. In other words, participation is valued by and valuable to the cultural community and other members, and "this recognition of the shared value and worth of what is being learned best explains the intrinsic motivation and desire to learn on which the effectiveness of this kind of learning in great part depends" (Paradise & Rogoff, 2009, p. 124). I qualify this by offering that this is not to say that this process is not without conflict or challenge; at the skatepark, as will be explored in later chapters, conflicts and practices of exclusion occurred.

Moreover, LOPI distinguishes between motivation for participants who are more and less experienced within a cultural community. For more experienced participants, their motivation tends to connect to the desire to accomplish something particular. For more novice participants, their motivation stems, in large part, from their interest "in contributing to and being part of valued activities of their families and communities" (Rogoff et al., 2016, p. 372). In other words, an important aspect of motivation for less experienced participants is the desire to belong to the larger group. This facet is a clear example, too, of how the prisms of LOPI are interrelated, as, in this instance, the community organization of learning (Facet 1) directly connects with the motivation to learn (Facet 3), as well as the central aims of learning (Facet 4), which will be explained next.

As will be explored in Chapter 9, as well as implicitly throughout the book, this type of intrinsic motivation permeates the experiences of the participants of Franklin Skatepark. Though multidimensional, their motivation for learning emerges from a desire to be part of something beyond themselves, particularly something that both matters to them and where they matter, and they recognize that connections with other participants are vital to this motivation. For example, in the previous chapter, Derrick articulates how the park is someplace where he can "get his word out," whereas at school, he can't teach teachers anything.

By contrast, in assembly-line instruction, motivation for less experienced participants is typically organized by and through the seeking and collecting of *extrinsic* rewards (e.g., grades, graduation). For instance, young students in elementary schools are often rewarded for "appropriate" behavior by getting stickers and other such items; the skateboarders at Franklin Skatepark often discussed how their main goal in school was to not get in trouble. Within ALI, for the more experienced participants or experts—in the case of schools, this would be teachers—the motivation for participation is to teach or instruct and sort learners. In LOPI, the motivation of experts is to accomplish a task important to the cultural community, and this may or may not directly involve guidance of novice participants.

FACET 4: GOAL(S) OF LEARNING. The primary aim of learning in a LOPI framework is to transform one's participation within the cultural community. The purpose of this transformed participation is for participants to increase their role in and contribution to the community. As explained in the previous facet, participants, over time, go from pitching in to community endeavors to trying to accomplish the endeavors of the community. Through transforming their participation, they also learn "to collaborate with consideration and innovation, as well as gain task-specific information and skills" (Rogoff et al., 2016, p. 372).

By understanding the goal of learning as transformed participation, developing knowledge and/or skills is always occurring within the broader aim of and as part of the process of participation within a cultural community, or, as I think of it, learning these things occurs *along the way*. Among the participants at Franklin Skatepark, as they transform their participation within the cultural community over time, they acquire (necessary) declarative and procedural knowledge about skateboarding culture in general, about skateboarding at the park, and particular skills to skateboard (e.g., how to ollie). For example, in Chapter 4, I discuss the practice of "snaking," which is one way participants learn spatial awareness of the park and cultural norms around turn taking, which thereafter enables participants to participate differently in the park. In this way, learning discrete bits of information and/or skills are done alongside, in the service of, and motivated by transforming their participation within the group. These new skills and knowledge, then, enable transformed participation. Also, since learning knowledge and skills occurs within the context of participation, there is often a contextualized temporality, or timeliness, to learning—it happens *in and on time.*

Because learning these skills and this knowledge is connected to participation within a cultural community, all of this learning, too, is inextricably linked with identity and learning to be a certain type of person in the cultural community. As Gee (2003) explains, "Any specific way of reading and thinking is, in fact, a way of being in the world, a way of being a certain 'kind of person,' a way of taking on a certain kind of identity" (p. 3–4). This is clearly evidenced among the skateboarders at Franklin Skatepark where learning to skateboard and be a skateboarder, particularly as it involves learning how to be particular types of raced, classed, and gendered people, are inextricably linked. In these ways, "what" is being learned, or the "content" of learning, is multifaceted, as it comprises knowledge, skills, and *ways of being.*

In many respects, transformed participation serves an almost über function as it subsumes various other key aspects of learning. Thus, transformed participation can be seen as a litmus test for assessing or evaluating learning rather than the acquisition of decontextualized skills and knowledge as the end goal or product of learning. This starkly contrasts assembly-line instruction models of learning where the overall goal is "to transmit isolated pieces of information and skills, for the purpose of certification, which is prerequisite for learners' eventual inclusion in society" (Rogoff et al., 2016, p. 372).

The Means of Learning: How Learning Happens

FACET 5: MEANS OF LEARNING. Unlike assembly-line instruction, where learning is designed to happen through "lessons, exercises, and tests that are outside the context of accomplishing something productive" (Rogoff et al., 2016, p. 372), learning through LOPI occurs by various means of observation (and "listening in"), participation (and "pitching in"), and guidance from/by other participants engaged in a shared activity. What is important here is that observation is not a passive process but rather carried out with great concentration and purpose and is often self-initiated. Guidance from others, which may be direct or indirect, may involve other participants offering pointers, suggestions, or critiques. Moreover, guidance comes, too, via the broader cultural community's expectations, values, and norms.

Within LOPI, learners are largely responsible for taking initiative to help facilitate their participation, which is led by their desire to contribute and belong to the cultural community (as discussed in Facet 3).

This facet of LOPI is the one most focused on throughout this book, especially in Chapters 5–8, as a main purpose of *Dropping In* is to understand *how* learning occurs among the cultural community of/at Franklin Skatepark. For instance, Chapter 6 explores how observation allows participants to learn footwork as well as exposes them to different possibilities for tricks and utilizing features of the park. Chapter 6 also explores how skateboarding with others in a "session" engenders a set of learning practices whereby participants give and receive pointers, provide each other with motivation, and learn how to navigate failure and injuries.

FACET 6: FORMS OF COMMUNICATION. Though much learning happens by watching and doing, language and other forms of communication are key aspects of learning in the LOPI framework. Specifically, communication in the LOPI tradition "is based on coordination among participants that builds on the shared reference available in their mutual endeavors" (Rogoff, 2014, p. 74), which involves a balance of "articulate nonverbal conversation and parsimonious verbal means" (p. 74). In other words, verbal aspects of learning and instructing are used judiciously and are mostly "nested within the shared endeavors, providing information to carry out or understand the ongoing or anticipated activity" (p. 74). For instance, among the skateboarders at Franklin Skatepark, speech is used *in time* to offer praise, a suggestion for improvement, or encouragement. In this way, "guiding and directing comments augment rather than replace firsthand learning through observation and participation" (Paradise & Rogoff, 2009, p. 120). In the opening vignette of the book, for example, Kevin talks through how to do a trick while Houston is watching Hollywood do the move; the talk is supplemental to the primary focus of watching and then doing.

Less frequently, language is used for explanatory purposes within LOPI; for instance, there are times when one skateboarder might explain to another some aspect of a trick. However, the ability—or need—to offer in-depth explanation of what one is doing is not as valued within a LOPI framework (or the skatepark), as it lacks utilitarian or pedagogical value. Mastery and progress toward mastery are important, not the ability to explain detached from context. This was evidenced time and again during interviews when the skateboarders, trying to explain to me in words about a trick, would often say, "It's hard to explain . . . watch this instead," and then get on their board and show me by *doing it*. This use of language and communication contrasts with how language (verbal and written) is often implored within assembly-line instruction, where verbal and written explanations of decontextualized activities are highly valued and often the means of assessment.

However, within LOPI, storytelling, teasing, and dramatizations often function as important means of communication to facilitate learning. These formats "that bring remembered or hypothetical scenarios to life also guide learning and development in a way that contextualizes information and ideas in the service of skilled problem-solving and appropriate action" (Rogoff, 2014, p. 74). For instance, as explored in Chapter 6, participants share stories of past injuries, in part, to help other participants understand how to handle pain and failure in culturally "appropriate" ways. Also, as discussed in Chapter 7, the linguistic practice of "heckling," which is a way participants tease each other, functions as a means whereby participants implicitly teach and learn cultural norms regarding age, race, class, and gender. Significantly, these discursive practices are often used to instruct people how to behave and are contextualized within participation.

FACET 7: ASSESSMENT. In assembly-line instruction, assessments function to "test their [students'] receipt of the instruction, separate from the learning process" and aim "to sort learners into categories of quality" (Rogoff et al., 2016, p. 373). From these forms of assessment, notions of being "behind" or "advanced" become knowable and have material effects on people's lives and experiences of learning (Anderson-Levitt, 1996; Chudacoff, 1989). Often, feedback is given to learners through extrinsic rewards, commentary on written work returned after it was submitted, and by ranking learners against other learners.

From a LOPI perspective—as implicitly demonstrated throughout the explanations of the other facets—assessment, learning, and participation occur simultaneously, often spontaneously, and are designed to support learner's "progress toward mastery." Thus, the purpose of assessment is to aid participants' transformed participation and their (potential) contributions. As Santana, in Chapter 6, notes, providing each other feedback is meant to help other skaters progress so they can then develop skills, in part, so other skaters can learn from them.

Another important aspect of assessment in LOPI—and skateboarding—is that it occurs *during* the activity. Unlike an assignment in school, for example, that a student submits and then some time thereafter receives teacher's comments on, in LOPI, feedback is available and given *as* the learning is happening, in real time. Moreover, in addition to *when* the feedback is given, *where* it is given matters—in this case, within the contextualized cultural practice where it can be useful, which connects with the first facet of LOPI, the community organization of learning.

BUILDING ON AND EXTENDING LOPI

From the broad array of sociocultural approaches to understanding learning, I selected LOPI as the guiding theoretical framework for several reasons.[1] For one, I appreciate how the framework offers a way to attend to individual participants and their face-to-face interactions as well as broader structures that inform their learning. In this way, LOPI provides a way to examine the social and communal organizational structures within a learning environment and the "means" of learning, which facilitated my paying attention to the intersections between context, practices, and underlying principles. Analytically, the facets of the framework allowed me to disaggregate aspects of learning (e.g., assessment, means) to examine them as distinct elements *and* put them in relationship with other aspects of learning and participation (e.g., motivation for learning).

Another reason I selected LOPI is its origins and connections to learning within family systems. For participants of Franklin Skatepark, kinship-type relationships and imagery proved integral to their experiences with/in the cultural community—talk of the skatepark as a "second

---

1 Throughout this project, I debated whether to use LOPI as my central framework or Lave and Wenger's (1991) seminal work on situated learning with particular attention to "communities of practice" and "legitimate peripheral participation." I have found great value in these concepts—and have implored them previously in my own work (e.g., Petrone, 2010). Moreover, in their scoping review of "action sports," Ellmer, Rynne, and Enright (2020) explain how "communities of practice" was one of the more popular theoretical frameworks used. While my thinking has been greatly informed by theirs—and I draw on some of their ideas in teasing out several specific findings, especially in Chapter 6—I decided to use LOPI, for all of the reasons I outline in this section, as well as to work against what feels like a certain type of hegemony Lave and Wenger's work seems to hold in the field.

home," the other participants as a "family," and even explicit ways notions of "big" and "little" sibling dynamics factored into participation. In this sense, LOPI offered me a way to think more deeply about some of the relationships and, more significantly, emotionality within the cultural community.

Also, because learning to skateboard is so inextricably connected to a sense of participating in local and global "cultures," I wanted a framework that explicitly attended to the cultural nature of learning and participation. Finally, explanations of LOPI often draw on explicit contrasts with the assembly-line instruction found within most schools, which aligns well with my project's aims to similarly make visible how learning in schools is structured by illuminating purposive learning for a group of people whose experiences in schools were largely non-purposive. Toward that end, in considering an education audience, I appreciate how the clarity with which the framework represents many broad ideas related to learning, particularly through the prism, might facilitate a clear and structured approach to thinking about designing learning environments.

I also note several ways my work might extend the LOPI framework.

PLACING LOPI. By situating *Dropping In* within the context of Franklin Skatepark, I draw attention to how a particular place—its physical geography, and the broader sociocultural and historical community context—factors into participation and learning within a LOPI framework. More specifically, I explore the interplay between the participants, their social and discursive practices, and the architecture of the physical place, especially in Chapter 5. In this sense, part of this work explores how space gets produced and factors into social and discursive practices, participation, and learning. By focusing on the role of place and space in this way, this research expands LOPI's conceptualizations of the facets of "community organization of learning" and "the social organization of endeavors" to account for physical geography, place, and space, particularly in relation to not only the community and social organization of learning but also other facets, including assessment and the means of learning.

"OFF-SITE" LEARNING. Whereas my central analytical focus of examining learning for this study is what physically and discursively occurs at Franklin Skatepark, I also give attention to how the participants engage in myriad learning practices outside of this physical space that inform how, what, and why they learned at Franklin Skatepark. In particular, a range of literacy practices—including, for example, viewing skate videos, editing videos of their own, reading magazines, tattooing, listening to and producing music—functioned as important means of mediation for the skateboarders' learning and participation at the park even though much of the actual textual engagement may have happened outside the park. In this way, they were importing and exporting a range of participatory practices that were constitutive with learning and participation. Similarly, their skating at other parks also shaped their understanding of, attitude toward, and use of Franklin Skatepark. I draw attention to some of these practices in Chapter 8, where I focus on literacy as an aspect of learning how to skateboard and the linkages with participation at Franklin Skatepark. In doing so, I hope to extend the ways LOPI explores the linkages between, what I refer to as "on-" and "off-"site participation and learning.

POWER, AGENCY, AND CONSTRAINT. In recent years, scholarship in the learning sciences has drawn attention to the need within sociocultural perspectives to give more attention to issues of power, oppression, and ideology. In other words, there has been a push toward more "critical" perspectives to be layered into more traditional sociocultural theories of learning (Esmonde & Booker, 2017; Lewis, Enciso, & Moje, 2007; Philip & Gupta, 2020). Specifically, Esmonde (2017) notes that "one of the enduring challenges of sociocultural analyses of learning has been to identify the relationship of broad systems of oppression (macro-level), with moment-to-moment interaction (micro-level)" (p. 23).

Though not the book's primary focus, *Dropping In* heeds this call from recent scholarship by attending to various ways learning at Franklin Skatepark is informed by broader social categories and systems of social ordering, including age, gender, class, and race. Thus, my hope is that this book expands LOPI by giving some emphasis to how participants' overlapping identities and participation in other cultural communities come into conflict with and limit or expand learning opportunities at Franklin Skatepark. For example, in Chapter 7, I explore how the linguistic practice of "heckling" reveals ideological tensions and conflicts regarding class, gender, and race that simultaneously open and constrain possibilities for learning for participants at the park. In this way, I wonder how Franklin Skatepark, as a cultural community, functions as a space whereby not only learning but also social transformation is both possible and limited.

Related, I draw on, at times, Thornton's (1996) concept of "subcultural capital" to further make sense of the distinctions among participants and how these factor into their learning. In her discussion of music club youth cultures, Thornton focuses on the ways her participants develop hierarchies within their cultural communities and make distinctions between "authentic" or "legitimate" and "inauthentic" popular cultures. Drawing on Bourdieu's (1984) ideas of social and cultural capital, as well as status, she developed the idea of "subcultural capital," which she explains as the subcultural knowledge that functions to confer particular statuses and make distinctions within youth cultural communities.

LOPI WITHIN YOUTH CULTURES. Nearly all LOPI-related research focuses on the learning of children with familial and community contexts. *Dropping In* broadens this inquiry by exploring a youth cultural context in which various aspects of structuring social life and learning differ. In doing so, this book offers a window onto how LOPI may be used as a way to understand youth learning within contexts that exist in a liminal space somewhere in between schools, communities, and families. Given the emphasis on youth, the book offers implications for youth studies scholars and secondary schooling, whereas previous research LOPI has emphasized children and child-adult relational learning within elementary schools (e.g., Rogoff, Turkanis, & Bartlett, 2001).

CHAPTER THREE

Behind the Bowl
A DISCUSSION OF RESEARCH METHODOLOGY

> As critical scholars of education and culture we also note that we often live a contradiction. In our research and writing, through our own ethnographic practice, we may valorize "popular" knowledge and values. We often serve as advocates of subordinated groups, attempting to show the logic, vitality, and dignity of their cultural worlds. We serve, in other words, as vehicles of what has come to be called a counter-hegemonic discourse. Yet we also stand at the top of dominant educational institutions. We are the products of their knowledge-making machinery. However much we may have "resisted" this machinery, we bear the handiwork of its imprint. (Levinson, Foley, & Holland, 1996, p. 23)

ALTHOUGH WRITTEN IN an authoritative style and tone, this book, like all knowledge, is constructed. Therefore, the purpose of this chapter is to explain the systems of reasoning and particular mechanisms I drew on to design and carry out this study. In this way, my aim is to let my readers in behind the curtain, or, as I refer to it for this study, "behind the bowl." Specifically, I discuss my rationale for selecting Franklin Skatepark as a research site, my choice of critical ethnography as a methodological approach, and the analytical apparatuses I developed and used to generate and analyze data. I also provide a more practical discussion of methods of data generation with particular attention to my process of gaining access to this cultural community.

To situate these aspects of my methodological approach, I first explore the politics of representation and various aspects of my positionality, including my relationships to popular culture, schooling and higher education, adulthood, dis/ability, place (rural [sub]urban), race, class, socioeconomics, gender, and masculinity, and how these, as best I know, factor into my processes of research. Drawing on Reyes's (2020) notion of an "ethnographic toolkit," which "consists of researchers' social capital and backgrounds, among other characteristics, and shapes field access, field dynamics, and data analysis" (p. 221), I offer this analysis to locate various ways I "actively and strategically" drew on, leveraged, and/or downplayed aspects of my "visible and invisible traits" to design, carry out, and write about this research. In doing so, I hope to contribute to methodological understandings of how in-depth, nuanced considerations of reflexivity can move from renderings of one or two aspects of positionality that relate to experiences in the field to "understanding the mechanisms underlying under which circumstances researchers use certain tools over others" (p. 227).

Finally, while I recognize that methodology chapters are important moments in research reports to establish trustworthiness between the researcher, researched, and reader, I hold as my main audience for this chapter novice ethnographers. For this reason, I prioritize a descriptive, detailed style of explanation (rather than over reliance on theoretical language) throughout the chapter. As a doctoral student, I loved reading methodology chapters and found concrete explorations of how to "do" ethnography particularly generative. They helped demystify the processes of ethnographic research and offered me practical strategies and considerations. I especially appreciated how these explorations—and what I hope this chapter does—raised my awareness to how everything, even the seemingly trivial, is consequential to and for the research. As Reyes (2020) explains, "As qualitative scholars, our bodies, racial/ethnic identities, gender, sexuality, appearance, backgrounds, educations, citizenship, and social networks, among others, all matter and are used to gain access and understand the field" (p. 225). In general, these explorations helped me understand and think through ethnographic work as embodied, idiosyncratic, and quite taxing physically, mentally, and emotionally.

POSITIONALITY AND THE POLITICS OF REPRESENTATION

We don't see the world as it is; we see the world as we are.
—Anaïs Nin, *Seduction of the Minotaur*

Positionality is vital because it forces us to acknowledge our own power, privilege, and biases just as we are denouncing the power structures that surround our subjects. . . . When we turn back, we are accountable for our own research paradigms, our own positions of authority, and our own moral responsibility relative to representation and interpretation. (Madison, 2012, p. 7)

This book took me many years to write and have published—even after the bulk of the initial data set was generated. My delay—my fits and starts, doubts and uncertainties, thoughts of abandoning the writing entirely—was rooted in the quandary of how to write a book about a cultural community and group of people from my vantage as an "outsider." As the person contracted with a publisher and whose name goes on the cover of this book as its "author," I wield quite a lot of power in representing the participants of Franklin Skatepark. This position—this politics of representation—is fraught with challenges and concerns, as it ought to be, particularly given the ways in which I differ from the young men portrayed in this book and operate as a visitor to their cultural community.

Moreover, given my positionality as an able-bodied, white, heteronormative, cisgender adult male who works in academia, I recognize—as best as I can—how my vantage, my training, and my "power, privilege, and biases" (Madison, 2012, p. 7) produce particular frames of reference and limitations in understanding and representing the participants of this study and Franklin Skatepark more generally. This is especially true when it comes to the racialized experiences of the participants who self-identify as Hispanic—Luis, Derrick, Santana, and Matt.

In more recent research, I have collaborated with an Indigenous community, emphasizing Native American youth development through storywork and cultural practices (Petrone, González Ybarra, & Rink, 2021; Petrone & Stanton, 2021; Petrone & Rink, with Speicher, 2020), and this work has powerfully forced me to contend with the complexities of carrying out and writing about research from the vantage of (white) outsider, including, retrospectively, this study on skateboarding. In particular, my current work has helped me understand how research carried out by cultural outsiders can do real harm as it often distorts perspectives, misuses culturally sensitive knowledge, causes or compounds trauma, and promotes deficit-based and "damage-centered" perspectives (Smith, 2012; Tuck, 2009).

Conversely, this work has also helped me understand the importance of long-term relationality as a cornerstone for ethical and responsible scholarship, reciprocity as integral to the research process, and how none of these matters if the work is not approached with a "good heart" and "clear spirit" (Smith, 2012, p. 10). Though these principles for research are discussed within the context of Indigenous-focused work and collaborations, I have come to view them as litmus tests for all research in which I engage.

In many ways, this more recent collaboration and the consequent methodological understandings have helped me navigate with more consciousness the writing of *Dropping In*. Thus, I'm grateful for the time and distance between generating data and publication of this book, as it opened new possibilities for not only me as a scholar to learn and develop but also for the book to be a more nuanced and carefully constructed text, especially as the time has afforded more opportunities to engage the participants of Franklin Skatepark in reviewing, updating, and discussing the study's findings and book production process more generally. Specifically, through the writing process, I visited with many of the focal participants to revisit their experiences, the findings, and the representation of them and the cultural community—a process that also enabled opportunities, inadvertently, to generate new data focused on retrospective perspectives, as well as a longitudinality to trace imprints of participation in the cultural community on later life outcomes, experiences, and perspectives.

Having the distance between data generation and publishing also illuminates an inevitable tension for me between carrying out a study and developing new theoretical and/or methodological understandings and insights that may trouble or complicate what it is I have already done. Here, I am reminded of first reading Django Paris's retroactive reflection on previous research he'd conducted whereby he, based on new understandings of researcher responsibility, wonders if he went far enough in his advocacy and reciprocity; he writes that having had communication with a participant from a previous research project left him with "that nagging feeling that I did not do enough with and for the youth of South Vista" (Paris & Winn, 2014, p. 127). Reading these words filled me with relief and helped me accept (at least more so) the human, dynamic, complicated, and often messy process of research and being a researcher.

In looking back on my own study at Franklin Skatepark, I can see how, at times, I adhered to and practiced—sometimes unwittingly—many of the principles I have since come to see as foundational, and how at other times, I did not do so as well or as much. Moreover, the time and distance has helped me better recognize how my own unconscious biases at the time factored into my process of designing and carrying out this study, especially regarding race, gender, and ability. All of this brings certain degrees of discomfort and uncertainty for me, and though I desire a neat and clean narrative and polished representation of myself as a researcher, what I offer is a frank and transparent discussion of the moves I made in this study. Thinking here of my intended audience of novice ethnographers, my main hope in doing so is to help humanize the research process—and perhaps provide a bit of relief, as Paris did for me.

Popular Culture, Familial Influence, and Dis/ability

When I was eight years old, I bought Bruce Springsteen's album *Nebraska* for my brother Michael's 16th birthday. At the time, I didn't realize the purchase would have enduring effects that, in some ways, led me to research Franklin Skatepark. Late in the night I gave *Nebraska* to my brother, he woke me and invited me to his room. Music I'd never heard was playing, and as I settled onto his bed, he handed me the liner notes from the album. He told me to read along as we listened to "Atlantic City," a song about a guy who, despite having a job, still had "debts that no honest man could pay," and so decided he was going to "do a little favor" for a guy he knew to make some money (Springsteen, 1982).

From this introduction to Springsteen's music, I would often sneak into my brother's room when he wasn't home and play his records, strumming my air guitar to "Rosalita," using my hockey stick as a microphone to sing "The River," or just lying on the floor, staring at the ceiling to "Johnny 99." At first, I didn't really care much about the words except to be able to sing along. Eventually, however, I paid more attention to the stories, the images, and the characters, and while it would take me years to grasp some of the deeper sociopolitical meanings of Springsteen's music (e.g., Wolff, 2018), this entry into popular culture was not merely entertainment for me even then—it politicized me long before the novels, films, and music of other great American artists such as John Steinbeck, Richard Wright, Spike Lee, Michael Gold, Leslie Marmon Silko, Alice Walker, Bernard Malamud, Public Enemy, and Woody Guthrie later would. More significant than anything, though, Springsteen's music—and the host of other literacy practices his music gave way to or "sponsored" (Brandt, 1998)—connected me to other people, most notably my brother, and their stories as vehicles of learning about the world. Springsteen's music became a space I would return to time and time again to make sense of the external and internal experiences of my own life, especially as they involved issues of masculinity and class.

I mostly grew up in a suburb of Long Island, just outside New York City, after my parents packed up my four siblings and me into our jalopy of a station wagon and left behind the only spot in the United States—Brooklyn—they, or their parents and grandparents who had first traveled there from Italy, had known. Our departure from Brooklyn was brought on by the need to find housing enough for the seven of us, the youngest being just two weeks old, that we could afford. A short time before our move, my father had been diagnosed with a neurological disorder that prevented him from ever working again after leaving the doctor's office that day, diagnosis in hand.

From that moment forth, my childhood and adolescent years bore the imprint of my father disintegrating before my young eyes. I watched his disease strip him of his ability to walk, then talk, and, eventually, use his body at all beyond a head movement and blinking eyes. By the time I was gearing up to go to college, my dad was being taken, as an early 50-something-year-old, to a nursing home against his will. It wasn't until years later, when I heard Springsteen's homage to his own dad, "Walk like a Man," that I first found my tears of sorrow for my dad's plight: "Well I was young and I didn't know what to do / When I saw your best steps stolen away from you" (Springsteen, 1987).

From the onset, my father's disease and lost ability to work quickly catapulted my family into the world of food stamps, social security checks, and all of us having to find work as children to pay our way for clothes, school-related activities like sports, and just about anything else we wanted. On Long Island, my father's wobbly body became our caretaker at home, something that was not without its many hardships for all involved, so my mom could go to college to become a middle school special education teacher to support our brood.

These particular circumstances and the relationships and experiences emergent from them configured a constellation of ways of thinking, feeling, seeing, and being that are elemental to how I move about the world to this day—personally and professionally. In particular, these experiences immersed me in notions of dis/ability, masculinity, and class long before I had the theoretical training to name them as such. Normative ideas around able-bodiedness, for instance, came into sharp relief for me through the embarrassment I felt and the stares from others that accompanied me when I pushed my dad in his wheelchair along a sidewalk in our hometown. Ideas of middle-class normativity became visible for me, too, when, for years, I would cover my mouth when I laughed to hide the half of a front tooth I had after an injury that couldn't get fixed because we couldn't afford it. And normative ideas related to masculinity revealed themselves anemic as I helped my dad's struggling body cook in the kitchen while waiting to watch my mother shoulder her book bag from her car after breadwinning all day for the family. As a child and adolescent, I learned fastidiously about critiques regarding dis/ability, class politics, and gender norms, and this set of experiences became the taproot not only for my interest in songs, films, and books, as I knew, in story, there was a space for emotionality, connection, and humanity, but also for my "critical" orientation toward the world—one that recognized politics of representation, conflicting ideologies, and power dynamics between what was understood as "normal" and what was just your real life.

Growing up in a house where we didn't talk about any of this, I turned to Springsteen's music, and eventually to certain films, other music, and books to try and make sense of the dissonance between my experiences and what I was coming to understand through school, certain media, and other people how things were "supposed" to be. Together, this engagement with popular culture facilitated a space unlike any other for pleasure, escape, connection, intellectual engagement, sociopolitical critique and action, psycho-spiritual development, learning how to "walk like a man," and fostering a creative outlet in more meaningful ways than formal school ever did. In this way, like Springsteen sings, "I learned more from a three-minute record than I ever learned in school" (Springsteen, 1984).

And it was this engagement with these cultural and literacy practices that set me on a course—intellectually, politically, emotionally, and spiritually—that I am still traveling, first in my decision to become a high school English teacher, and now as an educational and youth studies researcher writing this book to understand how and why the cultural community of Franklin Skatepark means as much as it does for a group of "failing" young men—and likely, trying to learn a bit more about myself, past and present, in the process.

I offer this introduction to establish that for me, popular cultures—whether it be through media consumption or face-to-face interactions—have never been frivolous sites of fleeting adolescent pleasure but rather significant spaces of meaning making, identity formation, and connection. And so I entered this research project with this bias, and in many regards, it is this bias that initially drove this entire project, as, in the end, so much of ethnography is, in some way, a way of coming to know oneself, sometimes even more than the so-called other.

More, though, than this bias, my engagement with pop culture was my initial point of connection to the participants of this study. Though skateboarding wasn't my particular thing, I shared with these participants the deep connections to popular cultural practices that cohere around making sense of one's place in the world. And as a researcher, I strategically drew on this facet of my positionality and my experiences to build relationships and trust with the participants. In many respects, it was the closest I could come to being an "insider" to this group, and I leveraged it for access and data generation. Thus, discussions with participants often included references to and sharing of music, films, TV shows, concerts, documentaries, and books that extended well beyond skateboarding culture.

Working-Class Politics, Formal Schooling, and Being an Academic
In addition to engagement with pop culture being a point of convergence, so, too, was class. I grew up with a working-class sense of myself and my family, in large part, due to the aforementioned socioeconomic circumstances. Money was tight, and my family relied on social services throughout my childhood and youth. For this reason, I could relate to the participants of this study and their economic situations and their need to get jobs early in their lives to pay for necessities (in the case of Derrick's case, rent money for a place to live), which is much different from their middle-class and more affluent counterparts, who may have worked to acquire stuff they wanted but didn't necessarily need for sustenance, or to help support their households. The participants' ideas for careers and future lives were familiar to me, too, as I had not only put myself through school doing manual, hourly waged labor but was also meant to partner with my brother in a business rooted in laboring for rich folks all over

Long Island—building and then servicing swimming pools in their back-yards and pouring concrete patios to make spaces of entertainment for them and leisure for other wealthy people.

Here, though, was a stark point of divergence between me and the participants, and, in many respects, between me and my brother, who always supported but never truly understood my desire to not only go to college to be a teacher but also eventually to go on for a Ph.D. to be a professor. The fact that those decisions cohere around reading novels, writing articles, and teaching other people to do the same only furthered the chasm between my brother and me and between me and the guys of Franklin Skatepark. "Why you wanna read all those damn books, Rob-ert?" was a popular refrain I heard when I first told my brother I was leav-ing Long Island to go to college to study English and become a teacher, then later when I left the high school classroom to get a master's degree in literature, and then again when I moved on to a doctoral program in literacy education. In fact, he and my cousin Thomas, even still, usually refer to me as "college boy."

I was a schooler and eventually read my way up and out of my working-class roots to the middle-class trappings of the professorial life, even before I actually had one. Going to college and then on to pursuing graduate degrees and working at universities amid Ph.D.s changed me. It changed not only how I came to think about my future life but also about my past life and my family. I heard myself slough off my New York accent; I started wearing clothes I knew would get me made fun of by my friends from home; and I started writing things I knew my family would never read or understand if they did. And so, as I observed and interacted with the skateboarders in this study, I could recognize their working-class ethos and aspirations but I couldn't *feel* them that much anymore, much in the same way I can't when I am with my brother, who, now at the age our dad was when we put him away, is still laboring in rich folks' backyards on Long Island.

For all intents and purposes, as a high school student, and later as a teacher, I bought into the achievement ideology and rewards of formal schooling. Growing up, despite the economic circumstances of my fam-ily, it never crossed my mind that I wouldn't go to college right out of high school. I was good at school and reaped the rewards of it. And so, when I began teaching and meeting students for whom college, the achievement ideology, or the rewards of the corporate structure of schooling (Eckert, 1989) did not make sense, I had difficulties working with them in ways that honored where and who they were. I built solid relationships with my students, and we laughed and learned a lot, but I wasn't really helping them in the ways they wanted and needed. And in some sense, I see the exigency for this entire study stemming from those earliest experiences I had as an educator.

Through this research, I grew in my own understanding of schooling and the ways the mechanisms of social reproduction and hegemony, including racism and classism, operate to reify the distance the participants of this study felt to school. Though I had been primed by my formative experiences for a critical orientation toward many aspects of social structures in the United States, I had significant unconscious biases when it came to schooling. In this way, the young men highlighted throughout this book have been some of my greatest teachers, as they helped facilitate my own critical consciousness regarding schooling. Whereas I entered this research project intent on understanding how these participants' cultural practices might engender strategic connections for teachers to make between their "funds of knowledge" (Moll et al., 1992), I exited the project critiquing the very foundations of schooling that marginalize these and many other young people—especially as they linked with the aims, means, and organization of learning.

I highlight my positionality as both a former teacher and an academic for several reasons. For one, it seems rare in educational research for scholars to hover on their roles as academics and their affiliations with institutions of higher education. Too often it seems that this facet of positionality is rendered invisible and normative, which is problematic, especially given how detrimental university-based research has been for various groups of people, especially minoritized youth and communities (Paris & Winn, 2014).

In my research at Franklin Skatepark, academia was definitely neither the norm nor the aspiration, as my participants didn't care much at all about higher education in the ways I did, and in many regards, this aspect of my positionality had potential to be a hindrance, as it marked me as not only an outsider but also linked with an establishment from which the participants felt alienated. For this reason, I often downplayed my role as an academic, never wore clothing attached to any institution of higher education, and didn't mention my past role as a high school English teacher unless asked about it. I attempted to distance myself, at least in the eyes of the guys, from formal schooling, though, of course, they knew through my initial explanation of the project and me, and the institutional review board (IRB) forms they signed, that I was affiliated with a university.

Interestingly, when interfacing with city officials, parents, and others involved in this research but less directly with the skatepark, this aspect of my ethnographic toolkit was one of the *first* I made visible to help establish authority and access. This was a hard lesson learned, when one day, hanging out at the park and first meeting Santana and explaining my project and the need for IRB consent and parental permission, his mother drove into the parking lot. He invited me to meet her, and before I could barely get past my explanation of the project, she stared me in the eyes and said with force, "I don't know you. How do I know what you're telling me is legitimate? How do I know you're not a pedophile?" From that entry, the two of us had a lengthy conversation, ending with me sharing the consent forms and the contact information for the institution's IRB chair, and her demanding concrete reciprocity from me in the form of tutoring her son.

From that experience, I always made sure to carry my university identification and be available (including giving my cell number out) to parents through all facets of the study. This particular mom ended up becoming an important participant in the study, as she offered a much-valued parent perspective, as well as inviting me to various family events, including birthday parties and church services; she also read and provided feedback on this book.

Age, Adultism, and Place

Entering this research site as a former teacher with the aim of writing for other people in education also proved to be one of the most generative aspects of my positionality in terms of data generation and analysis. Specifically, because I entered the site with many preconceived ideas about youth, learning, and teaching from my own preparation as an educator, I was filled with "surprises" at nearly every turn. Finders (1998/1999) explains how "surprises" for researchers or observers are useful, as they help reveal one's implicit assumptions about the phenomenon they are examining. For instance, on first entering the park, I was surprised at the ways participants of many different ages shared the same space and engaged each other. As someone entering the park with experiences of schools, I was accustomed to learning environments being segregated by age. Over time, the age heterogeneity at the skatepark proved not only a significant component of the learning environment but also became one of the most fascinating areas of inquiry for me. In this way, my surprise opened up a way to understand myself, how my prior experiences filtered my observing, and the skatepark. Over time, I came to rely on these moments of surprise to focus my attention, observation, and inquiry.

Though I highlight the role of surprises pertinent to the organization of learning within schools and the skatepark, my surprises and reliance on them was not limited to these. For example, I found myself surprised in many instances in which teenage boys were behaving "well." I had been socialized into understanding adolescence/ts through the psychological developmentalist paradigms that dominate education and often position young people as deficit, deficient, inherently disabled, rebellious, and desiring distance from adults (Elman, 2014; Lesko, 2012; Petrone & Lewis, 2012), and so I found myself operating from a particular brand of *adultism* that eventually cracked open as the construct it is after my "surprises" of observing patterns of competency, care of others, and connections with adults mounted throughout data generation and analysis.

One area in which I had to fight against my own prejudices was related to *place*, particularly regarding rurality. Growing up in and around New York City, I very much operated, prior to this research and other research in rural communities (Petrone & Wynhoff Olsen, 2021), from a *metrocentrism* that located urban places and viewpoints as normative and rural as "other." When discussing this aspect of my positionality at talks and conferences, I often reference the book *When Brooklyn Was the World, 1920–1957* and the Jay-Z song "Empire State of Mind," explaining how the titles of these texts capture the metrocentric sensibility many New Yorkers I know carry: that the rest of the world revolves around, as we say, "the city."

Unlike my social location as an educator, though, I openly utilized my New Yorkness to my advantage throughout the research process. Specifically, I used it to help orient myself to the rural community (Finley) and the guys' lives from a place of curiosity, which was authentic, by explaining how different things were in New York and then asking them to help me understand how things in Finley and their lives worked. I also found the participants were largely curious about New York. Like many people without excess financial resources, these guys did not travel much beyond the state's borders, and so they were piqued by my New York connection and posed questions based on things they'd seen in movies, heard in songs, or read about in books regarding their favorite musicians, graffiti artists, or skateboarders. This back-and-forth exchange both enabled me to develop understandings of their perspectives on their community and identities as "rural," as well as build rapport, often through banter and the occasional debate over the best pizza in town—something I assured them was a waste of time as there was no truly good pizza anywhere outside of New York!

Masculinity and Race

Remaining aspects of my positionality essential to explore are *race*, *sexuality*, and *gender*, particularly related to notions of *masculinity*. As a heteronormative, cisgender man, I operate from myriad unconscious biases when it comes to gender and sexuality. As a younger person growing up in the 1980s and 1990s, particularly through organized athletics, I was socialized into dominant norms of masculinity of the time, which consisted of various forms of what today would be referred to as "toxic masculinity." Specifically, I spent time in locker rooms and among male peer groups and knew how the free-flowing and rampant language of aggression, misogyny, dominance, and homophobia could permeate those spaces.

Alongside this broader socialization, I grew up in a female-dominated home, where, as previously mentioned, my mom was the primary breadwinner and my father a stay-at-home parent. I am also graced with three sisters who powerfully shaped my gender consciousness from an early age to recognize patriarchal oppression and women's capacities and rights to engage the world and have control of their bodies in all of the ways I want and feel entitled to as a man. In the end, my heteronormative, cisgender identity undoubtedly facilitated my access to the core participants, all of whom identified similarly, and, at times, I drew on these facets of my ethnographic toolkit to "relate to" the participants, though so much of this was unconscious for me at the time.

Given my explicit initial research interests on masculinity and class emergent from my background, issues of race were not paramount for me or even readily accessible to me when I began this research. In fact, I recognize that my own whiteness and the ways in which white suprem- acy was operating in me rendered issues of race marginal at first. The process of engaging this research (and the ways in which the participants and the data compelled) brought race more directly into the study and facilitated my own shifting awarenesses and understandings of race, racism, and white supremacy—how these operated both within social structures and in myself. Over time, issues of race, particularly through language use, as discussed in Chapter 7, became an area of inquiry for this project, particularly under the broader interest in understanding how this cultural community functioned as a site of opening up *and* constraining opportunities for participation and social transformation. This issue is particularly significant given how, as I mentioned in the first chapter, there was a disproportionately high representation of Latino young men at Franklin Skatepark in relation to the community writ large.

Moreover, in retrospect, I can see how my being white most certainly facilitated my entry and access into the cultural community, though I was mostly unaware of that and of how it was happening. During the study, I was cognizant, though, of how I navigated talking about race and rac- ism differently with Latino and white participants, especially early in the research process. With white participants I felt much freer to ask them questions about their uses and understandings of racialized language, whereas with the Latino participants, I stepped much more cautiously due to my concern of triggering harmful or traumatic experiences, par- ticularly given my lack of experience and awareness. Over time, as rela- tionships developed, talk of race with Latino participants increased, often initiated by them or in relation to some of their literacy practices (e.g., tattoos). Interestingly, the relationships I developed with the Latino par- ticipants have proved, over time, to be the most in-depth and sustained across all the participants.

In thinking across my relationships with race, dis/ability, class, place, age, affiliation with schooling and higher education, sexuality, and gen- der, my aim in this section is to move beyond the typical approach of locating one or two facets of research positionality and instead to explain how and why I "actively and strategically" drew on and utilized or did not utilize particular aspects of my "ethnographic toolkit" for this research project, which, as Reyes (2020) says, "highlights how these traits shape the ways we view the world and the ways in which the world views us" (p. 225). In doing so, I also hope to highlight the various ways my own intersectionality reveals my own "power, privilege, and biases" (Madison, 2012, p. 7), affords and limits my understandings of the lives and learning practices of the diehard locals of Franklin Skatepark, and informs the design and processes of data collection, analysis, and representation— aspects I explore next.

CRITICAL ETHNOGRAPHY AS AN APPROACH
TO RESEARCHING FRANKLIN SKATEPARK

To develop a deep understanding of how Franklin Skatepark functioned as a cultural community and context for learning, I utilized ethnography as a research methodology. An ethnographic approach enabled me to develop understandings of Franklin Skatepark's web of relationships, including interpersonal dynamics, roles and statuses of participants, and the historical formation of the park and its role in the community writ large. In addition, because LOPI requires the ongoing presence of all facets of the framework rather than just the occasional occurrence of some of them, a long-term investigation allowed me to understand how the various features of learning functioned as a whole.

While grounded in ethnography's use of data generation through long-term participant-observations, in-depth interviews, and document and artifact analysis, this study was guided by a "critical" approach to educational research (Carspecken, 1996; Morrell, 2008)—one that purposefully aims to locate sites and sources of knowledge from places and people not normally legitimized as such. More specifically, a critical orientation moves from a stance of "ventriloquism," in which the ethnographer is simply trying to "transmit" information, toward a stance of "activism," "in which the ethnographer takes a clear position in intervening on hegemonic practices and serves as an advocate in exposing the material effects of marginalized locations while offering alternatives" (Madison, 2012, p. 6). (See Fine, 1994, for a more thorough explanation of these different stances in ethnography.)

In addition, a critical ethnographic approach seeks to understand, along with cultural norms, power relations occurring within the research site and among participants. This emphasis is particularly important given the call within sociocultural scholarship for increased attention to the various ways macro-level systems of representation and oppression inform learning within particular contexts (Esmonde & Booker, 2017; Philip & Gupta, 2020). A critical ethnographic approach also promotes attention to power dynamics between researcher and researched, including emphasis on transparency of how the researcher's own various positionalities function as discursive filters for and during the research process to help work against extractive research practices and toward reciprocity and respect.

For these reasons, this project was guided by "relational" (San Pedro & Kinloch, 2017) and "humanizing" (Paris & Winn, 2014) methodological perspectives—both of which emphasize "the building of relationships of care and dignity and dialogic consciousness raising for both researchers and participants" (p. vxi). Moreover, these research approaches align well with methodological considerations raised within Critical Youth Studies that emphasize the need for "radical reflexivity" (Best, 2007) on adultist lenses, representation, dialogue, power, and "radical love" (Ibrahim & Steinberg, 2014). To address these concepts, this study focuses on a small number of participants, a long-term investment of time and resources to establish and sustain relationships, emphasis on participants' stories and perspectives, and an overall goal of contributing to the cultural community and lives of the participants. In this way, the cornerstone of this research was cultivating "relationships of dignity, care, and respect" that engender participants "'feeling valued' by a 'worthy witness'" (Paris & Winn, 2014, p. xvi).

This relational ethos is perhaps most clearly exemplified in this project through the participants' responses to being in communication more recently, years after the initial research. Specifically, during the development of this book, I reached out to the participants to let them know I'd received a contract for the book and wanted to revisit the project with them. Frankly, I was taken aback by their responses of excitement, gratitude, and willingness. One participant, who had moved away from the community, expressed an eagerness to fly back to visit face to face with me, and another participant messaged the following to me in response to my inquiry in reconnecting: "That's wonderful news [about the contract], btw! Aside from the Dogtown and Z Boys documentary, I don't think anyone else has really given a shit about some small-town skateboarders, let alone kept in touch over the years. It means a lot."

SELECTING FRANKLIN SKATEPARK AS A RESEARCH SITE

Prior to researching Franklin Skatepark, I conducted an 18-month collaborative research project with a teacher at Finley's high school. During that project, I carried out extensive research in the community, including examining official city documents, interviewing community members and city officials, and participating in various community activities (e.g., city meetings, police ride-along). This research provided me with a deep sense of the community that would later enable me to contextualize Franklin Skatepark and the skateboarders within the broader social, cultural, economic, and political dimensions of Finley.

Shortly after this research, I taught a university student, Sandra, who, for a project in my class, spent time at Franklin Skatepark and interviewed a few of the skaters. Sandra lived in Finley, and her husband, Crazy K, was a long-time skateboarder and a frequent participant at the skatepark. Knowing I wanted to study a group of "failing" young men in an out-of-school context, having previously researched the community of Finley, and discussing the idea with Sandra and Crazy K, both of whom were excited about the prospect, I decided to study Franklin Skatepark.

As much as I'd like to say I selected skateboarding because of its rich cultural practices, countercultural attitude, and aesthetic sensibilities (all of which I came to quite admire through this research), the reality—though I feel somewhat sheepish admitting this—is that my decision to study skateboarding was motivated more by convenience and availability— that is, having familiarity with a community, having at least two people who would grant me access and introduce me to others, knowing many of the participants at the park were young men labeled "at-risk," and so on. At that time, I had a neutral to a somewhat negative attitude toward skateboarders, and I had very few, if any, expectations going into the work. That skateboarding is such an intense activity to watch, do, and study— and that this particular park proved to be so rich in cultural practice and personalities—was more luck than my purposeful strategizing.

It turns out that, methodologically, Franklin Skatepark was an ideal site because the nature of the park is such that spectators, and even people taking photographs and shooting video, are an acceptable and expected part of the culture. This feature allowed me to conduct observations with less chance of standing out as peculiar or intrusive. Related, because of the age heterogeneity of the participants at the park (including several who were my age or older), my adult status was not entirely anomalous. Theoretically, Franklin Skatepark provided an opportunity to observe a youth-dominated learning environment that was not overtly supervised or controlled by adults, coaches, or by an institution such as a school (though, of course, there were ways in which the town government, and at times, police and/or parents/adults, inserted themselves into the governance of the park).

Also, since most of the research on skateboarding has focused on urban and suburban spaces and participants, especially middle-class white youth, I selected Franklin Skatepark because of its geopolitical location as "rural" and because the vast majority of its local participants identify as working-class and racially as a combination of Latino and white. These factors enabled me to more closely examine how class, place, and race, in addition to gender, inform processes of learning within a cultural community. Related, likely due to its rural context, Franklin Skatepark had a smaller number of participants who regularly frequented the park than other parks I had visited in urban and suburban areas. This stability of regulars enabled me to build deeper relationships with participants over time, which aligned with my ethnographic, relational, and humanizing approach.

In addition to providing theoretical and methodological connections and rationale for my decision for site selection, I note these particularities of Franklin Skatepark and its participants to draw attention to the distinctiveness of this park and group of skateboarders. My aim with this research is not to claim generalizability to other skateparks or skateboarders, though there will likely be many points of similarity with other parks, but rather to understand how learning and participation occur at this particular park, and the factors that inform that learning.

ENTERING FRANKLIN SKATEPARK AND GAINING
ACCESS TO ITS DIEHARD LOCALS

Selecting Franklin Skatepark as a research site in no way meant it was actually going to be the site for my study. I still had to gain access to the site to carry out the research, which, particularly as a non-skateboarder and a schooler, was no easy feat. Prior to this study, I had only ever involved people under the age of 18 in research through their engagement in schools and roles as "students." In such research, I was introduced by school personnel (e.g., teachers, administrators) and was buoyed by the infrastructure of schools wherein being a former teacher interested in students' experiences was not a particularly peculiar phenomenon. In contrast, being a middle-aged non-skateboarder who doesn't really look all that "alternative" and rocking up to a skatepark to ask youth about their experiences didn't exactly have much of a precedent.

From the start, I presented myself as someone interested in learning about how learning happens at the park and was hoping to turn my research into a book. Eventually, I became known as the guy writing a book about the skatepark, or as one participant said, "They know your name is Rob, and they know you're trying to write a book. So they respect that because you're doing something, you're not sitting here causing problems. If no one wants to cooperate with you, you pretty much say that's fine. You're not ragging on people, so people respect that."

Over time, I earned a spot in the community unlike anyone else—I was not a skateboarder, parent, or friend. I became an interested observer who mainly participated in the non-skating aspects of the community. (During the third season of data collection, I did start skateboarding. I had purchased, with the help of two participants, a board, and eventually began skating during my visits. This portion of my research proved invaluable as it gave me intimate access to the experiences of newcomers.) I did not become friends with the participants though I became friendly with them. I never attempted to or desired to be one of them, nor did they wholly adopt me as one of their own. More than anything, I functioned as a listener to their stories, someone who sought to understand what they did, and how and why they did what they did. Over time, many of them expressed surprise and appreciation for my sustained interest, which is not to say the participants may not have had ulterior motives in working with me; they very well may have—whether it be the promise of being written about, getting rides, or some special recognition within their local cultural community.

Cultivating the relationships, access, and status I did within this cultural community took a long time, constantly changed and got renegotiated, and relied on some good old-fashioned luck. As mentioned, when I entered this research site, I did so with the intention of wanting to study it and write about it, not to become a skateboarder. For this reason, I approached the site slowly and cautiously. At first, I visited the park for short amounts of time, did not initiate eye contact or communication with anyone, and did not take any notes while within visibility of participants. Because the nature of the skateboard park is such that spectators, and even people taking photographs and shooting video, are a more or less normal part of the community, I was able to do this observation without much notice or disruption to the typical ongoing activities.

During this phase of my research, and really through the first two seasons of data generation, I wore nondescript clothing that marked me as an outsider to the community but not "too much" of an outsider, with the exception being my footwear—a pair of Chaco sandals. Specifically, I wore worn blue jeans or worn shorts, plain white or colored T-shirts, and sometimes button-down plaid flannel shirts. I never wore clothing that displayed name brands, attire that affiliated me with a sports team or university, or the clothes I would wear to teach at the university. Also, I always wore my clothing "messy"—my shirts untucked, for example, and I kept my hair as unkempt as possible.

In addition to these clothing choices, as I began to interact with participants, always at first in response to their initiation, I tried to maintain a sense of neutrality and non-judgment. For example, it felt imperative I not comment or convey judgment about their smoking cigarettes, swearing, talk about each other, sex, drugs, and drinking, or their homophobic language. I wanted them to feel free in front of me to talk about and do what they would do if I was not there, and I took it as a good sign in terms of access when they would spark cigarettes in front of me and talk about their drinking and other activities. This is not to say this was easy or without ethical dilemma for me, especially as someone who, as a younger person, struggled with alcohol and tobacco consumption. In some instances, participants tested me by explicitly asking me if I would call the cops if they lit up a cigarette (to which I said, "No") or implicitly discerning my interest in purchasing them alcoholic beverages. Over time, I established a boundary that it was okay for them to talk with and around me (in fact, I would ask them about these things and share my own past experiences) about these types of activities but that I would not join in them.

Along with this more or less neutral ethos, I attempted to convey a genuine sense of interest and curiosity in the particulars of the participants' lives, especially related to their skateboarding practices. Given that I was genuinely interested, this was not difficult, though I did need to constrain myself, particularly early on, from asking *too many* questions. In fact, at first, I did not ask many questions at all and answered their questions honestly and straightforwardly.

For several of my earliest visits, no one acknowledged me, but soon thereafter, several participants, particularly younger, less experienced skateboarders inquired into my presence, asking questions such as "Who are you?" and "What are you doing here?" Over time, as who I was and what I was doing circulated among the participants (which did not really take hold until toward the end of my first season and beginning of my second season of data generation), inquiries such as "How's the book coming?" increased for a while. My entry into the park during this time was often disrupted quickly by a younger participant coming up to me and asking about the book, if I had a title yet, and how many chapters it was going to be. They would sometimes stand by me for some time, offering advice on who I should talk to or what I should write about. Eventually, these inquiries abated, and there came a point in the middle of my second summer of data generation where my entry into the park was a normalized occurrence in which I could walk in, say hi to people I knew and who knew me, sit down, and just hang out.

In addition to these deliberate moves I made as a researcher negotiating site entry, several other factors, including preexisting relationships and a sense of "right time, right place," made the access I eventually got possible. To start, Sandra and Crazy K proved to be invaluable points of contact for me, especially in helping to establish contacts with participants of the park. Specifically, at the annual skate contest during my first summer of data generation (discussed in the next chapter), Sandra and Crazy K introduced me to several participants who, although I would have to put in the legwork to build rapport, recognized and associated me with

Crazy K, who was held in high regard at the park. In this way, I had some street cred with prospective participants, and to some, I became known, at first, as "Crazy K's friend." In fact, I would use this to my advantage during my early contacts with participants, saying things like, "Hey, I'm friends with Crazy K" or "I remember when Crazy K introduced us."

Perhaps the greatest single factor in my access, though, had to do with TS. During my previous research at Finley High School, TS was a student in one of the classes I researched; he was taking a 10th grade English class for the second time and barely passing it. During that semester, TS got his first tattoo, and shortly thereafter the local free newspaper in the town where I lived had a cover story on tattoos. Seeing it, I thought of TS and decided to bring it to him the next day. I did so, and he and I developed rapport—not a particularly deep or intense one—but one that had not been there prior to me giving him that article. It turns out, and I did not know this prior to starting my research, that TS was an avid skateboarder, and, in fact, one of the key people behind the development of Franklin Skatepark, as well as one its most respected participants.

On one of my early visits, I noticed TS skating, and after some time, he noticed me. In fact, it was one of the most nerve-wracking experiences I had during my early visits. He had just stopped skating and stood about eight feet from where I was at the picnic table; he looked at me, did a double take, pointed his finger at me, and then smiling and shaking his finger, said, "You look familiar." He paused and then said, "Teacher!"

I smiled weakly, terrified that I would be forever associated with being a teacher in the eyes of the skateboarders, and I muttered, "No, no, not a teacher. I know you from Ms. Cassidy's class. I'm a researcher."

"Yeah, that's right," he said, "I knew you looked familiar."

Over time, TS became one of my key informants and most helpful guides, as well as providing me access to many other participants. It seemed all I had to do once I had TS's approval was mention I knew him and others would agree to help.

It turns out that the reason TS was so willing to help me was because of the article on tattooing I had given him. In one of my final interviews with TS, I asked him why he was willing to help me. He said, "Like when you were in Ms. Cassidy's class you were always helping me out with stuff, so it's like, I don't know . . . You showed me that kind of solid stuff. Like, I'd be a dickhead to just be like, 'No' [I'm not going to help you out]."

AN ANALYTICAL APPROACH TO MAKE SOME SENSE OF FRANKLIN SKATEPARK

Given LOPI's theorization of learning as a process of transformed partic-ipation, I developed the analytic of *participatory events*, which are those instances when participants partake in the activities of the park. This analytic focused my attention for data generation and analysis on the activities, social arrangements, and forms of participation developed and practiced by the participants. For instance, over time, I came to under-stand that there were "non-skating" and "skating" activities participants took part in that were integral to both learning and the cultural life of Franklin Skatepark (e.g., hanging out at one of the picnic tables within the skatepark, skating alone, skating within a small group). (Chapter 5 discusses these forms of participation.)

For each participatory event, I noted the following (modified from Hymes's idea of "speech events," 1972): purpose (goals and outcomes of participatory event); setting (time and place); participants (e.g., age, class, race, gender); mood (or "key," the tone, manner, spirit of the event); norms of interpretation (belief system of the community of the event); and norms of interaction (rules governing the event). By noting these aspects of participatory events, I was able to chart particular prac-tices and patterns across these different structures of participation. For example, as I looked at sessions as a form of participation, I located the various ways skaters interacted with one another, including the following eventual codes: "soliciting assistance," "giving unsolicited assistance," "teasing someone about their clothing," " discussion of costs of boards and clothes," " slapping board on ground while watching others skating," and "saying 'you're gay' when someone lands a trick." Once I compiled a list of hundreds of these codes, I linked them together under broader headings. For example, two of the headings that emerged in relation to these open codes discussed above were "teasing" and "giving feedback." As I developed this list of codes, I reread the data to develop connections among these smaller notes, start to notice potential linkages across broader codes, and generate interview questions that would help me ascertain participants' perspectives on these issues.

Because of my interest, too, in literacy and the roles of texts in meditating participants' experiences of/at Franklin Skatepark and broader contexts, I also utilized the analytic of *literacy event*, which, for this study, is a specialized type of participatory event that specifically involves texts and textual activity (e.g., reading magazines, tagging, shooting videos). Building on the seminal work of Heath (1982, 1983), Morrell (2004b) defines a literacy event as "a communicative act in which any text is integral to the nature of the participants' interactions and interpretive processes" (p. 11). For this study, I focused on instances in which participants accessed, consumed, evaluated, produced, and/or distributed texts as part of their participation within Franklin Skatepark (even if the textual activity did not physically occur at the park) and related cultural communities (e.g., tattooing, graffiti artistry). Due to its emphasis on the contextual features of literacy activities, this analytic enabled me to gain an understanding of how, when, and for what purposes participants engage in literacy activities, what meaning these activities have for the participants, what roles literacy plays in that context, and how those literacy events represent, reflect, and/or shape the participants and their social and cultural context. In particular, I focused on how textual activity functioned as part of learning how to skateboard and be a skateboarder at Franklin Skatepark. (See Chapter 8 for more on literacy.)

DATA SOURCES AND PROCEDURES FOR DATA GENERATION

Participant Observations and Field Notes

During my early participant observations in the first summer, I focused on "casting the net wide" and getting as broad a sense as possible as to the happenings of the skatepark. During this time, I attempted to suspend all judgment and not take anything happening for granted. For example, these early notes contain information on the physical description of the park and the participants, including hairstyles, clothing, and equipment. These notes also focused on how they used the park, including how and where they arranged themselves physically within the space. For these early observations, I relied on the newness of the environment to document those activities that would soon become "invisible" to me as my familiarity with the park and cultural community developed.

A difficulty I had during this phase of my data generation was describing the skating activity that I observed. Other than basic terms such as "ollie," "bowl," and "quarter pipes," I had no schema or lexicon to describe skating activities. Over time, as my knowledge of skateboarding increased and my relationships with the skateboarders developed to the point where it was normalized for me to ask them about different tricks, I was able to write about what I was seeing using their language. Related, I often used my ignorance to build rapport with participants by asking them to explain things since I wasn't a skateboarder.

As my research progressed, my field visits and data generation procedures became more focused. Once I had a sense of the general organization of the park, I focused my observations on particular elements to generate a more robust data set. For example, as I came to understand that one of the ways skaters participate is by skating alone, I focused several observations on individuals skating alone.

For the first few visits, I spent only about 20 minutes observing before I would leave to make my jottings and write field notes. On several occasions, especially during these early visits, I would leave the parking lot to get something to eat or write out my field notes and then return to the park for more observation. This was helpful for me to gain a sense of the relationship between time of day and activity level, who spent time at the park during which times, and how long people typically spent at the park. Once I became more familiar with the users of the park and they me, I was more visible with my jottings in the park, and I became more mobile in the park, physically positioning myself wherever would enable me to best capture what I was observing.

I always carried out fieldwork when I knew I would have adequate time to write field notes immediately after my visit, as I wanted to be as fresh as possible in recalling what had happened. I typically blocked out about an hour for every 20 minutes of observation. Concretely, after leaving the park, I would drive two blocks away to a dead-end street, and sitting in the driver's seat, I would type field notes on a laptop. On those occasions when my laptop battery drained before completing my field notes, I audio recorded my reflections during my drive home (approximately 30 minutes) or went to a coffee shop, where I could continue to write. The day after writing field notes, I would reread them, edit them, and then generate an analytic memo as appropriate.

Interviews

While participant observations and consequent field notes served as the foundation of my study, especially during the first summer of data generation, formal and informal interviews were essential, especially in the subsequent summers. By the second summer, as I became a known entity at the park, interviewing began in earnest. I conducted formal interviews with 16 of the participants of Franklin skatepark (several of whom I interviewed formally on more than one occasion), a parent of one of these skateboarders, a teacher of two of the skaters, two city officials who had a part in establishing the park, and several other non-focal participants, including a professional skateboarder, industry-related people, and skateboarders from other communities. All formal interviews were audio recorded and transcribed. Informal interviews were not typically audio recorded, as the spontaneous nature of these conversations made it difficult, if not impossible, though there were instances when it was possible. When I could not record the conversation, I would recount the conversation in my notebook as soon as possible, and, when available, I'd check for accuracy, qualification, and/or expansion with the participant.

In most instances, I conducted interviews at the skatepark, at one of the picnic tables, in other areas of the park (e.g., ledges, grassy areas), or outside of the gated area of the park at an outlying picnic table or standing near or sitting on cars. Sometimes interviews moved as the conversation did. For example, during one interview, the interviewee began talking about his music endeavors and asked if I wanted to hear some of his songs, so our interview moved from a picnic table to his car to later sitting on the trunk while he played guitar. In other interviews, participants would leave the table and skate a section of the park to demonstrate what they were explaining to me.

The majority of these interviews, though, were at the picnic tables, making them visible to others, which sometimes created situations whereby others would come over and sit with me and the interviewee and sometimes enter the interview. At first, I found these interruptions frustrating, especially since I was an outsider trying to tread lightly, and I did not know how to stop this from happening. Eventually, if I wanted to talk alone to the interviewee, I would ask the person interrupting to leave us alone for a bit, saying something like, "Hey, is it cool if we talk alone for a few minutes, and then you and I can talk when we're done?" In some instances, the interviewees themselves would say something like, "Can't you see we're doing an interview?" or "Get the fuck out of here."

In a short time, though, these interruptions became an important aspect of my own awakening to the cultural community. Specifically, these intrusions forced me to recognize that group conversations and disseminating information collectively was an important part of how the cultural community operated, and, in a way, my individualizing these interviews at the park was not fully aligned with the overall vibe of the cultural community. As I became aware of this, I eventually opened up these individual interviews to be more group-oriented. In doing so, these small group discussions became key opportunities for me to capture the very phenomenon related to relationships and social arrangements I was studying. These conversations took on a life of their own, and my "interview" often turned into a group discussion or debate about an aspect of the cultural community or skateboarding in general.

Because I still wanted the opportunity to speak individually with some participants, I interviewed each of the focal participants at least once alone, away from the park. I wanted to make sure they each had a chance to speak to me without the dynamic of others around. These interviews took place in a range of locales depending on the interviewee (e.g., place of work, home, coffee shop, tattoo parlor), and the format of these interviews more closely resembled a semistructured, in-depth interview format. Once I formally interviewed a participant, subsequent conversations happened more spontaneously, were conducted less formally, and typically lasted shorter than the initial formal interview.

Similar to participant observations, the interview protocols changed over time, as did my understanding of and familiarity with their participants and their cultural community. At first, the formal interview protocols consisted of questions designed to learn biographical information, including involvement in skateboarding, as well as their perspectives on school, learning, literacy, and work. As my research progressed, I drew on my field notes and emergent themes to create interview protocols designed to ascertain participants' perspectives on particular facets of their cultural communities. For example, as I came to understand that one of the forms of participation at the park consisted of skating with others in a "session," I would generate questions related to sessions, such as the following: When do people skate in sessions? Can you tell me about a time when you wouldn't skate a session with someone? Is the game of "skate" considered a session? In this way, as my understanding and analysis became more focused, so did my protocols.

In addition to formal interviews, I carried out dozens and dozens of informal interviews. These interviews were spontaneous and brief conversations—sometimes occurring at a picnic table, sometimes while skateboarding—and my goal in conducting these interviews was usually to build rapport, seek some clarification, or find out what a participant thought about a particular aspect of the community. In some instances, these casual conversations transitioned to formal interviews. Messaging via social media and texting also functioned as a type of informal interview whereby I might pose a question to participants. This form of communication proved particularly useful as I wrote this book and had focused questions.

Photography and Video Documentation

Throughout data generation, I captured particular moments at the park by shooting video and photographs. With the exception of the skate contest and instances when no one was at the park while I was, I did not capture digital images during the first summer of fieldwork. In fact, even after the first summer, I was very selective in capturing digital images because of the way it brought attention to me and whatever activity I was capturing. Notable exceptions included when participants were already capturing digital imagery, at which point my doing so would be less obtrusive, or when participants requested that someone capture something that is happening. By the third summer, it was not uncommon for a participant to say, "Hey Rob, you got your camera on you?," at which point we would set up a shooting session. In addition to furnishing the photos to the participants, I used these photos and videos for my own data purposes, especially in helping me reconstruct field notes and make sense of different moves and tricks and the ways my participants use space within the park.

As I got to know participants and would capture video and photographs of their skating, I would send them to them, which would facilitate our digital communication beyond the park. This video work functioned, too, as an easy way to conduct a quick interview, as I could ask questions while engaging in the shared activity. Over time, these interactions enabled me to have a lived experience of "symbiotic learning partnerships" that occurred at Franklin Skatepark; Hollett (2019) explains that such symbiotic learning partnerships often emerge between skateboarders and videographers through their "vibing" with each other, whereby the two establish "collaborative, rhythmic cycles" (p. 753). In this way, the act of shooting photos and videos functioned in myriad ways—as sources of data, a means to relationality and reciprocity, and a way to elevate the participatory aspects of my participant observations.

Cultural Artifacts

Finally, I collected a variety of participant-created and industry-created texts, including books my participants read (e.g., *Scar Tissue, American Hardcore*), skateboarding magazines (e.g., *Thrasher, Transworld*), videos (e.g., *Dogtown and Z-Boys*), tattoos (through digital photography), and songs my participants listened to and/or wrote. Though I asked each participant direct questions about their textual activities both related and unrelated to skateboarding, these artifacts often emerged as data sources through more organic means—through spontaneous conversations at the park or overhearing others talking about texts and then asking them about the texts. In addition, social media functioned as an important text for the skateboarders, and so my research also involved observing and engaging them on social media. In fact, I sometimes used what I observed on social media as cues to inquire into the participants' activities and perspectives.

EXITING FRANKLIN SKATEPARK

Figueroa (2014) notes that, while qualitative researchers often give extensive attention to entering a site in their writing, they typically give less or no attention to their "departure" from their research site and the lives of participants. For me, there were two key facets of my departure I was not prepared for. The first was the emotionality of the leave-taking, and the second was the overwhelming sense of responsibility I felt upon exiting the study.

Concluding the acute data generation portions of this study was both relieving and deeply sad for me. I was relieved because the process of data generation was intense, but it was also this intensity that amplified my emotional connection to the work. Spending several years getting to know people and building relationships with them does not occur, at least for me, without emotional bonds getting formed. I became deeply invested not only in the study but also in the lives of the people I'd come to know, the broader community of Finley, and Franklin Skatepark.

In addition to this simultaneous sadness and gratitude, I also felt an overwhelming sense of responsibility. As it should be, I felt accountable to those who'd given me their time, offered me their perspectives, and entrusted me with their stories. Leaving the site meant it was time to write this book—and to do so in a way that had integrity to the research and the participants, anxieties I discussed at the beginning of this chapter. Having said that, as I think of my exit from the site, I note that I have also maintained relationships with many of the participants, following their life paths and engaging them on various occasions. In this sense, the formal research has been completed but the relations forged there continue for me.

CHAPTER FOUR

Entering the Bowl

This is my favorite skate park. This is home. I love this park. I mean I've seen a lot better parks, you know, but this is my home. Nothing will ever beat Franklin Skate Park . . .

—Hollywood

RP: So what was that like when the park was finally opened?
Luis: It was like heaven . . . but made out of concrete and coping.

THIS CHAPTER INTRODUCES Franklin Skatepark, the town where it exists (Finley), and the group of young men highlighted throughout this book—the "diehard locals"—with particular emphasis on five focal participants among them: Luis, Crazy K, TS, Derrick, and Matt. As mentioned in previous chapters, an important aim of this book is to humanize and story a demographic who typically exist as statistics of so-called failure and crisis, and so I implore, at times, a narrative approach in this chapter. Specifically, I draw on the annual skate contest at Franklin Skatepark from my first summer of research as a narrative frame. I use the contest as a frame, in part because it is such an unusual activity, and so it reveals, through juxtaposition, a sense of how the park typically operates.

Stylistically, I toggle throughout the chapter between first-person ethnographic description of the contest and third-person explanation of various aspects of life at the park and broader community. This approach is meant to offer a window onto the processes of fieldwork explained in the previous chapter, to provide pertinent contextual information, and to lift from the pages and render into 3D, as much as is possible through words, the young men and their engagement at Franklin Skatepark. Also, this chapter uses this description and introduction to highlight various features of the park and learning that will be picked up throughout this book. From a theoretical perspective, an important aim of this chapter is to explain some of the ways Franklin Skatepark operates as a "cultural community" (Rogoff, 2003).

EN ROUTE TO RESEARCH

Beads of sweat cascade down my forehead as I walk to my car to head to Finley for the annual contest. I shoulder two bags—one with my laptop, the other with my research equipment: my digital voice recorder, camera, notebooks, and consent forms. Before I put my bags in the back seat, I check out my look in the reflection of the window—a plain white T-shirt with a few visible stains, untucked and hanging loosely over a pair of torn gray shorts, and a pair of open-toed sandals. As I nestle into the driver's seat, I muse that this business of trying to fit in without seeming a "poser" is a more arduous task than finding key informants.

Pushing 80 on the open road, I hit a crest on the highway that always marks the midpoint in my 30-minute journey to Finley, and I think back on the night before, when I ate dinner with Crazy K, a 30-year-old self-employed tile contractor who has been an avid skateboarder since he was an early teen, and his wife, Sandra, who is a former undergraduate student of mine and now works as a high school English teacher. They are residents of Finley and spend quite a lot of time at Franklin Skatepark. Over dinner they assured me that at the contest they would introduce me to some of the other skaters they know, regulars they think will be generative for me to know. Thinking of our conversation, I soon pull off the highway and enter the stream of traffic that will take me to Finley.

WELCOME TO FINLEY, A TALE OF TWO CITIES

Located about 30 miles from a micro-urban area (Liberty) and the main campus of a major university, Finley has historically been a relatively remote, rural, and light-industrial community. As a hamlet of approximately 8,500 people, the vast majority of whom are white, Finley serves as the county seat to a predominantly rural constituency. Economically, Finley has relied on local manufacturing companies, the largest of which typically employs approximately 10 to 15 percent of the town's population, and agriculture is another key, though shrinking, aspect of the local economy.

In an interview, a city official described a certain "tension" that exists within what he referred to as "a tale of two cities": between those community members who consider Finley a "bedroom community" for Liberty and those who view Finley as a self-contained entity separate from Liberty. In fact, by some of its residents, Finley is described as a "small metropolitan area," serving as a residence for university and government employees for nearby Liberty. By others, it is considered a "blue-collar town" serving as a hub for small manufacturing companies. Still others think of Finley as "a small hick town," meant to signify it as a rural, agricultural community. One of the participants of this study describes Finley as a town that "wants the image to be white-collar but it's not." This confluence of varying and sometimes conflicting identifications has become especially visible as Finley, which has been deeply embedded for generations in traditions of agriculture and the automobile industry, both of which have undergone major changes in recent years, has had to find new ways to reinvent itself.

With a classic main street connected to an old county courthouse, Finley's downtown has the feel of a Hollywood film set in small-town (white) America. The courthouse building, erected in the late 1800s, serves as the symbolic heart and geographic hub of the downtown and the county at large. The town's main street has resisted being overrun by chain stores and still consists of mostly locally owned businesses, including a pharmacy, pizzeria, movie theater, gun shop, tattoo shop, and microbrewery. With "for rent" signs in some storefronts, a recent phenomenon that many in the community attribute to the recent opening of a Wal-Mart and a major regional chain supermarket, has raised concerns in the community about a possible "empty downtown," as one community member termed it.

As part of its recent attempts at community revitalization, the town passed a bond for a multimillion-dollar performing arts center connected to the high school. Built with the expressed intention of not only serving the public schools and community at large but also drawing in people from the surrounding region, the arts center regularly hosts a variety of national touring acts. In addition, the community built a new sports complex and middle school complete with an aquatic center. Hoping to revitalize its community through support of its public education, the town paid for billboards on the highway promoting Finley schools as ideal places for young people to learn.

THE ANNUAL SKATE CONTEST

As I pull into the parking lot at Franklin Skatepark, I am taken aback by the rows of vehicles crowding it. More a dirt and gravel patch of earth than a paved area with designated spots, the lot typically hosts five or six vehicles, or, on a busy evening, nine or ten. Yet today I have to make a three-point turn and find a spot on the adjacent street because of the overflow of more than 50 vehicles.

Franklin Skatepark sits on a 20-acre plot of land known more generally as Franklin Park, which, in addition to the skatepark, has a sand volleyball court and a disc golf course. Situated on a rectangular corner lot, Franklin Park is bordered by rows of houses on two sides, a quarry on a third, and on the fourth, a sunken open field where whitetail deer can often be spotted on summer evenings. Railroad tracks run parallel to the park, and the sounds of trains blaring through are a familiar accompaniment at the park.

When I walk toward the skatepark, I am surprised by not only the powder-blue converted school bus that fashions a "Congregation of Christ" display on its broadside (the church is sponsoring the contest), parked dead center in the main grassy area of Franklin Park, but also the smell of hot dogs cooking on an open grill. Normally, bags of chips, fast food, bottles of water, cans of soda, and the occasional pizza pies are found at the park, and it is rare to ever smell food prior to sitting at one of the picnic tables where it is being eaten. And though music sometimes communally plays through a portable speaker or car stereo, it is never as loud as it is today—two massive speakers bookend a makeshift stage set up near the school bus. A range of heavy metal, hardcore, and hip-hop music blasts through the crowd. While I weave in between people congregating on the grass, I snap photos of the carnivalesque scene and do a quick head count. Stopping at 200, I muse to myself that this is much different from most afternoons, when, at most, I am one of 20 or 30 people at the park.

Eventually, I enter the gate of the fence that rings the skatepark, and when I do, Crazy K, a stocky, white male with a crew cut; an array of tattoos on his back, legs, and arms; and a five-o'clock shadow walks toward me and tells me that Sandra, his wife, went home to get his helmet. He explains that the judges are going to let him compete but that helmets are mandatory. At our dinner-interview the night before, Crazy K had explained that because he was over 25 years of age, he was ineligible to compete, which irritated him, since the categories for the contest—beginner, intermediate, and advanced—are not age-specific. Later, when I checked the official entry forms to the contest, several of the advanced participants were in their early teens while several intermediate participants were in their late teens or early twenties. Within a minute of us talking, Sandra walks up to us, gives Crazy K his helmet, and says to me with a smile, "I've got a kid for you!" As we maneuver together through the mass of people, I snap pictures of the action, taking advantage of the large crowds and flurry of activity to blend into the scene.

THE ROLES AND STATUSES OF THE DIEHARD LOCALS

The vast majority of the people who use Franklin Skatepark are young men who live in Finley. Despite the socioeconomic diversity of Finley—and how skateboarding, in general, cuts across socioeconomic status (Atencio et al., 2018; Borden, 2019)—the guys of Franklin Skatepark are firmly on the "blue-collar" side of the town, aspiring to find jobs in the manufacturing industry when they can, through various trades such as welding and auto mechanics, or by doing something related to skateboarding, tattooing, or music. Of particular significance is that, though the majority of Finley is white in terms of racial demographics, a high percentage of the regular participants of Franklin Skatepark identify as "Hispanic" or "Mexican." These young men, three of whom are highlighted in this book as focal participants (Derrick, Luis, Matt), proved central figures in the cultural community of Franklin Skatepark.

From this large group, there is a smaller inner circle of participants, "the diehard locals," which is a core group who live in Finley, skate there frequently (some every day), and are committed to the well-being and upkeep of the park and cultural community. These locals assume control and responsibility for the park and act, as one participant said, as "park bosses." One of the guys explains how this is actually a common practice at most skateparks: "No matter what park you go to, there's always a group of locals that just kind of keep order in the whole thing. And they're always the ones that usually have the seniority when people are going and stuff." It is important to note that not all skateparks are governed by such a group of locals. This is increasingly true, particularly at larger parks in urban spaces that are sponsored by private and nonprofit entities and coordinate various programming, including camps and coaching sessions (Atencio et al., 2018). I draw attention to this to point to how Franklin Skatepark is a unique cultural community, particularly given its rural context, which, in relation to urban skateparks, has distinctive factors that contribute to the social organization and learning at the park.

In many respects, this small group of diehards at Franklin Skatepark is analogous to what Dupont (2014), from his research of two larger, urban skateparks, refers to, within what he calls the "hierarchy of the skateboard scene," as the "core skateboarders." He explains how these core skaters "were not simply trying on a subcultural identity; their membership was more permanent and would have lasting effects on their lifestyle" (p. 564–565). Given the longitudinal nature of this project, I can attest that this sense of enduring impact is consistent for the locals of Franklin Skatepark, as their intense participation in this cultural community continues to reverberate in their lives, whether through their actual skateboarding, jobs, literacy practices, friendships, or just overall lifestyles.

Among these Franklin Skatepark locals, several distinctions exist. The terms used here are the terms used by the participants to delineate different roles and statuses. There are "old guys," such as Crazy K and Thurman, who function as almost "elders," as TS says, in that they do not get too involved in the day-to-day particulars of the park but take part in some of the group decision making and help maintain a sense of responsibility for the well-being of the community. For example, Thurman sometimes brings a push broom to sweep out the bowl and on one occasion paid a visit to city hall on behalf of the park. These "old guys" function as important players in the learning community, too, particularly given their more extensive experiences with skateboarding.

In this sense, these participants have accrued a "temporal capital," which speaks to the ways age and time have an "important currency" in skateboarding and afford these participants a "subcultural authenticity" (O'Connor, 2018). This notion of temporal capital is key, as the "old guys" designation is not automatically linked with someone's age; for example, in instances when biologically older participants are new to skateboarding (as was the case with me), they would not be considered one of the "old guys," though they might be referred to something like, "an older guy who is just getting into it." In this way, the designation of "old guy" signals age to some extent (someone in their early 20s, for instance, would not be considered an "old guy") but has to exist alongside an accrued or earned reputation from extensive previous participation.

Another designation is the "regular skaters." These participants, such as Luis and TS, are those typically in their late teens and/or early twenties and have been skateboarding since at least their early teens. These "regular skaters" have deep understandings of the cultural community, are often quite skilled, and have an identifiable "style." (The concept and significance of style is discussed in Chapter 9). This group of participants is the closest to day-to-day leaders; though ages span in this group, many of them are recently out of high school, have relatively more resources (e.g., money, car) than younger participants, and a fair amount of clout among the other participants. In other words, this group has high levels of subcultural capital within the cultural community and social capital (in comparison to younger participants) beyond the cultural community (Dupont, 2014).

Another category of participants within the broader "locals" or "core" participants is the group known as the "next generation." These participants (e.g., Derrick, Matt, Archie, Santana, Houston) are typically younger (middle and high school age) than "regular skaters," have not developed the same level of subcultural capital, and do not have access to the same types of resources or social capital as the "regular" skaters or "old guys." However, the hallmark of the "next generation" is that they are highly dedicated to the cultural community and learning to skateboard. This dedication and commitment are primarily evidenced by the consistency of their showing up to the park and the time they put into their skateboarding. To a certain extent, these skaters have been primed by the regular skaters and will replace them in due time. Within the "next generation" group there is quite a wide variance on ages, ability levels, and potential outcomes regarding their future status in the group.

The following table (Table 1) provides an overview of these locals, including their age, race/ethnicity, academic standing and/or occupation, and status in the cultural community. The participants with an asterisk are focal participants, and the quoted words and phrases are from the participants.

Table 1. Overview of Participants

PARTICIPANT	AGE	RACE/ ETHNICITY	SCHOOL SUCCESS/ OCCUPATION	STATUS
Houston	12–15	White	"Not the best student"; gets Cs and lower; dropped out of high school	Next generation
*Matt	13–15	"Mexican-American" "Hispanic"	Does "OK" in school; wants to go to college; graduated though alternative high school	Next generation
Archie	13–15	White	Cs, Ds, or Fs	Next generation
*Derrick	13–15	"Mexican"	"Not the smartest in the book"; gets Cs and lower; dropped out of school	Next generation
Santana	14–16	"Mexican"	Dropped out of school	Next generation
Hollywood	17–19	Native Hawaiian & Filipino	Expelled from regular high school and graduated from the alternative high school; tattoo artist and piercer	Next generation
Larry	19–21	White	Dropped out of HS; perfect score on verbal section of GED; moved to CA to make a living in the music business	Regular skater
*TS	19–21	White	5 yrs. to graduate HS; tattoo artist apprentice	Regular skater
*Luis	19–21	"Hispanic" "Mexican"	5 yrs. to graduate high school with a 1.4 GPA; became a welder	Regular skater
Thurman	Mid-30s	White	Self-employed contractor	Old guy
*Crazy K	Early 30s	White	Struggled in school but did graduate; self-employed tile contractor	Old guy

Though this book primarily focuses on this core group of "old guys," "regular skaters," and "next generation" locals, it is important to provide a sense of others who spend time at the park. For example, "little ones" are typically younger participants who have not yet learned the implicit rules of the park, nor have they proven themselves, and while several of them will eventually become "next generation" skaters and then "regular skaters," some of them will fade away before achieving that status. These little ones are often seen as nuisances by the core skateboarders until they prove their commitment, at which point they gain access to more resources, including pointers from more experienced participants. There are instances, however, as discussed throughout this book, whereby the core skateboarders and the "little ones" engage with one another in quite generative ways.

There are also more casual participants who skate on a regular basis but do not get too involved in the doings of the park or the people. These participants are typically older skaters who are looking for some recreation and fun without, as one of them says, "getting caught up in the whole thing." As one local says of another skater who is in his early 20s and primarily skates alone, listening to music through his earbuds, "You watch, and you can see he's just skating for himself. He just sort of hangs out and does his own thing." There are also participants who never seem to coalesce with the cultural community at large and maintain "asshole," "weird," or "poser" status.

In addition, skaters who do not live in or near Finley also use the park. These participants, known by the locals as "outsiders," are quickly marked by not only their clothing, style, or vehicles but also because the group of locals is small enough that they all know or at least recognize each other. These "outsiders" are either accepted, which does not necessarily mean that they are folded into the cultural community but that they are allowed access without any trouble, or are viewed as "disrespectful," and indirectly, or sometimes directly, confronted. In these instances, those skaters are rarely seen again.

In addition to those who are at the park to skateboard, many people who do not skate also use the park. Though not nearly as common as in larger, urban skateparks with more structured activities and programs, parents, especially those of very young children, spend time at the park. More so than these adults, other youth from Finley use the skatepark, more or less as a "hangout." These people include friends of skaters or just others looking for a place to spend time away from direct adult supervision. These non-skaters are perceived by the skaters differently depending on their affiliations with skaters. For example, people who hang out at the park without knowing or closely associating with skaters are generally perceived as being in the way or "losers," whereas non-skaters who have affiliations with skaters are more accepted as spectators and interlocutors. These non-skating participants are not necessarily the "consumers" noted by Dupont (2014) but rather other youth from Finley who don't necessarily have any interest in or affiliation with skateboarding but want a place to hang out outdoors, away from direct adult supervision. I note this, in particular, given the rural context of Finley and limited places designated for youth there.

Throughout my research, it was rare that any female skaters participated at Franklin Skatepark, and I did not have occasion to interview any of the few I did observe; from my data, Franklin Skatepark existed very much as a male-dominated space, which, despite changing gender demographics within skateboarding (Atencio et al., 2018; Corwin et al., 2019), remains quite common (Dupont, 2014; Carr, 2017). Though there was never explicit behavior that overtly excluded female participants (in fact, many of the male participants explained they'd like to have a romantic partner who skateboarded), the way in which this cultural community is intensely gendered seemed to make the possibilities for female skaters to fully participate quite limited.

Related, Dupont (2014) explains how women who wanted to engage in the parks he studied "ran into a series of roadblocks" and were only accepted as either "invisible girls" or "ramp tramps." "Invisible girls" refers to women who were meant to be "invisible but supportive spectators," whereas "ramp tramps" were young women at the park "in the pursuit of obtaining status through sexual affiliation with a skater" (p. 575). Similarly, it is not uncommon for several young women to be at Franklin Skatepark at any one time, though not as skaters. Typically, these young woman fulfilled one of the two roles noted by Dupont (2014): they are either girlfriends of a male participant, a friend of a "girlfriend," a sister, or a "ramp tramp," which is, as described by one of the participants, a girl who hangs out at the park "to flirt with guys and cause trouble." In these ways, whereas some skateparks have been instrumental in opening up participation for female skaters (Atencio et al., 2018; Borden, 2019), Franklin Skatepark seemingly constrains opportunities for female skaters. Moreover, throughout my research, I was not aware of any participants who identified as queer, which is not to say there aren't any but only that I am not cognizant of any. (Chapter 7 addresses intersections of participation and issues of gender, masculinity, and sexuality in more depth.)

The Significance of Commitment and Respect for Status

Respect is a key factor in determining one's status in this cultural community, and respect is earned by and bestowed on participants in several ways, including the ability to perform certain skills or tricks, age (as mentioned above), and one's style. However, when it comes to respect at Franklin Skatepark, what matters equally, and perhaps even more, is one's devotion to the skatepark, commitment to learning how to skateboard, and overall respect and "heart" for the cultural community. As Luis says, "As long as you're trying real hard and giving it all you got, you're just as good as anybody else." In kind, TS explains how Luis, while not the best skateboarder from a skills perspective, is a well-respected participant since he is dedicated:

> When you skate, I think most of the respect from the skatepark comes from being down there. Like even if you aren't that good a skater, like I know kids who like, look at Luis. Luis has never been that great of a skater, but the fact that he's down there constantly skating, people respect the fact that, you know, that he's committed to something. And it doesn't matter how many times he fell the day before. He's going to be back up there and whatnot. So that's like the really cool thing about it. You just kind of build, I don't know, a reputation for the way you skate—like the way you hang out with people, the way you treat people, and you just build a respect level on that.

Here, TS explains how respect comes from "being down there [the park]" and one's commitment, which are valued above being able to skate well. In this sense, one of the ways skaters derive status is through their "time spent within the skateboarding field" (O'Connor, 2018, p. 928) and "commitment to the activity" (Dupont, 2014, p. 564). Interestingly, TS suggests that one's reputation is built on "the way you skate" but qualifies this not by discussing ability or even style but rather "the way you hang out with people, the way you treat people." In this sense, respect is not just *that* you spend time at the park but *how* you spend that time there.

Conversely, it is possible for a participant to be both an excellent skateboarder in terms of skills and style *and* "an asshole" who is not truly respected. One local says, "The ones that are really good [at skating] tend to get a lot more respect. There are a couple that don't, but that's just because their attitude is bad."

DERRICK: "I THOUGHT I'D JUST GO WITH THE FLOW"

After taking a series of photos to document the flurry of activity, I reconvene with Sandra, who is standing on the grass just off the concrete edge of the park. As we watch, she points to a skater—a tall (approximately 6'2"), lean, brown-complexioned young man with shaggy brown hair. I recognize him from previous visits, and his attire—a tan Hurley T-shirt and darker tan shorts down to his knees—is consistent with what he normally wears. Sandra explains to me that he, Derrick, is the "kid" she mentioned the night before during our dinner-interview; she tells me that she spoke with him before I arrived, and he is interested in talking with me. She goes on to tell me that he is 14, going into eighth grade, has "lots of family problems right now," and would be "a great person to talk to about skateboarding."

From getting to know Derrick over the following several years, I came to understand that for him, skateboarding feels like "freedom" and the skatepark specifically a place where he can be in control of his life. Feeling caught between his divorced parents and his responsibilities as the second-oldest sibling (and oldest son) of four children, Derrick turns to the park and his friends there to "get away" from the pressures of his day-to-day life, "relax," and take his mind off "other things you have to deal with," like parents, home, and school. During the second summer of research, Derrick was spending a great deal of time "couch surfing" at friends' homes and, at the age of 15, had begun to seriously consider moving out on his own, possibly with a friend, much like his sister had already done at 17.

By my third summer of research, Derrick was living full-time with a friend's family and was working to save for an apartment. Self-reported as "not the smartest in the book," Derrick explained early in our interactions that he was committed to finishing high school. In one of our first in-depth interviews, he said, "It [graduating from high school] shows that I try hard for what I've got. It makes me feel better, showing that, yeah, I finished high school, you know, I've got my diploma." Within two years of this initial discussion, Derrick dropped out of school and began working full-time in a local factory. Despite the difficulties he faced with his family, Derrick, at the time, planned on—and eventually got—a tattoo of what he refers to as "Mexican prayer hands" in honor of his Mexican heritage and family. The tattoo includes a ribbon that wraps around the hands three times, each with one of his sister's names on it, and then his parent's birth dates on either side, so, as he says, "it'll have my whole family."

Consistently touted as the best bowl skater at the park, Derrick has a smooth skating style, making the skateboard look like a natural extension of his feet and catching air look like surfing a wave—an aesthetic that would more easily place him in southern California than the Midwest. Probably the only skater at the park with a legitimate shot at doing something more with skateboarding, Derrick was "not sure" when I first met him as to what extent skateboarding might fit into his future, since, as he says, "I could possibly break a leg" or it might get "annoying to me." He says about his future related to skateboarding, "I thought I'd just go with the flow. Whatever happens, happens, I guess. Try to make the best of it." In many regards, Derrick's relationship with skateboarding demonstrates how vital notions of pleasure, fun, and participant control and power, among other things, are for the young men of Franklin Skatepark.

TS: "I'M REALLY PSYCHED ABOUT THE FACT THAT THESE KIDS NOW HAVE SOMEWHERE TO GO"

As Sandra and I stand next to each other, nearly 20 skaters skate all at once. As we watch this free-for-all, Crazy K takes a cigarette break and joins us. Soon, TS comes over to him, smiling, and says, nodding to Crazy K, "I want to hang out with a *geezer*." Sandra, also smiling, retorts, "You're kind of a geezer yourself," and the four of us laugh.

Plastered with tattoos, which seem to increase on a daily basis, TS's pale-white, lanky frame protrudes from his long black shorts and plain white T-shirt. Although his light brown hair is still long enough to warrant the use of a brush this first summer, by the dawn of my second summer of research, TS had shaved his head to help display the tattoo he had inked on it. At 20, TS became a high school graduate, taking five years to barely earn his diploma, and then transitioned to be an apprentice for a local tattoo artist. In a later interview, TS shared that he wishes that when he was in high school, teachers had been more encouraging of his artistry and skateboarding, explaining how he used to be forced to go to career days every year but never once had the opportunity to talk with a tattoo artist to learn about that potential career path—and instead had to network outside of schools, primarily with other skateboarders, to learn more about tattooing as a career.

TS's efforts at helping to make Franklin Skatepark a reality are unsurpassed among the users of the park, so much so that his name is on a plaque in the park. Frank Rodgers, the city councilman who spearheaded the development of the park, said that TS was "amazing" when it came to helping out with the park and that the process "completely turned him [TS] around." In many regards, TS is the most respected skater at the park—in part for his ability but even more so for his commitment to the park. For TS, the park is one of the things he is most proud of in his life. As he says, "If I can say that all I've really done through skateboarding is put that park there, like I did something that not many people get to say they've done. And not many people get to be responsible for [something like that]. And I'm really psyched about the fact that these kids now have somewhere to go." As discussed in Chapter 9, TS's sentiment regarding his role in the development of Franklin Skatepark speaks of how powerful the idea of being a contributor to the welfare of others is—in the language of LOPI, to be able to meaningfully "pitch in."

"DERRICK IS *GOOD*": THE CONTEST BEGINS

As Crazy K, TS, and Sandra talk, the MC of the contest announces that open skate time is over and it's time to start the advanced category of the contest. For this skate contest, which is organized around self-determined ability levels, not age groupings, participants have the option of self-selecting into one of the following three categories: beginner, intermediate, and advanced. Contestants in each category get a total of three "runs," during which they are scored by judges based on the difficulty of their tricks, style, number of tricks landed, and variety. Starting with the beginner category, each contestant gets two minutes for a run, followed by the next person, and so on. Once everyone in the category has had the opportunity for a first run, they each go on a second run, and then a third. Once all of the beginners have gone, the intermediate contestants perform in the same way, and then the advanced contestants.

Derrick is called as the first advanced candidate. As Sandra, Crazy K, TS, and I stand together waiting for the announcer to release Derrick to begin his timed run, Crazy K says to TS, "Derrick is *good*," to which TS replies, "Yeah, Derrick *is* good. He's improved *a lot* since last summer." Derrick starts his run by dropping into the three-foot bowl, doing a rock and roll, then a rock to fakey, before gliding down the waterfalls into the nine-foot bowl, where he carves its deepest section, pumping his legs by bending his knees and crouching down a bit. Generating momentum, Derrick rides out of the nine-foot section, over the waterfall, into the six-foot bowl, where he rides up the wall and grinds on the coping. It is at this point that both TS and Crazy K loudly smack the tail of their boards on the ground, an act known as "board slapping," which is the skateboarder version of congratulatory clapping. (I note that TS and Crazy K's behavior—both their celebratory board slapping and their talk about how good Derrick's gotten—illustrate some of the ways in which participation at Franklin Skatepark is not only communal but also heavily reliant on keen observation and participants *noticing* each other.)

As he drops back into the bowl, Derrick's mouth is slightly open, his eyes completely fixed on the upcoming concrete, his helmet, although buckled, sitting on the side of his head as if it is ready to fall off at any moment, and he looks as if he is surfing the concrete. Derrick's intensity and focus demonstrate what another skateboarder would later explain to me as "having a lot going on" when one is skating:

> There's a lot to think about, man. You're flying through a concrete bowl, and there's a lot of concentration involved. Getting on that rail and doing a certain trick—there's a lot of concentration, there's a lot going on. The more technical you are, the more you've got going on. There's more working, and there's a lot of skill involved doing it. I mean, something like that [hitting a rock with your skateboard] could happen at 15, 20 miles an hour, and you could slam face first into a concrete wall.

Derrick ends his run with a "big air" out of the deeper bowl and an ovation of board slaps and whistles from the spectators encircling the park.

LUIS: "SKATEBOARDING'S MUCH MORE THAN JUST A HOBBY—IT'S A CULTURE, A WAY OF LIVING"

After Derrick's run, TS goes, followed by Crazy K. Crazy K's run marks the end of the first round of the advanced category, and as soon as his run is over, skateboarders rush the bowls until there are close to 40 people skating at the same time. Crazy K, while standing near Sandra and me, is greeted by Luis, a 19-year-old skater who competed in the intermediate category. Luis initiates the conversation by saying, "Nice run, man. I've never seen anyone try to catch air on that hip before." The two talk for a few minutes, mostly Crazy K explaining his run and Luis asking questions. I stand near them, and when a lull enters the conversation, Crazy K says to Luis, "Hey man, this is Rob. He's writing a book about skateboarding and wants to talk to the guys." I turn toward them, and Luis introduces himself, putting out his hand. As we shake, I tell him he looks familiar, that I've seen him skating down here before, and I ask if he is friends with TS, to which he says, "We're roommates."

Luis, shirtless, wears camouflage shorts that run just past his knees and a black bandana over his shaved head. One of the very few skateboarders at the park whose physique does not fit the prototypical thin, lanky frame, Luis looks better equipped for a football field than a skateboard park. His dark-brown complexioned skin serves as the canvas for an array of tattoos, many of which he designed himself and all of which have political, communal, familial, and/or aesthetic value for him. Similar to Derrick, Luis has several tattoos related to his Mexican heritage and identity. One such tattoo, the word "Familia" scripted over a Sacred Heart and sparrows, pays homage to his mother. He explained to me, in one of our many interviews, that he got that tattoo for her "because I figured it was the least I could do since I played around with a lot of shit while I was in school. So, that little bit of pain was the least I could do. I was into drugs; I was all around not a very good kid."

I explain to him that I am working on a book project about skateboarding and he tells me to "shoot" with questions. Over the course of our conversation, he tells me that he's been skateboarding since seventh grade, recently graduated high school with a 1.4 GPA at the age of 19 after five years, since he failed his "first" senior year, and he is currently working as a welder, a trade he feels lucky to have picked up during his time in school. Initially drawn to skateboarding because of its "subversive attitude," Luis explains that skateboarding is "much more than just a hobby—it's a culture, a way of living." After recounting his injuries, which include ankle, knee, and wrist sprains, he explains how he reads skateboarding magazines, like *Thrasher*. As our conversation winds down, he tells me whenever I am down there and he is there, too, to feel free to ask him questions. He says that skateboarding is "accepting of anyone who wants to skate," and that he is interested in my project because he is interested in "getting the message out there."

MATT: "THE PARK KINDA RAISED ME"

As the advanced competition ends, the focus of the festivities shifts from the park to the makeshift stage set up on the grassy area outside of the skatepark. As the crowd transitions from one locale to another, a group of people, including Crazy K, Sandra, and TS, congregate right outside of the gate by the parking lot—some leaning up against or sitting on the hoods of cars, others sitting on the ground. In addition to the aforementioned people, Matt sits nearby on the deck of his skateboard, which he slides slightly back and forth as he picks at the grass. Matt neither looks up much from his downward gaze nor enters the conversation. Matt did not enter the contest but was present as a spectator.

Sometimes referred to by others at the park as "Mexican Matt," Matt identifies as "Mexican-American," and he is a dark-complexioned 14-year-old ninth grader whose black bushy hair frames a broad, warm smile that was rarely revealed at the park during my first two summers of observation. In fact, during the first summer of my fieldwork, Matt rarely spoke to anyone at the park and mainly skated by himself. He also spent a great deal of time watching others during this summer and typically skated only when very few people were at the park.

Although his family lived in Finley (and very close to the skatepark), he and his sister attended the public schools of a neighboring town. Hence, Matt did not know many of the other participants at the park who lived and went to school in Finley. By the second summer, however, Matt had both improved a great deal in his skateboarding skills and began to more visibly forge relationships with the other guys; by the third summer, Matt was a fairly well-known participant at the park. Given that Matt's first summer of skating at the park was my first summer of data collection, methodologically, tracing Matt's journey provided important insights into his learning process and trajectory of participation at Franklin Skatepark.

Interested in finishing high school and going to college to become a pharmacist "'cuz the money," Matt earned mainly Cs and Ds in school and, prior to my third summer of data collection, was finishing his tenth grade year (and first year in Finley public schools—he ended up transferring to Finley schools, in large part due to the friendships he developed with the guys at the skatepark) at the community's alternative high school because he missed too many days of school during the fall semester. Eventually, Matt graduated from the alternative school, though not without struggle, and had no prospects or interest anymore in college. By that point, he began considering military options, none of which worked out.

"EVEN IF I GET A TROPHY, I'M STILL GOING TO FEEL UNSATISFIED": THE AWARDS CEREMONY

The conversation among Luis, TS, Crazy K, and others eventually shifted from recapping the events of the contest to the large boulder that was cemented just outside of the skatepark two days prior and has since been covered with graffiti. TS, pointing to it, says, "Has anyone seen the rock? It's only been in for two days and it already has graffiti on it! People think it's a graffiti rock, but it's *not*. It's for landscaping."

No one says anything as he pauses for a few seconds. "Frank [Rodgers] is going to have something to say about this for sure. The city is going to want to shut down the park."

At this point, Crazy K jumps into the conversation, "The city spent $600,000 on this park—they're not going to shut it down!"

TS holds up five fingers and says, "500 grand. I was on the committee; my name's on a plaque," as he points toward the park wall with the plaques on it. TS says to no one in particular, "Don't think they won't [close down the park]. Don't think they won't."

Just as Crazy K is about to say something in response, there is an announcement that the awards ceremony is going to start, and everyone in the group begins to gather themselves to make their way toward the stage. Throughout the awards ceremony, I sit with Sandra and Crazy K, just in front of Derrick and Matt, and I find myself surprised by the anticlimactic nature of the event. Though everyone clapped as each recipient got called up to receive their trophy, it all felt very lackluster, and, as a former competitive athlete through high school, I was surprised by the seeming lack of enthusiasm in the participants' responses to their trophies and even overheard one say to another, "Even if I get a trophy, I'm still going to feel unsatisfied."

I was also surprised by the collaborative attitude of the skaters, especially when it involved people against whom they were competing. For example, both TS and Crazy K encouraged another skater in their category to "keep going" toward the end of his run during the contest. Derrick and TS, both participants within the same category, helped each other plan out their runs, and Crazy K, TS, and Derrick even collaborated to think about how they could each improve their performance to impress the judges. In this way, the awards ceremony—through its emphasis on ranking the skaters and judging them against one another—highlights a way the annual contest stood in contrast to the normal workings of Franklin Skatepark, where competition was present to some extent but was mostly done to push each skater to improve and was supplanted by a collaborative ethos among the participants; in this way, the participants' responses to the awards ceremony can be understood as a form of "resistance" to dominant social relations and norms of competitiveness, particularly in sports contests (Beal, 1995).

"A COMMUNITY WITHIN A COMMUNITY": LEADERSHIP AND GOVERNANCE OF THE PARK

Although there is no formal, organized leadership or governance for the park, there exists a complex set of social arrangements among its participants. One explained how the participants at the park have created "a community within a community where everyone knows each other" that "has its own energy to it" and works together to take care of problems. For instance, during my second summer, the park was vandalized by a group of kids who identified themselves as a gang from another town. Late one night, this group poured motor oil into the bowl and wrote their gang name near it with latex paint.

By the next afternoon, the locals of Franklin Skatepark had organized cleanup efforts and had begun to plan how to respond to the incident. When I showed up at the park that afternoon, several of the locals, mostly the "regular skaters" and the "next generation" participants they had recruited, were in the bowl, scraping the paint and/or cleaning the motor oil with materials they purchased on their own. Many more were at the park on their phones communicating with other locals to see what they might, as a community, do. Eventually, they called the police, and after being told to take care of the situation themselves, the locals contemplated the idea of organizing a brawl with this other group. While there were reports of smaller groups of participants threatening members of the alleged vandals, no large-scale rumble ever manifested.

One of the "old guys" of the park, Thurman, went to city hall to speak to public officials about the incident. Also, several locals "stood guard" at the park for several nights. This type of group collaboration and distributed problem solving, although not officially governed, was common when conflicts arose at the park, whether with people "disrespecting" the park, issues related to graffiti, or people sustaining serious injuries at the park. The discussion about the graffiti rock, for instance, provides another glimpse into this type of distributed problem solving and community-based participation.

This type of organization is also made visible in the ways participants "look out" for one another. For example, one local explains how there exists a certain kind of "trust" between participants. He says, "You find you're almost a family there. Like, you know, people up there I trust more than I trust some family members with, you know?" Similarly, another participant explains how this trust works at the park:

> People leave their cars unlocked and windows down, they leave their boards laying out while they go to the store for 20 minutes just because there's that commonality that, you know? Even if a dickhead comes up and decides he wants to be like that, they will protect it. They'll recognize it. Nobody is afraid to ask if you're using somebody's board and they've never seen it before.

In addition to the locals maintaining control of the park, another form of governance is through a 24-hour camera that is always focused on the skatepark. According to a city official, the camera, which is accessible on the Internet, was installed primarily as a way to advertise the park as a feature of Finley and for users to see if their friends are up at the park. The users of the park believe that the camera was installed to monitor their behavior. Interestingly, many of the diehard locals appreciate the video camera and wish it was more effective at stopping people from tagging at the park, especially since the skateboarders themselves are often blamed for the graffiti. In fact, they often threateningly invoke the camera whenever something illicit or controversial happens at the park. For example, in one instance several users were smoking pot at the park (before marijuana was legalized), and a group of locals called out to them to stop and said that they would not be surprised if the police were going to head down to the park to arrest them because they were watching them via the video camera.

Beyond graffiti, which is a concern at other skateparks (Taylor & Marias, 2011), controversy about the park involves litter, underage smoking, and noise, especially the playing of music. In fact, threats that the park will be closed down for any of these or other reasons often circulate among its users. This self-policing among the participants at the park and the constant threat of the park closing is particularly curious considering that, as one city official says, threats to shut down the park have never come from "credible local officials with any real responsibility for the operation or maintenance of the facility." He explains, "It's inconceivable that we [the city] would devote so much money and so many resources to this park's creation and then shut it down over some spray paint." In these ways, panoptic surveillance (Foucault, 1975) functions—for better or worse—as an additional means of "governance" at the park, which, as noted in Chapter 1, contributes to continuing debates about the spatial politics of skateparks.

THE CULTURAL COMMUNITY OF/AT FRANKLIN SKATEPARK

After the ceremony, as everyone disperses, I walk to the parking lot, say goodbye to Sandra and Crazy K, and get into my car. I drive to a nearby dead-end street, turn my car off, and start typing up my scratch notes into more cohesive field notes. As I type for nearly three hours, the glow of the computer screen the only light amid the encroaching darkness, my mind fires with connections between what I had just observed and previous visits to the park.

Still early in the research process, this site visit catapulted this study—not only relationally and in terms of access but also conceptually and analytically. Questions in brackets filled my field notes: What is the role of competition—and, more importantly, collaboration—in learning to skateboard? Do people teach each other how to skateboard? What if someone gets hurt? Who is "in charge" of Franklin Skatepark? Do people of all different ages skate together? Why is it that there is such a disproportionately high number of Latino young men at the park considering the racial demographic of Finley? Why aren't there any female skaters? What about talk—how does talk function in learning and engaging each other, especially teasing each other? How do tattoos and literacy more generally factor into learning how to skateboard? And what does any of this have to do with schooling and teaching?

As this experience opened up this study, I hope this chapter functions for this book—that it opens up many of the topics and inquiries that the remainder of the book picks up. Theoretically, this chapter explores, to a large extent, how the park operates as a cultural community, including how it is situated within a broader sociopolitical context (Finley) and involves particular people. Toward this aim, this chapter provides insights into the web of social relationships that exist at Franklin Skatepark and factor powerfully into the social and communal organization of participation there. More specifically, the diehard locals as a group of people who are in relation not only with each other but also with the skatepark and the broader community are "trying to accomplish some things together" and have some "common and continuing organization, values, understanding, history, and practices" (Rogoff, 2003, p. 80). As highlighted, these participants have different roles and responsibilities within the cultural community, as well as different levels of involvement and statuses. Furthermore, the interactions and relations among the participants are, at times, congruent, and, at other times, conflictual.

Beyond locating the various key players in this cultural community, the chapter addresses some of the underlying values and principles of social and community organization that necessarily inform all other facets of participation, including the means, motives, and goals of learning, as well as how assessment occurs and the types and roles of communication—all of which will be addressed in subsequent chapters. In other words, understanding the structures by which the community and social activities and interactions are organized helps illuminate how and why learning occurs within a context.

As explained throughout this chapter, Franklin Skatepark is organized in such a way that participants across multiple ages and skill or experience levels are able to participate at any one time. Even during the contest, which is an unusual event in that it allows only one person to skate at a time and is organized by skill level, participants who are not skating are actively participating in the cultural community through observation, words and sounds of encouragement, and dialogue with others. We see this, for instance, with TS and Crazy K watching Derrick skate and encouraging him. Even in the moment toward the end of the chapter when the group begins discussing the rock that has graffiti on it, Matt is there, listening in. In this sense, Franklin Skatepark nearly always affords opportunities for learners to be involved in some capacity in the ongoing endeavors of the cultural community.

These social and community organizational structures also facilitate distributed and collaborative decision making and problem solving. This underlying principle and value of the cultural community is evidenced at a micro-level when Luis and Crazy K talk through their runs, and on a broader level when the entire group collectively brainstorms ways to deal with vandalism. In this sense, Franklin Skatepark, as a cultural community, values participants taking an active role in shaping the direction of the cultural community; hence, the park doesn't just exist as a place for learning but is constitutive with the people and practices that are part of it.

While more can be teased out regarding how Franklin Skatepark operates as a cultural community, a key takeaway in moving forward is that underlying structures of social and community organization of a learning environment make available and/or delimit particular processes of learning, types of talk, forms of assessment, and so on. One inquiry to ponder, as we explore these relationships within the cultural community featured in this book, is wondering about the underlying structures of social and community organization within schooling contexts.

Drawing on Franklin Skatepark as a point of comparison, for instance, we might wonder: In what ways do the structures of social and community organization of schooling enable and/or constrain participants' opportunities for shaping the direction of the learning environment in meaningful ways? Is collective and distributed problem solving supported by underlying organizational structures? How are participants afforded opportunities to take up various roles and responsibilities within a network of others who are trying to work toward some common goals? What types of talk, participation, embodied experiences, assessments, and means of learning make sense or seem peculiar given how participation is organized and structured in schooling? How might shifting organizational structures make new types of talk, participation, assessments, and learning practices make sense? Not meant to be exhaustive, I offer these questions to help draw attention to the ways underlying structures of organization of learning in schools promote particular types of learning practices, assessments, motives, talk, and goals.

PART TWO
CARVING THE BOWL

CHAPTER FIVE

Participation Structures and Spatial Production of/at Franklin Skatepark

Spaces like grocery stores, skateparks, and classrooms are not merely static contexts in which activity takes place. Instead, over time and within a given activity, they are continually and repeatedly (re)produced. . . . As individuals use the skatepark in particular ways, in pursuit of practical goals (e.g., learning a new trick), they edit the park for themselves, constructing the setting. Certain physical features are salient and meaningful in particular ways for ongoing activity, whereas others fade into the background. As individuals engage in activity together, in the same arena, the ways they edit the space necessarily affect the possibilities for others' activity. (Ma & Munter, 2014, p. 242)

BUILDING ON THE previous chapter's exploration of Franklin Skatepark as a cultural community, this chapter focuses on the ways participation is structured at the park. As discussed in Chapter 2, paying attention to structures of participation is important given how integral context is to learning. I specifically attend to participation frameworks by exploring social practices related to non-skating activities (e.g., hanging out at picnic tables) and skating activities (e.g., skating alone, in small "sessions"), including the practice of "snaking," which is a way whereby participants learn and teach spatial relations at the park.

By addressing these social practices, I do not, as Ma and Munter (2014) say, "reduce skateparks to containers constituted by their physical features" but rather "consider how skateparks are produced in socially negotiated activity" (p. 239). In other words, Franklin Skatepark, as a context for learning, does not exist "a priori, as a given, or as a container for action" (Vadeboncoeur, 2006, p. 247–248) but is produced in relation to the participants through their engagement in various practices. In this way, Franklin Skatepark is a space that "is both constitutive of, and constituted in, social practice" (Hirst & Vadeboncoeur, 2006, p. 206). An important aim of this chapter, then, is to explore the interplay between the physicality and materiality of Franklin Skatepark and the social practices that (co)produce space at the park.

Toward this end, this chapter opens with an explanation of the physical layout of Franklin Skatepark, including how the participants repurpose material objects to facilitate their engagement. The chapter then explores how participation is structured across skating and non-skating activities, and explains the social practice of snaking. This type of spatial analysis is particularly salient with respect to skateboarding since, as Carr (2017) explains, "Performances of skateboarding are inseparable from and always defined by their environments. Skateboarding is inherently 'about' a specific site and its terrain, as no two skate spots are the same" (p. 27). For this reason, this chapter serves as an important foundation for the remaining chapters that explicitly address learning practices and principles.

(REPURPOSING) THE PHYSICAL AND MATERIAL LAYOUT OF FRANKLIN SKATEPARK

Franklin Skatepark is a concrete area that consists of two main concave sections, one known as the "bowl" and the other "the street"; in this sense, it is a "hybrid" (Ivarsson, 2012) skatepark, meaning it mixes street and "transition" (e.g., bowl) elements together (see figures 2 and 3). The bowl section consists of three separate pool areas that are connected by what the skateboarders refer to as "waterfalls," which are sloped declines from one area to another that provide smooth transitions. These three areas have various points of entry with different heights from which to drop into the bowl, including four, six, seven, eight, and nine feet. In the space where the walls of the bowl meet the concrete flat surfaces rests a circular coping from where the skateboarders drop into this bowl.

The street side is a mostly flat surface save a "pyramid" with a "fun box" on top of it positioned on one side. The entire street side of the park sits three feet below the level of the flat areas of the park and is accessible by several smooth points of entry as well as a six-foot roll in and a six-foot quarter pipe. The cement areas around and in between these two main areas of the park (bowl and street sections) consist of flat surfaces as well as a range of street-style obstacles, such as stairs, rails, and ledges.

FIGURE 2. Bird's-eye view of Franklin Skatepark. Map data © 2022 Google.

FIGURE 3. Field view of Franklin Skatepark. Reprinted with permission from Dan Hughes.

Small grass areas line the fringes of this concrete structure, and the grass and concrete areas are all enclosed in a three-foot-high fence with two gates. Several picnic tables and garbage barrels are also within these parameters. In fact, virtually every time I showed up to the skatepark, these movable material objects were in different locations than they had been during my previous visit. The reason for this was that skateboarders often integrated these objects into their skateboarding. For instance, they would put barrels on their sides, place them where they wanted them, stick a rock against them to prevent them from rolling, and then they would utilize them for a trick they wanted to perform or as part of a game of skate or for theatrical effect for shooting video. Picnic tables, too, were carried about and placed at different locations to create new opportunities for participation and utilization of space.

On some occasions, other skateboarders themselves were similarly used as part of the action. For instance, on one evening, during a whole-group session, Derrick wanted to see how far and how high he could catch air. He had already jumped four barrels, and without any more barrels available to test his limits, he asked other participants who had been watching and cheering him to lie down so he could jump over them. One of the less experienced skateboarders volunteered, and eventually four participants were lined up for Derrick to try to jump over. Video cameras rolled as Derrick first jumped over one, then two, then three, and finally four people lying side by side on the edge of the street side of the skatepark.

This repurposing of the material features of Franklin Skatepark demonstrates how the participants quite literally extended the park and reimagined novel uses for aspects of it. This spatial production not only illuminates the constitutive nature of interaction between physical place and participants' social practices but also how integral innovation, creativity, and imagination are to the practice of skateboarding. In many regards, it highlights how skateboarders see the world, particularly the material objects and spatial relations in it, in unique ways, what Borden (2019) refers to as the "skater's eye." To accentuate this point, during an interview with TS, when I asked about places to sit and hang out at the park, he said, "I've always thought they needed to have bleachers mainly because of the fact that I think that would be fun to drag them up and use them as a obstacle, you know?"

In many regards, this repurposing and production of new spatial relations speaks to a fundamental essence of skateboarding—whether it be in relation to empty swimming pools, park benches, or, in this case, garbage barrels, picnic tables, and human bodies. According to photographer and artist Craig R. Stecyk, whose skateboarding photography in the 1970s generated attention of the ingenuity, skill, and attitude of skateboarding culture, "Skaters by their very nature are urban guerrillas: they make everyday use of the useless artifacts of the technological burden, and employ the handiwork of the government/corporate structure in a thousand ways that the original architects could never dream of" (Peralta, 2002). To this point, a recent *New York Times* article (de Luca, 2020) offers a snapshot into a skateboarder's view and spatial production of New York City during the COVID-19 pandemic—a time the article describes as "an opportunity, even of liberation."

I pause here to note, too, how, in skateboarding, bodies are central to spatial production. While not central to my analysis, others (see, in particular, Borden's [2019] discussion of "super-architectural space") have theorized how space gets produced by skateboarders "out of the dynamic intersection of body, board, and terrain" (p. 177). Borden (2019) explains how skateboarders engage a form of "bodily questioning" whereby "the body interrogates architecture as another body in relation to their own actions" (p. 180). In this sense, different parts of the park—flat bottoms, wall edges, transitions, drop-in points—all demand a degree of reciprocal engagement (and involve quite a lot of physics). In other words, the architecture of the park—as a physical setting—does not dictate how skateboarding—or learning—occurs there; rather, the bodies of the skaters in relation to each other, the social and discursive practices, and the architecture produce the space and the learning together.

Moreover, this attention to bodies as key aspects of spatial production also speaks to skateboarding scholarship that explores the role of embodiment and sensory experiences (e.g., sound, feeling vibrations through the board) as aspects of participation and learning (e.g., Bäckström, 2014). These ideas are well illustrated in the example from the last chapter when Derrick was skating and had "a lot going on there." In that moment, Derrick's participation involved a complex body-board-mind-place set of relationships and spatial production whereby, as Borden (2019) explains, "intense bodily and mental processes become as one"

(p. 181). This moment of Derrick's participation can also be understood as a "multisensory emplaced learning that acknowledges how situated learning is embedded in specific environments, as well as in embodied learning acts" (Bäckström, 2014, p. 755).

FORMS OF PARTICIPATION

As explained in Chapter 3, I developed and utilized, from the theoretical orientation of LOPI, the analytic of *participatory events*, which focuses on instances when participants partake in the activities of the park. This analytical focus allowed me to map how and where and for what purposes people at the park engaged in the community. Specifically, in broad terms, I organized participation into "skating events" and "non-skating events." Skating events involved people actively skateboarding and/or directly observing, photographing/videoing, and talking about skateboarding that was happening in real time. Non-skating events included "hanging out" in one of the following areas: the parking lot, on the grassy areas within or outside of the gated area for the skatepark, or most commonly at one of the few picnic tables within the skatepark.

Skateboarding Participation

When it comes to participating directly in skateboarding, there are four central forms of engagement that structure participation at the park: (1) skateboarding alone; (2) skateboarding in a small group (approximately two to six people), which is known typically as a "session"; (3) being part of a large group who are skateboarding the entire park or section of the park together—the most extreme example of which is the annual contest; and (4) standing or sitting at one of the areas of the concrete section of the park (e.g., on a ledge, box, or the coping). Additionally, there are two other participation structures: the game of "skate," which is a specialized version of a session, and what I refer to as "explicit instructional sessions," which are much less common than these other forms of participation and consist of instances in which one or two skaters are providing extended, overt demonstration with explanation to another skater (this form of participation is discussed in Chapter 6). These forms of participation often occur simultaneously at the park.

SKATING TOGETHER IN A "SESSION." The most popular form of participation at Franklin Skatepark is the small "session." A session is when a small group of skateboarders skate together, taking turns skating a bowl or another area of the park, such as a rail or the steps. TS explains, "A session is just a general term for like you and a bunch of friends going out and skating. Most of the time you call it a session when you've got two or three friends with you at bare minimum."

At the park, sessions develop either through the deliberate coordination of skaters going to the park together, or they happen more spontaneously whereby the people at the park, although not there to skate with each other specifically, will create a session together, oftentimes through one skater asking another to skate the bowl with him. In other instances, sessions will form simply by the fact that there is limited space to share with one another, which facilitates a necessity of skating with others, even those you do not know. For example, one participant, when asked how he got to know the guys at the park, explained that he "just skate[d] with them." He then pointed to another skater at the park at the time and said that he did not even know who that guy was, that he was from another town, but that he would probably skate with him by the time he left the park that day.

As discussed in more detail in Chapter 6, from a learning perspective, sessions are important forms of participation for many reasons, including how they provide skaters with inspiration, instruction, and opportunities to learn from and contribute to the learning of others. Sessions also have important social functions, including opportunities for participants to have fun with each other, build and/or deepen relationships with known friends or new ones, and index statuses and reputations within the cultural community.

THE GAME OF SKATE. "Skate" is similar to the game of "horse" found in basketball. Essentially, a small number of skaters will take turns performing a certain trick. The person whose turn it is selects the trick and performs it. If he performs it successfully, the other participants take turns attempting to "land" the trick (which means completing the trick successfully). If a participant does not land the trick then he receives a letter, starting with s and moving through the spelling of the word *skate*. As people spell *skate* they drop out of the competition, and the last person left is the winner.

While games of skate are sometimes played for money or to test one's ability against another's, they are engaged mainly for fun and as a learning activity in which skaters have to push themselves to experiment and take risks. It is also a venue through which participants get exposed to new tricks. For example, Matt explains how a recent trick he learned, a "double kickflip," emerged from a game of skate: "I was playing a game of skate with a friend and he did it, and I didn't know how to do it so then after the game I just kept on tryin' it and I landed it not too long after it." The game of skate differs from more traditional sessions as it draws explicit attention to competition and places emphasis on successfully landing a trick, though this competition is better understood as more about pushing oneself to improve than it is about competing against someone else—what I refer to as a "collaborative competition."

WHOLE-GROUP PARTICIPATION. On occasion, several small sessions will be occurring at one time and will sometimes merge into a larger session, sometimes consisting of up to 20 skaters and even more observers. These "whole group" or "large" sessions operate in many of the same ways that smaller sessions do but differ in several significant ways, too. For one, they involve a larger number of people, oftentimes all the users of the park at one time, either as participants or as observers whose attention coheres around a particular activity. It is also the time when digital video and photography are more likely to be used at the park to capture a moment.

As discussed in the next chapter, these forms of participation often function to offer opportunities for "performative moments" (Jones, 2011), which not only provide "verification" (Donnelly & Young, 1988) of one's accomplishments but also engender participants' status in the cultural community, since these are instances in which feats are on display and are more likely to resonate throughout the park's oral culture and lore, as well as on social media. Other than the skate contest, whole-group sessions are the largest public peer performances these skaters get. In other words, whole-group sessions are not necessarily the times for practicing or giving explicit instructions, they are for "showing what you got," as one participant put it.

Because this form of participation often includes most if not all the participants at the park at the same time, the majority of the participants do not actually skate. This participatory structure is typically reserved for more advanced skaters, whereby less advanced skaters participate as spectators. These whole-group sessions operate, then, as important learning opportunities not only for those skateboarding but also for those observing, as watching and listening are key aspects of learning within this cultural community. In many regards, these whole-group sessions are the closest the skateboarders get to a "summative" assessment. In the most extreme example—the skate contest—trophies are bestowed on participants for their performance, though, as demonstrated in the previous chapter and as others have noted (e.g., Beal, 1995), these external rewards are not typically valued by skateboarders, which, again, connects to ways competition and collaboration exist within this cultural community.

SKATEBOARDING ALONE IN "SOLO SESSIONS." In addition to small and whole-group sessions, participants also engage in the skating portion of the park activity by skateboarding alone in what I refer to as "solo sessions." The majority of solo skaters I observed were either out-of-towners who came to the park alone and didn't know other participants, or younger, less experienced skaters who were still working on some of the basic moves (e.g., ollie, dropping into the bowl) that would enable them to participate more fully in sessions with other, more experienced skaters. For novice skaters in the cultural community, solo skate time was necessary to advance their skills, work on tricks, and develop a certain level of comfort in order to be ready to more fully participate in skate sessions with other participants.

More experienced skaters typically use the solo skating time to practice and refine what they already know, and took bigger risks and worked at learning new tricks when skating with others. Derrick explains how skating alone is about "trying to do stuff by yourself . . . when I skate by myself I just try to practice the same tricks that I do, try to make them better." Though participants are always, to some extent, open to being observed by others, these "solo sessions" are opportunities for skateboarders, particularly those not as experienced, to practice without (much) external review of their peers.

While more experienced skaters skate alone on occasion, the majority of their skating time was done with others. The exception to this was the "old guys" at the park. For these participants, solo skating at the park afforded them "alone time," which functioned as a time for "getting grounded," a space for emotional or stress relief, and, for some, skating alone had an almost spiritual aspect to it. These solo sessions are oftentimes accompanied by listening to music through earbuds. As Larry says, "It's like when I skateboard, you know, I could totally go out all by myself and put on some headphones and be by myself all day long. I know there's a lot of people that call each other up and they get a group together, and that's cool, too, but I find my serenity in just keeping it to myself." He goes on to explain how skating alone helps him take his mind off stuff "that's getting at you, you know?" He says, "There's nothing better than being pissed off at something, trying to get away from it, and getting on your skateboard. And there's two ways you can go about forgetting about it: you can either land a bunch of tricks and feel good, or you can crash a lot. So either way it's a win-win situation, I guess. [*Laughs.*]"

SITTING OR STANDING ON THE CONCRETE. For participants who take a break, one of the more popular areas for them to sit or stand are in various spots in close proximity to where people skateboard. For example, after making a few runs, a skater might sit on one of the "boxes" or "ledges" on the street side of the park or on the coping on the bowl side and watch others while taking a drink of water. Participants' time spent in these resting spots are typically shorter in duration to non-skateboarding forms of participation (e.g., sitting at picnic tables), as participants who are sitting or standing on the concrete are very much still participating in the activity of skateboarding and often rejoin after a short break to get water or cool down.

In this way, even though people are not actively on boards and literally skateboarding, they are still participating in skateboarding through observing, listening (Fors, Bäckström, & Pink, 2013), congratulating others, and engaging in dialogue with other skaters as they skate, which, as explored in subsequent chapters, are key aspects of learning (and teaching) how to skateboard. Likewise, these spaces were often utilized by participants who shoot photography or video of the action, often in explicit, ongoing communication with those being photographed or videoed.

In such instances, these participants, as Ma and Munter (2014) discuss, strategically positioned themselves in the park to "seek teaching": "Skaters at times positioned themselves to learn from others (seek other to teach them) and other times positioned themselves to help others (seek to be teachers)" (p. 254). What becomes interesting, I think, from a spatial practices perspective is that as participation and engagement in the cultural community changes through things such as the development of subcultural capital, relationships, respect, status, and skills, so too does participants' spatial production of the park. In this regard, as participants transformed their practice and connection to the cultural community, the park itself became almost a different place for them. With each shift in participation, the participants sought teaching and learning opportunities differently and in new ways than they were able to previously. In other words, as the skateboarders learned and transformed their participation within the cultural community, each time they went to the park, it became different—even though it was physically the same as it was at that last visit—and they were different participants, particularly in their ability to produce space at the park. In this way, as Ma and Munter (2014) explain in their research on skateboarding, "Settings are experienced and (re)edited individually, continually, and repeatedly" (p. 242).

Related, the concrete area to watch the action also functioned methodologically for me, as I would often conduct informal interviews with participants during these instances so they could point out various things happening in the park while we talked. In this way, my own participation in the park repurposed and produced spatial relations within the cultural community—and my spatial practices, too, changed as my engagement with the community did, including as I transitioned to skateboarding as part of my research.

Non-skateboarding Participation

During the times when skateboarders are not actively skating (or watching), their participatory activities include "hanging out" in one of the following areas, each of which has its own functions: at one of the few picnic tables within the skatepark, in the parking lot, or on the grassy areas within or outside of the gated area for the skatepark.

PICNIC TABLES. The most prominent form of non-skateboarding participation was hanging out at the picnic tables. Situated within the fenced-in area of the skatepark where one could still observe the skating happening but be more distanced from the areas where skaters taking a quick break might stand or sit on the concrete, the picnic tables functioned as a space for the skateboarders to get away from skateboarding and shift their focus and conversations to things beyond skateboarding. As TS explains,

> When you're up by the coping all you talk about is skateboarding and stuff like that. When you leave, it kind of gets left in the park. Like you know when you're talking at the picnic tables, it's always about completely different topics. That's more like, I don't know, that's almost more like gentlemen's club time where you just sit there and talk about . . . shoot the shit about stuff that's going on.

Practically, the picnic tables served as a space for participants to take a break from the action, relax, eat and drink something, smoke a cigarette, and/or talk with friends about stuff other than skateboarding.

In addition to these practicalities, the picnic tables operated in other important ways, including as a site for relationship building, job networking, and learning. For instance, on several occasions, I observed a participant receiving a job offer or referral from another participant while sitting together at a picnic table. It was also a space in which cigarette smoking not only happened but also was policed and monitored (who was allowed to smoke at the park was not governed by state laws but rather by a more or less shared sense of who was old enough or mature enough to smoke).

As explored in Chapter 7, talk and discursive practices at the picnic tables also revealed various ways in which norms regarding class, gender, sexuality, race, and age were developed, reified, policed, and transformed. At this time, I draw attention to TS's likening of time at the picnic tables to "gentlemen club time" only to underscore how this particular space, like the park as a whole, was very much a heteronormative, masculinized space.

Also, though the picnic tables were mostly the domain of the skateboarders, this was the space most popular for interfaces between skateboarding participants and non-skateboarding participants, whether that be parents, friends, girlfriends, or other observers. As mentioned in Chapter 3, the picnic tables functioned, early in my research, as one of the key spots for me to observe and conduct interviews, something I realized after some time may have, at times, violated ways in which that space was normally produced by participants.

Though TS explains how at the picnic tables people talked about things other than skateboarding, while true to a large extent, there still was quite a bit of talk about skateboarding that did occur there. However, this talk was rarely related to what was actually happening in real time at the park but rather about what had happened at other times or among participants while skateboarding elsewhere. In this way, the picnic table, as it related to skateboarding, functioned as a discursive space whereby participants could narrativize and dramatize (Paradise & Rogoff, 2009) their prior experiences, including injuries they'd endured or feats they or others had accomplished. In other words, the picnic tables were a space for stories—often prompted by the introductory "Remember when . . ."— that functioned as opportunities for teaching and learning cultural and interpersonal aspects of skateboarding (e.g., how to handle injuries), "verification" (Donnelly & Young, 1988), disseminating information, and distributed problem solving. Related, discursive practices at the picnic table also included gossiping about others, as well as promoting and indexing other people's statuses within the cultural community—for better or worse, including recounting accomplishments of others or behaviors subject to criticism.

OUTSIDE THE GATED FENCE. Beyond the chain-link fence that surrounded the concrete skatepark and picnic tables was the broader community park. For the skateboarders, this space was utilized the least and functioned mostly to deal with people and/or issues unrelated to the activities at the park. For instance, they talked on their phones in this area, smoked pot (for those who did), or hung out with people who were not affiliated with the skatepark or skateboarding, including girlfriends (though girlfriends sometimes were welcomed participants in the gated areas, primarily at the picnic tables). The areas beyond the gated fence were also where greetings and partings occurred, communal music might be playing (from someone's car), and other transactional activities might occur. This area was the one where most interactions occurred between skateboarding participants and non-skateboarding participants, and it was not uncommon for a non-skateboarder to drive or walk to the park, call a skateboarder over, engage with them for one reason or another, and then leave.

Participation "Off-Site"

In addition to being physically present at the park to participate, there was quite a lot of participation related to skateboarding (and Franklin Skatepark) that occurred "off-site" or away from the actual park. Specifically, the skateboarders read and viewed industry-produced magazines and skate videos; created and viewed participant-produced skateboarding videos; engaged in a variety of textual practices that involved and/or had been sponsored by their participation in skateboarding, including tattooing, music, and tagging; and skateboarded in their basements during the winters, in their neighborhoods, in town, and at other skateparks.

In addition to digital resources and texts (e.g., videos), social media was another significant way in which participation occurred "off-site" though often connected directly to the park. For instance, participants might record their participation at the park and then post it to their social media accounts, which enables other participants access to the cultural community of Franklin Skatepark as well as an entry point to engage (in) the community. In this way, even someone who does not actually skateboard or is a less active or peripheral participant can engage as a participant on some level.

Finally, for many of the local diehards, participation at the park also involved engaging in activities related to city officials. This is perhaps most obviously evidenced by the can drives and helping design the park, interfacing with city council and even the police at times. Though some of these forms of participation will be addressed in upcoming chapters, I draw attention to this facet of learning here, since, as mentioned in Chapter 2, one of the limitations of LOPI is that is has not adequately theorized how learning that occurs within a cultural community both informs participation in other cultural communities and is informed by participation in other cultural communities. In this study, for instance, skateboarding at other skateparks was not only informed by participants' experiences of Franklin Skatepark but also by how they subsequently participated at Franklin Skatepark, and, in some instances, how they felt about the park. For example, several skaters expressed "appreciation" for "their" park after having tried several others and were able to, in more nuanced ways, explain how and why they preferred Franklin Skatepark, as they now had points of comparison regarding both the physical park and the cultural communities and social practices at other parks.

LEARNING THE HARD WAY: SNAKING TO TEACH AND LEARN SPATIAL RELATIONS

Through teasing apart the participation frameworks of Franklin Skatepark, particularly as they exist across skateboarding and non-skateboarding practices, this chapter has, thus far, explored ways spatial relations are produced, and how Franklin Skatepark as a place and the social practices there are constitutive. In this section, I turn attention to the particular practice of "snaking" as one way in which spatial relations of Franklin Skatepark are taught and learned. "Snaking" is a practice in which a skater skates in front of another and cuts off the other skater, interfering with their run. Snaking is done both accidentally, usually because a skater does not have a sense of how the park operates, or deliberately to teach a lesson on how to use the park or to claim space.

As previously mentioned, at any one time, there may be multiple forms of participation occurring in/at the park, and along with this social arrangement, there are instances whereby people collide into or interfere with each other. When collisions happen, either between two skaters or because of a loose board, responses are mixed. When a collision happens due to "normal" circumstances, the two parties involved typically apologize to one another, maybe help each other, or at least check to see if the other is okay, and then move on once again to pursue their endeavors. For instance, skaters who fall often lose control of their boards, which becomes hazardous for other skaters. When this happens, they or others who are observing typically yell "Board!" to indicate to those skating that someone has lost control of his board and to be alert to that fact. In some of these cases, skaters actually stop skating to retrieve the other's loose board. In many respects, this response is embedded in the shared understanding that by virtue of sharing space, these types of occurrences are inevitable and part of business as usual. Thus, the social production of this space and the social practices within it determine the codes and language of the space (Lefebvre, 1991), such as, in this case, apologizing after collisions, retrieving boards, and yelling "Board!"

Responses look much different, though, when a collision is the result of a skater's irregular or irresponsible use of the space (e.g., dropping into the bowl when someone else is skating it). In these instances, the more experienced skater typically responds by tossing the less experienced skater's board out of the area where the collision happened, saying something like, "What the fuck are you doing?" or more subtly shaking his head or making eye contact with another more experienced skater and rolling his eyes. Crazy K explains an instance in which he was snaked by a less experienced participant (in this case, a biker):

> I don't remember if you were down here, but there was this biker. And I was in my run going, and he comes out of the blue. And I'm doing a front side grind, and he just goes *right* in front of me. I had to go flying off my board, and I had to basically go up to the guy and tell him to fuck off, you know? You don't do that shit around here.

In his response, Crazy K reveals how this instance of snaking not only caused him to go "flying off his board" but also led to a moment in which he directly confronted the biker who snaked him by telling him to "fuck off." His additional comment, "You don't do that shit around here" illuminates how Crazy K's response to this conflict served as a way for him to let the biker know about the norms of participation in this context. In this way, Crazy K's behavior and language is based on his reading and decoding the space the participants of Franklin Skatepark have produced. To him, the biker had transgressed the code of the space, leading him to use language that is produced in that space and for it. While I'm not necessarily endorsing Crazy K's particular approach for "teaching" in this instance, his response to being snaked reveals how conflicts create a way for participants to come to understand the norms of participation in this context.

More experienced skaters sometimes purposely snake less experienced skaters when the less experienced skaters are not using the space "correctly." In fact, the biggest complaint from the more experienced skaters at Franklin Skatepark involving the people who use the park has to do with the "little ones" who stand in the bowl, interfere with runs and sessions, and generally get in the way. Many of the skaters discuss snaking as teaching/learning how to use the park "the hard way," by, as Crazy K says, "maybe getting run over a couple of times." Luis says, "There is no easy way to learn that [the unwritten rules of how to use the park]. You have to get hit a couple of times." Below, TS explains his experiences of learning the hard way *and* his teaching of others at the park through snaking:

RP: So let me ask you, I mean you guys talk about these almost like rules at the park. I mean they're not written rules.

TS: Park etiquette.

RP: Park etiquette, yeah. How do you learn that?

TS: It's not so much something like you just get taught in the classroom or something like that when someone will pull you aside. I remember when I learned park etiquette about don't drop in on people. I was in California, and I got taken out by some guy who was just slashing every pool, and I came around the corner and he didn't see me, and I just got leveled.

CHASE: Any environment you're in. I've learned there's a respect at this place. I don't tell Chris this about him or he does this wrong. I don't tell him that because it's something you learn. You acquire it and feel it out.

TS: And most likely you're getting knocked back down to the bottom of the totem pole, you know? Like no one really gets kicked out of the park unless they're really screwing stuff up, but like most of the time it's just kind of like you go down a pay grade when you screw up. It's like, "Dude now people don't trust you as much." You gotta earn that trust back. You goof around one day, you know you shoot your board into somebody's ankle, that person ain't going to trust you that much anymore. It's more or less like you just gotta build it back up.

When I asked TS if he was angry at the other skater for leveling him, he explained that he was not because it was his own fault and that he was actually grateful he had that experience so he could become more aware of how participation occurs.

Although often painful and sometimes seemingly cruel, both these manifestations of snaking serve important means through which participants learn and teach terms of participation, namely how to use the park spatially. Moreover, both TS and Crazy K's responses illustrate a broader feature of learning among the skaters of Franklin Skatepark—that the learning of these norms has to happen within the context of participation, and not as TS alludes to in his classroom comment ("It's not so much something you just get taught like in the classroom . . .") or in an isolated or decontextualized way (". . . when someone will pull you aside"). In fact, in many instances, experienced skaters actually produce conflicts to teach these norms by deliberately snaking less experienced skaters. In other words, unlike the snaking that occurs when less experienced skaters interfere (due to ignorance of the norms of participation) with other skaters, more experienced skaters purposefully snake less experienced participants to convey to them that their use of the park and/or behavior is not acceptable and that they need to learn these rules to be respected and trusted participants of the community. Snaking, in these ways, points to how the social organization of the cultural community helps to shape the learning practices. Unlike school settings, for instance, where a specified authority (i.e., teacher) delegates turn taking or explains the rules, the participants at the skatepark have to work it out themselves (Ivarsson, 2012).

Furthermore, snaking not only teaches spatial and participation norms but also teaches participants *how* to pay attention and observe. In many instances of snaking, the body and board are used to communicate more so than words. People who are snaked as part of a teaching moment are beckoned to learn how to read body language and gazes, listen to the sounds of boards and bodies on the move, and recognize how the positioning of skateboards are conveying information; for instance, a board perched on the coping signals—through an "embodied spatial claim" (Ivarsson, 2012)—that that person is making a bid to go next. Given how pivotal watching and noticing is to learning how to skateboard, as discussed in the next chapter, snaking can be understood as a key way in which participants are taught how to skateboard and be a skateboarder within this cultural community.

TS explains how he teaches less experienced skaters about the norms of participation by "shooting" his board at them. He says, "It's like, you get the point across no matter what, and either they learn or they don't. And the ones that don't learn aren't going to be in skateboarding that long." Here, his discussion of snaking speaks to the mutually constitutive nature of learning to skateboard and learning to be a certain kind of participant within this context. For instance, people who violate the norms of using the physical space of the park get, as TS explains "knocked back down to the bottom of the totem pole," "go down a pay grade," and are not "trusted" as much in the cultural community. (I note here that this discussion of snaking could easily be part of the discussion of Chapter 7, as that one, too, through focus on discursive practices, emphasizes the role of conflict in learning both how to skateboard and how to be a certain type of participant at the park.)

I also note that one of the very first times I skateboarded at Franklin Skatepark, Luis deliberately snaked me by cutting me off and then nearly stopping his board a few feet in front of me. As he started rolling away, he looked back, smiled, and laughed at me as I struggled to keep my balance and not fall. In this sense, snaking functioned as a form of good-natured "ribbing" and initiation; in fact, later, Luis let me know with a broad smile that he snaked me to "you know, break ya in." In this way, and in other instances, mainly among close friends and skaters of equivalent ability levels, snaking was done in a more playful manner.

LINKING LEARNING TO STRUCTURES OF PARTICIPATION
AND SPATIAL PRODUCTION

Theoretically, this chapter most squarely addresses the facets of LOPI that focus on the "community organization of learning" and the "social organization of endeavors," though it also connects these with other aspects of participation and learning, including, for example, the means of learning as evidenced through snaking and communication. More specifically, this chapter explores the intersections of physical geography and architecture of place with the participants to tease out the ways structures of participation and spatial practices are produced at Franklin Skatepark. In doing so, this chapter demonstrates how the skatepark, as a place of learning, does not exist as a static, a priori structure that simply houses learning but rather is "produced," through relationship with the participants, over and over, often in dynamic ways. In this way, this chapter reveals the constitutive nature of interaction between people, place, space, practices (social and discursive), and participation.

Of particular significance in detailing these constitutive processes and practices is the ways they connect to learning. A key takeaway of this chapter, particularly for educators, is that spatial practices and the overall production of space within a place create, facilitate, and/or constrain learning opportunities. Ma and Munter (2014) explain, based on their research of two skateparks, learning opportunities "emerge" as a result of how skaters produced—what they refer to as "editing"—space at the parks. They also explain how spatial practices can shut down access to learning opportunities.

Exploration of the spatial practices at Franklin Skatepark reveal how participation is social and interactive while also allowing for individual participation and observation. For instance, whereas skating alone enables participants to practice, skating with others allows for opportunities for more direct teaching and learning from others, and whole-park structures of participation create opportunities for participants to observe and be watched by others. This learning opportunity for observing others is also created by virtue of having to share the park. This shared, communal nature of the park also necessitates collective and distributed problem solving, and provides access to the full range of activities of the park for all participants and varied, differentiated entry points for participation, as well as opportunities for cross-age and cross-skill engagement among participants. In these ways, this chapter reveals that spatial production shapes possibilities for learning opportunities. Thus, this chapter lays the foundation for subsequent chapters, especially the next one, which explores particular learning practices constitutive with the structures of participation and social arrangements discussed in this chapter.

In considering the complex relationships between place, space, participation, and learning at Franklin Skatepark, I urge educators to consider these connections in their contexts. What is the physical place where learning occurs—what are its features? In what ways are students in a dynamic relationship with that place and actively producing it spatially? How are some spaces students produce being shut down or encouraged? In what ways are broader organizational structures of schooling promoting or constraining particular types of participation and spatial practices? Put another way, what are the social practices and arrangements within schools that enable or constrain spatial production and, thus, learning? How does this spatial production open or constrain possibilities for learning? For particular types of discourse? Relationships between participants? In what ways might opportunities for shifting spatial practices occur? How are students' bodies invited to be mobile (or constrained), and in what ways does this impact spatial practices and learning opportunities?

CHAPTER SIX

"It All Goes Together, You Know?"

PROCESSES OF LEARNING HOW TO SKATEBOARD
AT FRANKLIN SKATEPARK

> RP: How does someone, let's say, someone walked in right now, has never skated before, how would they learn how to skate?
>
> Alex: You can't really be taught. People always ask me, can you show me how to do this? You can't . . . I mean, it helps a lot to watch people skate, so you can get an idea, but you really can't teach people how to skate. You've just got to get on the board, get comfortable, get a feel for it. You know, once you get to that point and you feel comfortable, you can ride around smooth. *Then*, after that, a little bit of insight helps learning tricks and whatnot, but for the most part, just for riding a skateboard you've just got to get out and fall a lot until you get comfortable.

THE PURPOSE OF this chapter is to explore particular learning practices that occur at Franklin Skatepark, paying attention to how these practices help transform individuals' participation in the cultural community. Theoretically, this chapter most directly addresses facets 4 and 5 of LOPI, which, respectively, pertain to the "goals" of learning (transformed participation) and the "means" of learning. Because learning is inextricably linked with participation, I draw attention, at times, to the participation structures mapped in the previous chapter (e.g., skating together in sessions, solo skating) to illuminate how features of the park and the participation frameworks found therein engender a set of learning practices. By focusing on processes of learning, this chapter shifts from *where* learning happens to *how* learning happens there, which, as discussed in the previous chapter, are constitutive processes.

Specifically, this chapter highlights the following practices: (a) "doing it," (b) "skating with others," and (c) "watching others." Each of these practices connects to a series of other learning practices and underlying principles of learning, which are also explored in this chapter. Though mentioned throughout this chapter, the roles of language and literacy in learning will be explored in more depth in the following two chapters, respectively.

It is important to note that though this chapter parses out particular practices and maps them onto structures of participation, these practices and forms of participation are, in reality, often interrelated and synergistic. As Alex explains in the chapter's opening quote, these learning practices go hand in hand—one watches to see what is possible, gets on the board to try it for oneself or to "do it," at which point "insight" becomes useful. This insight then facilitates "doing it" better, at which point watching others pushes possibilities to extend learning, and so on, ad infinitum. Likewise, Derrick, when explaining how he learns new tricks by watching other people and videos, trying things on his own, and asking other skateboarders, says, "It all goes together, you know?" In this sense, while drawing attention to discrete learning practices, this chapter also recognizes the interrelated nature of learning how to skateboard, which aligns quite well with LOPI, as it, too, recognizes that various facets of learning are interconnected.

"DO IT, DUDE. THERE'S NO MORE ADVICE TO BE GIVEN": LEARNING BY "DOING IT"

A central facet of learning to skateboard is that explicit instruction and talking about skateboarding are limited in their ability to teach someone how to skateboard, particularly early on in someone's process of learning, and that skateboarding is learned, in large part, by "doing it." When asked how they learned to skateboard, virtually every respondent explained that they got on a board and just started trying it. For them, learning *how* to skateboard was not separate from *actually* skateboarding, an aspect of learning that sharply contrasts with the structuring of learning in schools, whereby students are asked to learn knowledge and skills divorced from their actual application and utility in the world (e.g., learning math in school to help balance a checkbook at some later time in life). In other words, how to skateboard is not something that is learned *about* but learned experientially by *doing*. Crazy K explains,

That's the thing about skateboarding. That's how I learned it. I just got on the board and did it. I think that's what makes the attraction for some people versus other people. Because it's not something that you say, "Well, do this and do that." I mean, we talk among ourselves, like if there are skaters who are not better skaters, we'll say, "Okay, try this, or lean back," or whatever, but it still takes you *doing it* to learn it. A lot of muscle memory, a lot of falling.

Perhaps this sentiment is best captured in the words of a participant, who, during a direct instructional session (described later in this chapter) in which he and other more experienced skateboarders were teaching a less experienced participant, said, "Do it, dude. There's no more advice to be given."

As Alex explains, before assistance from others can be of real help, skateboarders "just gotta get on the board, get comfortable, get a feel for it. Once you get to that point and you feel comfortable, you can ride around smooth. *Then*, after that, a little bit of insight helps learning tricks and whatnot." In many regards, this getting a "feel" for it speaks to a certain type of embodied learning and kinesthetic knowing, which is always embedded and may determine how knowing is expressed (Bäckström, 2014).

Perhaps more than any other form of participation, skating alone (solo sessions) epitomizes the learning practice of "doing it." In the following vignette, Matt, during his first summer skateboarding at Franklin Skatepark, attempts a series of tricks he'd been working on the previous few days. At this point, Matt was still quite new at the park and did not yet have the type of social connections and access to "relational resources" (Nasir & Cooks, 2009) to facilitate his learning. For Matt, this type of solo skating was the predominant form of participation during that summer, rivaled only by watching others when that was available.

During my first summer of observation, it was not unlikely for Matt to be at the park for the better part of extremely hot and humid days, and often alone there for significant stretches of time. This vignette is typical for his participation during that summer:

> With one foot atop his skateboard, Matt leans over his knees, drops of sweat pooling at the peak of his forehead before falling to the concrete. After holding this position for about 30 seconds, he stands erect, lifts his shirt to wipe his brow, and then rolls

his board toward the coping before leaning his body toward the bowl, preparing for another attempt at dropping into the bowl—his 14th in a row. At this point in his learning trajectory, Matt has successfully accomplished how to drop into the bowl, although once he does so, he cannot sustain or generate momentum, and he always ends up having to climb instead of skateboard out of the bowl. In other words, his runs consist of him dropping into the bowl, riding up the opposite wall to the coping, turning his board around (without doing a particular move) and then riding back up the wall he initially dropped into but losing momentum before making it to the coping and, thus, sliding back into the bottom of the bowl.

He follows this same pattern eight more times, making slight changes with each run—bending his knees a bit more, attempting to "pump" with his body, and on two occasions even attempting a 50–50 when he makes it to the top after initially dropping in. Each time he places his board on the coping to drop in—tail down, nose popped up in the air—his feet twitch and move, almost in a dancing movement around the board, but seemingly unsteady and uncertain. He looks down at his feet and board frequently, something more experienced skaters do not do as much, and his eyes dart from his feet to the bowl back to his feet and then the bowl before he pushes his top foot down into the board and glides down the side of the bowl.

After his second fall, he climbs out of the bowl, hops on his board, and pushes into the street side of the park, where he floats across it, picking up speed both through the initial dip into that section and riding up and then down a "hip." He skates the street side and then the perimeter of the park, not attempting any real tricks other than one where, when leaving the street side, he bends his knees, lowers his body so he is nearly in a sitting position, grabs his deck with one hand and "hops" to catch some air—a move he has had mastered for some time.

After skating the perimeter and street side for a few minutes, Matt stops in a corner of the park, positioning his board parallel to a 15-foot straight stretch of flat concrete that ends in a slight crescent. With the ball of his left foot pressed into the back half of his deck, he kicks into the ground with his right foot until he builds enough speed to carry him atop the small crescent of concrete; he places his right foot back on the deck, quickly maneuvering both feet (while looking down at them) so they rest perpendicular to the direction his body travels. Nearing the small crescent of concrete, he crouches down, twisting one knee almost into the other and bringing his feet together by dropping his front foot to where its toes are almost touching those of the back foot. From this position he presses down and then quickly jumps up, sending the board spinning like a corkscrew, hoping it lands right side up as his feet come down. On his first attempt, the board lands on its side, and while his left foot lands on the side of the board, his right foot finds the cement, preventing him from falling or twisting an ankle.

He slowly rolls back to the point where he started and attempts it again. This time, the board shoots out from under him before he has a chance to spin it, and he falls backward, landing on his backside and hands stretched behind his body. He walks to the board on the grass, skates back to his starting point, and reattempts the same move. On this try, he gets the board to land on its wheels and his left foot to land on the deck. After this failed attempt, he moves more quickly back to the starting point to try it again.

Matt reattempts this move 11 more times, landing two successfully, although not fluidly, before he skates the street side and perimeter a few times as he had when he transitioned from skating the bowl to attempting this trick. He then packs his board into his backpack, hops onto his bicycle, and pedals slowly out of the park.

This description of Matt "doing it" during a solo session highlights several learning practices, including (a) the importance of repetition and practice; (b) the integral nature of falling and failing to learn, which, in part, alongside sustaining of injuries, demonstrates a necessary level of commitment for accessing resources within the cultural community; and (c) the participant-initiated, directed, and devised "curriculum" that is not only individualized for each participant but is also flexible in that it enables learners access to multiple possibilities for engagement at any one time. Moreover, this vignette illustrates how the skatepark, as a learning environment, affords participants opportunities to simultaneously demonstrate mastery while also being on their growth edge of learning. For instance, Matt, while learning—and failing at—new tricks can also engage in activities he has previously mastered.

This description of Matt also indexes him as a novice participant. His noviceness is evidenced by his lack of certainty and stability on the board and in his footwork, as well as his inability to generate momentum in the bowl after dropping in to move beyond an entry level of participation. At the same time, Matt's solo session reveals how he has developed some comfort on his board and is advancing toward more challenging tricks and uses/spaces of the park. In other words, Matt offers an ideal example of someone who, from a technical aspect at least, is on their way toward developing their own unique style and significantly transforming his participation within the cultural community, something that did occur over the course of this research. In this sense, solo sessions are, as mentioned, particularly generative for Matt and other participants at similar levels of participation and statuses, as they help participants both build skills and earn respect for their putting in time.

Repetition and Embodied, Kinesthetic Learning

Repetition and practicing things over and over is one of the key learning practices at Franklin Skatepark (Ellmer, Rynne, & Enright, 2020; Jacobson, 2019). In addition to the physical doing, this practice demands intense mental commitment, dedication, and discipline. On a physical level, many of the skateboarders discuss this facet of learning in terms of developing "muscle memory," which they explain as the ability to know in their bodies how to perform particular aspects of skateboarding without having to think consciously about them. For example, in the excerpt of Matt's solo skating, he attempts two different tricks more than 10 times each, which, based on other observations, is actually quite a low number of attempts for him and others when working on a new trick, and he would go on to continue these same moves hundreds of times prior to achieving a modicum of comfort and reliability regarding the tricks. Even years later, some of the skaters talked about how, though they didn't skateboard anymore, they would "remember" in their bodies how to do certain tricks.

Examining the integral nature of repetition and doing it over and over reveals how learning in skateboarding is a profoundly embodied experience whereby knowledge and skills live in bodies evidenced by kinesthetic demonstration, not verbal or written explanations detached from performance. This embeds a skateboarder's production of multisensory information that is built on the body listening, doing, and remembering (Bäckström, 2014). This multisensoriality, or the inseparability of the senses, speaks to the way skateboarders as bodies utilize the combination of all their senses simultaneously to learn (e.g., vibrations of the board are actually sound waves—listening—but they are felt through the feet and up through the full body) (Fors, Bäckström, & Pink, 2013). I draw attention to this facet of learning, in particular, given how deeply *disembodied* learning and teaching is in schools (Robinson, 2013).

Furthermore, by practicing over and over and developing the muscle memory to successfully learn, land, "know," and "feel," as Alex mentions, tricks, and the confidence to do so, this practice engenders rewards in that mastery of certain basic skills opens up more opportunities to skate with and learn alongside other participants, particularly those more experienced. In this way, practicing tricks over and over not only enables mastery over them but also begets new opportunities and access for participation to progress learning in the form of "relational resources," which are "the positive relationships with others in the context that can increase connection to the practice" (Nasir & Cooks, 2009, p. 47). Related, the dedication that is revealed through repetition aids in participants developing status and respect within the cultural community, which also has implications for learning and participation.

Failure, Falling, Injuries, and Taking Risks

In the description of Matt's solo skating, he never successfully landed the two tricks he worked on mastering. From one perspective, it could be argued that Matt "failed" in his endeavors. As a former teacher, I struggle when I think of instances whereby my students were given as many attempts to get something "landed" before I brought out the red pen to let them know what they were doing wrong and where they stood— either in relation to some criteria or compared to their peers—which was usually quantified by some type of number or letter grade. However, this is not the language or attitude any skateboarder I have ever met would use to characterize this moment in Matt's trajectory of learning. Instead, they would likely note the normalcy of not being able to land a new trick. In fact, they might point to the estimates that "success rates" for landing a new trick are about 100 attempts before landing a trick (Sagor, 2002). This seemingly low success rate means there are exponentially more instances in which someone "fails" then "succeeds."

In this context, failure often means falling, and this falling is understood as inevitable, necessary, and not something to be ashamed of (Dahlquist et al., 2019; Haines, Smith, & Baxter, 2010; Jones, 2011; Kim, 2011). As Crazy K says, "No matter *how* good you are, you *are* going to fall!" When asked what advice he would give someone just learning how to skateboard, Derrick says, "If you fall, get back up!" Santana, when discussing how he goes about learning new tricks he sees other participants landing, says, "And if we fall, it's not like an embarrassment. It's like, if you can't do the trick, you just gotta keep trying it. It's not like *they* could just do it right away. They had to practice."

Some of the participants talk about this recognition of generative failure as fundamental to the process of learning to skateboard in terms of an expectation. TS says, "You got to know you're going to fall, and you know, *you got to get used to that idea in your head.*" In this way, failure is a necessary *mentality* to and for learning. In fact, failure is more than just accepted as standard operating procedure—it is valued and valorized, as it indicates someone pushing themselves to their learning edge and taking risks rather than just staying comfortable where they are at (Ellmer, Rynne, & Enright, 2020; Haines, Smith, & Baxter, 2010). In this way, failure is a manifestation of dedication and commitment to one's learning. Moreover, the centrality of failure and falling speaks to how learning within skateboarding is often based on mastery rather than performance (though there are times where there are elements of performance, particularly in whole-group sessions). In this sense, whereas schools are designed to have students *perform*, skateboarding works toward *mastery* (Dahlquist et al., 2019).

In many regards, the cultural value of failure (and falling) is symbolically and physically manifested in the injuries participants sustain and their resultant scars. Injuries typically result from pushing oneself, taking risks, and attempting to advance one's learning; without this risk taking, skateboarders knew their learning and participation would not progress—and they knew this risk taking had its consequences. Although every participant I interviewed explained how they did not like or prefer injuries—either in real time or after the fact, a point made emphatically by older participants whose bodies were prematurely achy—they recognized how injuries indicated a sense of commitment and conferred status among other participants. Similar to how many of the participants who were interested in tattooing discussed their lack of trust in an artist without (m)any tattoos, they talked, too, about how they "trusted" other skaters more if they knew they'd sustained injuries from skateboarding. In this way, participants literally wore their commitment on their bodies through their scars. Thus, scars served as a form of "verification" (Donnelly & Young, 1988).

Talk of injuries—narrativizing and dramatizing individual's and other people's injuries, particularly at the picnic tables in the park—was a constant aspect of the discourse at the park and among the participants: the time Houston, while trying his hand at BMXing in the bowl and fell, got his finger caught in the chain shaft and nearly cut off; when Luis fell and smashed his tailbone on the coping; when one of the little ones hit his chin on the bottom of the bowl, and so on. At first, I understood recounting these incidents as part of a toxic or über masculinity, and while there may be some of that bound up in this talk, this discursive practice served several important functions in this cultural community, including teaching novice participants about the cultural value of risk taking and normalizing failure and pain as necessary aspects of learning.

Demonstrating Commitment

Another important aspect of Matt's solo session is that it demonstrates a level of commitment to his own learning and participation. As discussed, commitment to the park is a crucial aspect of being a member of the cultural community. Matt's commitment is revealed in two ways. First—and most immediately visible—Matt is at the park and "putting in the time," as some of the participants refer to it. Just by virtue of being at the park and pushing oneself to improve one gets noticed by others, particularly since, as discussed later in this chapter, watching and being seen by others are such integral aspects of learning within this cultural community. Rogoff et al. (2015) say, "Central to the pattern of cultural practices related to LOPI is 'being there' during valued activities and having opportunities to contribute" (p. 480). As a researcher, I had an analogous experience whereby my access to participants—their trusting of me and my work—was due, in large part, by my being there, too, to my "seen face" (Smith, 2012).

A second way Matt's solo session demonstrates commitment is in what it might produce—namely his ability to do certain tricks and an overall sense of developing his own style—something that, as discussed in Chapter 9, is vital not only to individuals but also to the vibrancy and health of the broader cultural community as it functions as a valuable resource for other participants. In this way, Matt's commitment will further be revealed, in time, by the fruits of his labor as they are seen by other participants. For instance, this type of demonstration of commitment is seen in Chapter 4, when TS and Crazy K, while watching Derrick skate during the annual contest, marvel at how much he'd improved over the summer.

In this sense, there exists a type of "noticing" that occurs at the park, particularly among more experienced participants in relation to younger, novice participants. This noticing is important since the cultural community is not a static entity, and new participants are needed to not only eventually take over important roles within the community but also push others, especially more experienced participants, to improve their own learning and participation. In these ways, the hard work Matt is putting into his practice during this first summer demonstrates his commitment in real time and may demonstrate his commitment of time put in in the future (which it, in fact, did).

Self-Initiated and Self-Directed Learning "Curriculum"

Solo sessions illuminate the individualized and inductive nature of learning how to skateboard. There is no coach or teacher with a set of prescribed lessons or drills for participants to engage on a preset timetable. Learning within the cultural community is self-initiated and self-directed, meaning the participants themselves (with some help from other participants, at times) have to figure out what to learn and how to go about learning it. For many participants, this type of individualized, self-directed learning is what drew them to skateboarding, and they often talked about this appeal in contrast to school-sanctioned or community-league team sports, where they were beholden to adult authority and team structures. One participant, for instance, explained how he quit playing basketball for the school because "kids are taking it way too seriously" and that "in skateboarding, you choose the tricks you do, someone won't get mad at you if you don't do something. You're more free, and it's so much more fun."

The self-initiated and -directed aspect highlights how the learning at Franklin Skatepark is, as Lave and Wenger (1991) explain, "an improvised practice" (p. 93). Not having a prescriptive set of precepts, the participants seek out resources (videos, other participants) and various means of learning (watching others, asking others for pointers) to build their own curriculum that is idiosyncratic. In this way, much of the onus of learning within this cultural community is put on and is the responsibility of the individual participant. While there is a modicum of social and collective responsibility for each other's learning within the park, as will be discussed, participants are largely, particularly early on, responsible for their learning.

Moreover, this individualized learning curriculum is shaped, in many ways, by the cultural community of Franklin Skatepark—from the physical structure of the park to the spatial relations to the social and discursive practices that occur there, as well as the broader community context. In this way, "a learning curriculum unfolds in opportunities for engagement in practice. It is not specified as a set of dictates for proper practice" (Lave & Wenger, 1991, p. 93). (It is important to note here that this feature of learning is inextricably connected to issues of "self-determined motivation," which will be addressed in Chapter 9.)

I draw attention to the self-directed and -initiated facet of learning within Franklin Skatepark to illuminate how proactive and complex a process of building one's own learning curriculum is for these participants. This is particularly salient given how these young men—and many youth labeled "at-risk" or "failures"—are often cast as indifferent, lazy, incapable, and the like. It may, in fact, be true that in schools students like the participants of Franklin Skatepark behave and feel in such ways. My hope, though, by highlighting quite a contrary perspective of these young men when it comes to engagement, is to shift the gaze from these young men themselves as the source of the "problem" to the broader structures of learning and schooling that may be producing these behaviors and attitudes (Golden & Petrone, 2021).

Moreover, I offer this section, too, to counter the normalized desire of future teachers with whom I work to help make their students "lifelong learners." These young men are *already* lifelong learners—and quite adept at it, actually; in fact, I would say that these young men are "gifted and talented"—not only in their skills but also in their understandings of learning and teaching. I wonder: What might it mean if the starting point for teachers was that all students, *especially* those labeled "at-risk" and "failing," are *already* expert, lifelong learners—and "gifted and talented"? In what ways might such a starting point reconfigure relationships, pedagogies, and so-called interventions?

Simultaneous Access to Multiple Levels of Competency

Up to now, I have focused my attention regarding Matt's solo session on his process of working on two new tricks. Here, I draw attention to what he does *in between* and *after* working on these tricks. After a string of unsuccessful attempts at the first trick, Matt leaves the bowl side of the park and skates on the street side. Specifically, he enters the area, picks up speed, skates it for a while, and does a trick he has long had proficiency doing before he sets himself up for practicing a next trick he hasn't yet mastered. He also concludes this set of failed attempts with a similar stretch of time and skating in the street side of the bowl.

In both instances, Matt engages in a set of practices he is more familiar and comfortable with and has more confidence and competency in. In this way, during his solo session, Matt vacillated between engaging in activities where he had mastery and those where he did not, using them strategically to bolster and prepare himself. From a learning perspective, I draw attention to this toggling back and forth to highlight how participants in this cultural community have access to, at any one time, multiple types of practices linked with various stages of competency and mastery. Except in cases when someone has no experience on a board, participants have some level of proficiency, and, while learning to improve their skills, they always maintain access to engaging in activities they are comfortable with and proficient at.

For some skateboarders, this opportunity may actually curtail their learning, as they can still participate within this safe zone and therefore may not "need" to push beyond it, though, as already explained, this will necessarily limit their overall participation and status within the cultural community, as it demonstrates a lack of risk taking and will limit their access to other participants as resources. At the same time, for skaters like Matt, this access to both practices that stretch them to their learning edge and those that are more in their wheelhouse and repertoire of established practices opens opportunities for them to restore a sense of competence and confidence after a series of "failed" attempts at a trick.

This access also always allows them to innovatively establish their learning curriculum at any time. If they show up to the park, for instance, and feel like they don't quite have the desire to push themselves, they can still participate in the cultural community. If they push themselves and fail, they can, as Matt did, shift their engagement toward something else for a while to take a physical, mental, and emotional break from the taxing demands and reset themselves to try it again.

In these ways, learning is structured at Franklin Skatepark in a way whereby participants are always able to feel both challenged *and* competent. Hence, learning at the park simultaneously enables Matt to exist *within and at the edge* of his "zone of proximal development" (Vygotsky, 1978). This access to practices of proficiency and mastery alongside learning new content and skills may have particular purchase for youth in schools who are labeled "at-risk" and the like; such labels and ordering in schools necessarily shapes self-efficacy, perceptions of self, motivation, and engagement. For such students, being able to tap into acts and feelings of competence, proficiency, and even expertise and mastery could engender a qualitatively different internal sense and external experience of being a "struggling" student within schools.

"YO, IT'S FRIENDS THAT TEACH YOU": SKATING WITH OTHERS

As a central facet of the social organization of activities at the park, skating together, particularly in sessions, establishes a set of social arrangements in which it is normalized practice for skaters to learn from and alongside one another. As Alex, whose words open this chapter, notes, once someone is on the board and developing some comfort they can benefit from gaining some "insight" from other skateboarders. Specifically, skating with others provides skateboarders opportunities to practice while getting support from others, learning new things from them, and even teaching others, which, as discussed in Chapter 9, has tremendous emotional and psychological value for these participants well beyond their own learning to skateboard. In short, skating with others provides one with motivation, as well as various forms of assessment and instruction.

In addition, skating with others provides participants access to other skaters, which is especially important for younger, less experienced skaters, as more experienced participants often support and challenge (Ellmer & Rynne, 2016; Haines, Smith, & Baxter, 2010); in this way, skaters themselves become important "relational resources" for learning, and, as Nasir and Cooks (2009) explain, through the relationships forged and emotional bonds developed, "a reason to learn" (p. 47).

"You Complain?": Giving and Receiving Motivation and Inspiration

Skating with others provides participants with a tremendous amount of motivation and inspiration to learn and, as TS says, to keep "pushing" oneself. He explains,

> The difference between skating and a session is when you're in a session, there's a lot more energy flowing around. There's a lot more, like *pushing*, like, you know, you can be out skating by yourself trying to land a trick, and when you fall, there's not much motivation to get up, but when you got your friends sitting there saying, "You got it. You got it," you know, it just adds to it. Plus, you land stuff a lot quicker. You get a lot more motivated. You can work through pain.
>
> But most of the time it's always somebody, like especially with your friends being with you skating. Like it was always motivational 'cause you see them start, especially when you talk about having a session together. Like they start doing something, they start getting a little bit more, you know, they start doing bigger airs or longer grinds, and it just makes you want to do that. So you start pushing yourself and keep pushing. And the best part is it's not like a team sport where you're required to progress. You can kind of just go at your own pace, but you just become comfortable with pushing and pushing and pushing . . .

Significant in TS's discussion is how skating a session with others helps him to "push" and "keep pushing and pushing" to "work through pain" and develop his skills. Implicitly, he suggests that without this motivation and support, he would not progress or want to progress as much as he does. Also, TS distinguishes two ways of receiving motivation. The first is through verbal suggestions and words of encouragement, such as "You got it, you got it." The second is through the power of seeing others push themselves— how seeing others "doing bigger airs" or "longer grinds" "makes you want to do that, so you start pushing yourself and keep pushing." As he explains, within a session, "energy" builds among the participants and motivates them to push themselves and each other to try things they might not otherwise try and in many instances "land stuff a lot quicker."

In this way, motivation is both an internal experience *and* a communal and distributed facet of this community. For instance, as explored in the aforementioned section on "doing it," one has to be motivated and disciplined to show up to the park, to practice, to fall and fail and potentially get injured; and, as TS explains, motivation is also something that emerges from participation with others, particularly as they work toward common goals. He says, while skating a session, "you want to see what everyone else is bringing to the table and you want to see if you can step it up and bring that, too." Another participant said in response to my inquiry into what role friends play in his learning to skateboard, "Full out motivation!" Related, skate videos and music also provide motivation, getting the participants "amped up," as one of them says, to skate harder.

Another practice related to giving and receiving motivation and encouragement is offering praise to one another. In general, participants at Franklin Skatepark offer each other quite a lot of praise through words of encouragement (e.g., "Come on, you got this," "Nice!") and "board slaps," which is the practice of slapping the tail of one's board against the ground, as illustrated during the skate contest and the book's opening vignette. TS explains how this is "like clapping, just our way of doing it." Another participant explains that board slaps "are like stomping your feet at football games. It's a different way of saying, 'good job' so they can hear you." In many respects, these modes of congratulating and acknowledging a job or effort well done illustrates how Franklin Skatepark is quite celebratory. I deliberately highlight how pervasive praise as a form of assessment is within this cultural community given how *uncommon* a discursive practice it often is within schools.

"Why Don't You Try It Like This?" Giving and Receiving Instruction and Assessment

In addition to motivation, the participation structure of skating with others, particularly in sessions, provide skateboarders opportunities for both giving and receiving assistance and feedback to improve abilities. For instance, in a session involving Derrick and Ricardo, a participant who, after the first summer of research, moved from Finley, the two take turns skating the deepest bowl, trying different moves, and talking to each other about them. What follows is a snapshot of their shared endeavor. (A note: in this exchange, there are instances of problematic language related to gender and sexuality, a topic I address in the next chapter.)

The two take turns entering the bowl one at a time, reconvening on the concrete deck after each entry. Their conversation continues even when one is in the bowl. For instance, at one point, Derrick rides up to the coping in front of where Ricardo is standing, and says, "I don't know what I'm doing here." He then slides back into the bowl, grinds the opposite coping, and slides back into the bowl.

"Nice, nice, nice!" Ricardo shouts to him while he lifts his board in both hands and smacks its "tail" on the concrete.

Once out of the bowl, Ricardo asks to try Derrick's skateboard, gets on it, enters the bowl, does a rock and roll, then a blunt, before skating down the waterfall into the six-foot section and into the second waterfall into the nine-foot bowl, where he skates up and down the walls, building up enough momentum to bring him back to where Derrick awaits him and his board. As Ricardo ollies out of the bowl, he exclaims, "That board rides tight," and he rolls it back toward Derrick.

Derrick, pushing his board toward the bowl, hops on it and says just as he is about to roll into the three-foot section of the bowl, "Try this." He rolls into the bowl, does a 50–50 on the opposite side coping, rolls back toward Ricardo, and, when reaching the coping, does a rock to fakey, slides back into the bowl, and does a 360 to dismount.

Ricardo, bringing his deck to the coping, yells across the bowl, into Derrick's back, "That's gay!" and then drops into the bowl himself, does a rock to fakey on the opposite side coping, slides back down the bowl, and tries and lands the 360 dismount, to which Derrick, now watching, yells, "You're a fag!"

Derrick rolls into the bowl, pops out on the side where Ricardo is standing, skates over, and stands next to him. The two peer into the bowl and talk about the graffiti, and how not only does it look stupid but how it makes the bowl "too slick."

They again take turns riding back and forth across the bowl, although at this point they ride much more slowly, talking back and forth the entire time they are skating. "Have you ever tried a 'double kick'?" Ricardo asks Derrick. Derrick says that he has not but he has been working on a "tail slide," which Ricardo claims are "scary" and explains how he does the trick with his hand, saying "Once you do it with your hand, you'll never go back to a regular ollie." Derrick responds, "You know what I am worried about?

Not being able to push out of the tail slide into the ollie," to which Ricardo responds, "That's why I came up with using my hand."

The turn taking and talking continue as the two skate for another ten minutes until they both take a seat at the picnic table to drink some water and watch the others in the park.

Throughout this vignette, the two ask each other questions, share their concerns, discuss riding conditions and equipment, and assess each other and offer suggestions. Moreover, the feedback the two are receiving and giving is, as is virtually always the case in this cultural community, both contextualized and "in and on time" (Gee, 2003). In these ways, the instruction and assessment are embedded in the broader participation in the cultural community, and there is no distinction in this case between participating and learning to participate. They are one and the same. Thus, this example illuminates how much of the learning and teaching that occurs through skating with others is an almost *indirect* pedagogy. This more indirect aspect of this exchange is due, in large part, to the fact that there is not a clear or drastic sense of hierarchy between Ricardo and Derrick—they are roughly the same age and at the same level of participation. In other words, there are fairly equilateral power dynamics between the two that enable them to be co-learners and co-instructors at the same time with one another.

In some instances, skating with others, even if not in a session but just in the same vicinity, serves as a way for less experienced skaters to solicit assistance from more experienced skaters by asking them how they do a certain move; as Derrick explains in response to my question about how he learns the tricks he knows, "It's not always videos, it's watching other people skate. You ask them, 'Oh that's a cool trick,' you know, and they'll say, 'Thanks, man,' and you'll be like, 'What is it?' and they'll tell you."

For example, in a session involving Derrick, Santana, and Brad, the three were attempting to jump two barrels as they came out of the street side bowl. Derrick was the only one who could do this when the group started, and throughout the session, he assisted the other two, especially Brad, who was the least experienced of the three regarding his ability to land this move. Derrick watched Brad as he rode his board into the bowl, approached the barrels, and made his attempt. Once Brad got back on his board, Derrick offered him suggestions based on what he observed. After one attempt, for instance, Derrick told Brad to try and lower his front foot on the deck to keep it closer to his back foot so he could get more "pop" out of the board. As he was talking with Brad, Derrick got on his board to demonstrate visually what he was talking about. Brad, after Derrick showed him, got on his board to get a feel for it, and Derrick, looking at Brad's footwork, confirmed that it looked good before encouraging him to try it again. After the next attempt, Derrick, watching again, said to Brad, "A little more speed, and I think you'll get it," to which Brad said, "That's what I was thinking, too."

In this instance, Derrick is a more experienced participant regarding that particular move and so is functioning in an almost coach-like fashion. Specifically, he is actively assessing Brad, and Brad is willingly accepting Derrick's assessment and feedback. Derrick's instructional approach emphasizes providing a demonstration with explanation as well as active feedback during and immediately after Brad's attempt. Related, Brad is self-assessing alongside Derrick, evidenced by his echoing Derrick's feedback as resonating with what he was thinking. This encounter is quite dialogic, as well, though there is a clear asymmetrical relationship here between "instructor" and "learner." In many respects, this type of learning moment is more *direct* in its pedagogical approach, whereby one participant is actively teaching another.

I deliberately selected examples of indirect and direct instances of learning and teaching that involved Derrick to illuminate how this learning practice of skating with others, and the connected practices of learning from and teaching others, enables participants to move across different social positions within the cultural community across time and space. They are "teachers" in one instance, "co-learners" in another. I could, too, have offered an instance in which Derrick was also the *recipient* of a more direct form of pedagogy (for instance, the time when Crazy K taught him a particular way to exit the bowl) to further illustrate this point.

Overall, these instances of giving and receiving instruction and assessment illuminate a central underlying feature of learning at Franklin Skatepark—namely how so much of the learning is done through *reciprocal relationships* and "joint activity" (Vossoughi et al., 2021) between participants. In so many ways, individual learning at Franklin Skatepark is constitutive with other participants' learning (Dahlquist et al., 2019; Derrian, 2019; Ellmer, Rynne, & Enright, 2020; Ellmer & Rynne, 2016; Haines, Smith, & Baxter, 2010; Jones, 2011; Ma & Munter, 2014).

It is important to recognize, too, that learning from and alongside one another is available to participants through relationships that are more equal regarding levels of participation and status *and* ones that are more asymmetrical.

More will be explored in Chapter 9 about "reciprocal relationships," particularly given how essential it is for this cultural community, but for now, I ask the reader to put a bookmark here until then, and also to keep in mind how the skateboarders themselves are "relational resources" (Nasir & Cooks, 2009) for each other—that they can draw on and be drawn on, sometimes in more and less symmetrical ways. This highlights the reciprocal nature of much of the participation that occurs among the skaters within the cultural community, as well as how learning and the responsibility for learning is distributed and operates in dynamic interplay between individuals and the collective. Highlighting this facet of the social and collaborative nature of learning at Franklin Skatepark is important as it helps to illuminate, through contrast, how learning within schools is so often individualized and competition-focused, even when it involves features like "group work."

Explicit Instructional Sessions

While most of the instruction that occurs within sessions is among skateboarders skating together, one of the variations of sessions found at Franklin Skatepark is instances in which there are explicit learning-teaching situations usually involving young, novice skaters learning or attempting a specific move, such as dropping into the bowl, for the first time. These instances, what I call "explicit instructional sessions," focus attention on one individual and typically involve more experienced participants instructing that individual. While there are instances during whole park sessions where someone attempting a move is the focus of everyone's attention, in these small groups, explicit moments constitute the actual substance and exigency of the shared experience. This differs, for instance, from the previously mentioned session between Derrick and Brad, because although Derrick was providing direct instruction, the two were skating together in a session that extended beyond that particular instructional moment. What follows is an instance of an explicit instructional session:

While a few small groups of skaters congregate at different areas of the park, a late elementary-aged boy stands with one foot on his skateboard near the coping of the bowl. He is fully adorned in helmet, knee pads, and wrist guards, all of which seem way too big for his small, thin body. Standing right next to him is an older (probably early 20s), more experienced skateboarder. Both stand with one foot on their respective skateboards, the younger boy with hands on hips, the older smoking a cigarette, peering into the bowl, watching an older, more experienced skateboarder cruise back and forth from one side of the bowl to the other displaying an array of moves each time he makes it to the coping.

When the skater in the bowl dismounts across from the two, they inch up to the coping. The older skater quickly maneuvers the tail of his board onto the coping so it is perched at a 45-degree angle, suspended in air. The young boy slowly follows the older skater's lead, awkwardly placing his board in a similar manner, having to reach down and use his hand to position the board. The younger skater has yet to drop into the bowl in his life, and the two older participants have agreed to show him how.

The skater who just dismounted from the bowl looks across at the young boy and says calmly, "Get your back foot comfortable on the board." The younger skater shifts his foot, digging the ball of his right foot harder into the grip tape. A third older skater is standing in the bowl at this time, looking up at the younger skater. The skater standing next to the younger skater, the one who has his board in the same position as the young boy's, says, as he moves his left foot to the nose of the deck, gently resting it on the deck, "Put your other foot on the board around here."

At this point, two of the smaller groups of skaters skate over toward the bowl and, in almost an instant, a crowd forms around the bowl, all eyes on the young boy.

Once the young boy stops fidgeting with his left foot and stands in the correct position to drop into the bowl, the older skater next to him says, "Put all your weight forward and then drop in." He pauses for a couple of seconds and then says, "Like this." He pushes down on his extended foot and drops into the bowl, rolls to the other side, and dismounts.

The little boy stands, looking intently into the bowl, but hesitates. The older skater across from him, the one who first skated the bowl to demonstrate to the younger skater how to drop in, says in a tone more assertive than the calm, coaxing tones the older skaters had used up to that point, "Do it, dude, There's no more advice to be given."

A few seconds pass, none of the other skaters saying anything, and the younger skater pushes his front foot down on his board, starts to roll into the bowl, and quickly hops off of his board, running to the bottom of the bowl as the board passes him. He leans down, grabs his board, looks up, and says, "I did it!"

One of the older skateboarders, looking down at him, says, "No, you didn't."

The boy climbs out of the bowl, carries his board over to the group of boys still standing watching him, and puts his board on the coping to make another attempt. As the young boy stands ready for his second attempt, one of the older skateboarders says assertively, "Just do it. Don't think about it. Just do it." His voice then softens, "Just lean into it."

Another skater says, "The easier way to do it is to 'roll in,'" to which another older skater says, "Fuck that. He needs to learn how to drop in." Again attention focuses on the younger skateboarder, and one of the older skaters provides some instructions on what to do in case he falls.

As evidenced in this excerpt, explicit instructional sessions consist of demonstrating and modeling a particular trick or move by more experienced skaters, accompanied with verbal instructions. For example, as one of the "instructors" demonstrates how to place his feet on the board, another of the instructors says, "Get your back foot comfortable." In addition to the combination of verbal explanation and modeling, these sessions function to demarcate norms of the cultural community, including, for instance, what constitutes landing a trick or successfully completing a move. For example, while the boy exclaims "I did it!" his instructors are sure to let him know that he, in fact, did not ("No, you didn't."). Also, these sessions can be pedagogical in the sense they teach novice skaters how to handle pain and "failure." In many of these sessions, it is common for the instructors, after the learner has fallen, to say things like "Get up" or "Stop whining." These are done, in part, to teach new skateboarders the appropriate cultural emotional responses to pain and failure, which are that they are inevitable and necessary aspects of learning to skateboard and not to be used as excuses for not landing or attempting a trick. These types of explicit instructional sessions flow from more experienced to less experienced participants whereby there are more unidirectional power dynamics.

Offering Unsolicited Assistance

One of the reasons explicit instructional sessions are available to participants at Franklin Skatepark is because of the normalized social practice of soliciting assistance from other participants. For instance, Crazy K explains, "You find it with the better skaters, they'll be skating . . . and you'll have other skaters who will walk up and start conversations, and once you get conversations going, they'll say, 'Oh, I've been trying this.' And the better skater will say, 'Oh, why don't you try it like this.'"

This is not to say that anyone can go up to anyone else and ask for help and expect to receive it. People's time and energy are not just freely given out, particularly flowing from more to less experienced participants. As already explored, these relational resources are often doled out as participants demonstrate their commitment and establish respect within the cultural community—both for it and from it.

At the same time, there is a regular practice of more experienced participants watching and noticing less experienced participants, getting to know them over time, and then providing unsolicited feedback and assistance to them. For instance, Crazy K, as one of the "old guys" at the park, explains he will watch skaters and then give them some help: "Sometimes what I'll do is, I'll see a younger kid drop in or something, and I'll kind of watch him and see if I can't give him positive feedback. That's usually with an older skater to a younger skater. When there's more of an age similarity, there's not as much talking." This practice illuminates how participants watch to facilitate other participants' learning. Ma and Munter (2014) explain, in their research, that some skateboarders "positioned themselves to help others (seek to be teachers)," including "watching and offering critique and encouragement, sharing experience, assessing and disciplining" (p. 254).

In many ways, this giving of unsolicited feedback is not only a common and accepted practice among the skateboarders but also one that is, to a certain extent, expected of more experienced participants, particularly if a less experienced skater is making a genuine attempt at learning to skateboard and is ready for a particular form of help. For example, while skating a session with a few people, Archie noticed a younger, less experienced skater consistently trying to jump a set of stairs. In between his turns, Archie observed this younger skater trying this move, and not getting close, and without being asked for help, said to him, "Billy, learn how to ollie first." When Billy recovered from his latest attempt, he looked at Archie, and Archie, rolling out on his board, performed an ollie, and said, "Practice that one first."

Similar to motivation, this practice of offering unsolicited assessment and/or instruction demonstrates how learning is distributed and characterized by a reciprocity between the individual and the cultural community's responsibility. The practice of snaking, as discussed in the previous chapter, also connects to this individual-collective connection, perhaps in a less savory manifestation, as spatial relations are the responsibility of individual participants to learn and know and act in accordance with but will be taught and policed by the cultural community as needed. In this way, in addition to learning how to appropriately use the park, snaking also teaches participants that they need to, and how to, pay attention to what is happening around them.

The Role of Language in Learning

Skating with others, more than other structures of participation, helps reveal the role of language and talk in learning at Franklin Skatepark. Though skateboarding is an intensely embodied and kinesthetic experience, verbal communication is ubiquitous and embedded in most of the learning practices highlighted in this chapter. Among other things, language is used to deliver instructions, provide motivation and encouragement, and discuss moments of learning. For instance, talk during sessions, as in the examples of Ricardo and Derrick, consists of the riding conditions (i.e., how graffiti makes the cement "too slick"), particular moves (e.g., "tail slide"), and the skaters' feelings about doing particular tricks (i.e., Ricardo says how a certain trick is "scary"). Participants also use talk to offer advice, suggestions, motivation, and words of encouragement and congratulations to each other. For example, Derrick pushes Ricardo to try a certain move ("Try this"), and Ricardo, acknowledging a good move by Derrick, provides him with congratulations ("Nice, nice, nice!" combined with a board slap). (Similar types of talk are evidenced in the skate contest explored in Chapter 4.)

In looking across these, and at other instances, it is important to note how talk, particularly as it intersects learning, operates in this cultural community in significantly different ways than it does within schools. In a broad sense, talk is used at Franklin Skatepark to encourage participation—to *support* the learning, not be the focus of the learning or participation. Participants are not assessed or evaluated on how well they can explain things verbally but by how well they try and can *do* what it is they are trying to do. As Paradise and Rogoff (2009) explain, talk within a LOPI setting, in contrast to school contexts, "is not used to explain and vicariously reproduce nonpresent phenomena or aspects of an activity that actually takes place in another physical and social context. Talk is not used in a way that attempts to *substitute* for involvement in a productive activity, but rather *in the service* of carrying out that activity" (p. 118). In other words, talk is not a primary means of instruction but is utilized to support participants' ability to observe, develop their own curriculum, receive encouragement, and "pitch in" to the cultural community. This type of situated, embedded, and judicious use of language "is quite different from providing a detailed verbal explanation of the steps, independent of carrying out the process itself" (p. 119), which is a discourse pattern more typical of schooling (Mehan, 1979; Michaels, O'Connor, & Resnick, 2008).

In sociocultural theory, language is a particularly salient facet of learning because it not only serves as an important tool that mediates participants' experiences of learning but also always carries ideologies (Cook-Gumperz, 2006; Gee, 2015). In other words, language, as a tool that mediates learning, is not neutral; it is always laden with ideologies and helps in the construction of reality—of how people come to understand themselves and their social worlds. For instance, uses of "gay" and "fag" in the exchange between Ricardo and Derrick carry meanings attached to discourses of sexuality and gender. Because of how significant language is in this way, the next chapter explores a particular linguistic feature of the cultural community—heckling—as it illuminates various ways that ideology, particularly linked with race, class, gender, sexuality, and age circulate and inform learning and participation.

"YOU TRY TO PICTURE IN YOUR HEAD HOW THEY WOULD DO THAT": WATCHING OTHER SKATERS

Paying attention and watching other people skate is one of the key practices (and one that every skateboarder stressed) in learning how to skateboard. As Alex says in the opening of this chapter, "It helps a lot to watch people skate, so you can get an idea." This notion of "getting an idea" is particularly salient, as observation provides less experienced skaters with models and examples of moves and tricks, many of which they may never have seen before. Also, through observation of other skaters, less experienced skaters see a range of ways to use the space and materials at the park.

It is important to stress here that watching others is not a passive activity but one that is honed over time and practiced with keen, focused attention that necessitates high levels of cognitive, physical, sociocultural, and emplaced involvement. As Paradise and Rogoff (2009) explain, within a LOPI framework, "The act of observing is often pursued with concentrated energy, attuned keen perception for finding out about the activity, to be able to participate" (p. 110). To build on the previous sections, to learn, participants must "be there," practice over and over, and also pay close attention—a skill and attitude they must develop.

To further illustrate these ideas, I draw attention to the previous chapter on spatial production. Linkages between spatial practices and learning are clearly exemplified by the fact that participants at the park must share space. This is particularly salient when it comes to skating the bowl, since having more than one person at a time can prove hazardous and disruptive. From this, practices of observation and the discursive practices of observers talking to one another and cheering on the one skating become a quite normalized way to participate and opportunity to learn.

Thus, sharing space facilitates particular ways of watching and "doing waiting," which is "carried out through postural, spatial, and material means" (Ivarsson, 2012). In a sense, participants who are watching other skateboarders are always also communicating to one another in a variety of verbal and nonverbal ways. For instance, when one person is skating the bowl and several others are on the coping, observing, some of them are more poised to take the next run than others, who may be more in a resting mode. This is often signaled by the positioning of the board: if it's perched on the coping or the skater has one foot atop it near the coping, these people are signaling a desire to be next; someone who has the board flipped up and is holding it with one hand is likely communicating that they are not making a bid for the next run.

Watching, then, isn't only about learning from the person skating but also being in communication and learning to observe and decode the symbols of participation from others who are similarly "doing waiting." In this way, observation isn't only about watching to learn but also learning *how* to watch—what to notice and pay attention to—to learn the underlying structures of participation and values of the cultural community. As Ivarsson (2012), building on the idea of "embodied participation frameworks" (Goodwin, 2007), explains, there are powerful linkages between the "interrelated phenomena of *attention* and *participation*" (p. 14).

Gaining Insights

Observing other skaters reveals particular insights, or "clues," as participants said, about how to do certain tricks. In watching others, skaters pick up on footwork, body movements, and other aspects of skating. For example, during one of his first summers of skating at Franklin Skatepark, Matt typically sat on one of the ledges or boxes in the park and observed the action when whole-group sessions occurred. He explains, "When I first started coming up here, I didn't know anybody, so I just sat around—I didn't talk to anybody. It's like you watch someone try to do something, you're like, you just think about it, and you're like, 'I can do that.'"

In addition to watching "live" skaters, the participants also learned a great deal by viewing skate videos and photography in skateboard magazines (Enright & Gard, 2016; Ellmer & Rynne, 2016; Ellmer, Rynne, & Enright, 2020; McDonald, 2017; Thorpe, 2017). As Santana says about him and his friends watching videos together, "Like we see the moves and we go out there and try them and stuff." Likewise, in response to my inquiry about whether he reads magazines, Terry explains how the photographs in *Thrasher* assist him in developing his abilities as a skateboarder: "I look at *Thrasher* 'cuz some stuff in there—like the photos are insane. Like, you try to picture in your head how they would do that." Derrick also explains how video images help him "see where to put your feet" on the board to do certain tricks. Related, in response to my inquiry about a recent trick he learned, Hollywood explained how he learned it from watching a video of someone landing the trick. He says,

> I envy a lot of people that can do some of the shit I can't, but, you know, I just watch them and try to learn it. Like the latest trick I've learned is an Indy boneless. It's where you grab your board, flip it around, stand on one foot and jump back in. I learned that by watching the *Mentality* video at least 20 times, just rewinding that part.

In these ways, watching is done *analytically*, meaning observation is meant to support learning not just be entertainment; Jones (2011), in his research on skaters' use of videography and digital media in learning to skateboard, explains that they "use the medium to understand the motions and timing that go into performing particular tricks by attending to what Ferrell et al. (2001) call the 'microphysics of representability'" (p. 600).

Whereas skating with others enables a type of "side-by-side" learning (Paradise & Rogoff, 2009), observation of live skaters in real time and watching videos of skateboarding (or looking at photos) functions as a form of "distal guidance" (Billett, 2006) that enables participants to learn from others they may not have a relationship with or even know at all. This opportunity for such distal learning also enables various geographies of learning, particularly in the case of viewing videos, as well as social media use. More specifically, participants are both exposed to different geographies of skateboarding and can watch them away from the park and practice their skills elsewhere. Thus, their distal learning both opens them up to a much wider range of potential mentors and places for their learning as well as opens possibilities for new ideas to be recontextualized in the cultural community at Franklin Skatepark, much in the same way skating at other parks informs participation at Franklin Skatepark. Theoretically, this learning practice is interesting, as it opens spaces to recognize how engaging different cultural communities may shape participation within a particular cultural community.

Imitation

Observation is also an essential aspect of learning how to skateboard, because as an early part of their development of a unique style of skating, the skaters at Franklin Skatepark often imitate other skateboarders. In fact, imitation is seen as a normal aspect of learning how to do a certain move (e.g., one imitates another's way to do a move to learn how to do it and then do it uniquely). Imitation is a phase or stage of development virtually everyone goes through on their way to developing their own unique style. In this sense, imitation is not meant as a destination but rather as a stop along the way that the participant can move beyond and individualize. TS explains how observation of others functions to help skateboarders to learn how to perform certain tricks and how skaters imitate others as they work toward developing their own style:

RP: So when you think about where you were in fifth grade and I don't know how old you were when you started, and you look at yourself now like how did that happen this 8 or 9 or 10 years? I mean now that you step on a board, how does that happen? How does someone move from point A to point B?

TS: Like I said it just kind of consumes you. Like you start seeing videos and stuff. Like when you start skating, you're really, like you know you have a Walmart board or something like or a World Industry, something that you know you thought it was just cool to have one.

And then when you start getting into it, you start watching skate videos and stuff, and you start seeing all these pros doing all these crazy tricks that you had never even thought of. Like all you were thinking about was riding off the curb and maybe doing little slappy grinds everywhere. And all of a sudden you start seeing them doing that and you start trying to figure out how they do that, how they position their feet.

You start adapting to styles, like to stuff you like to see. . . . And you know you just kind of start finding that through stuff you watch or stuff you see friends do.

As TS explains, one aspect of watching others is to learn footwork and imitate them—or, as he says, "You start adapting to styles, like to stuff you like to see." In his explanation, TS explains how watching others skate—either friends or skaters in videos—pushes skaters to try different things by helping them to conceptualize beyond what they are doing or even know what was possible. He says, "You start seeing all these pros doing all these crazy tricks that you had never even thought of." In this way, observation of others helps one build their individualized curriculum by opening up new possibilities for things to learn and how to use the space of the park (or cityscape). Therefore, the types of texts and other resources one has access to affects how they will develop and learn.

Being Watched and Performance

Observation—who observes and who gets observed—serves important functions, especially when related to whole-group sessions. Whole-group sessions enable more experienced participants to perform for others by showcasing their moves, which in turn builds their status as participants in the community. For the majority of skaters who participate in whole-group sessions, the event provides an opportunity for them to both push themselves to try and land more difficult tricks and to be recognized doing so. During these whole-group sessions, participants have all eyes on them. As one skater said to another during one whole-group session, "The stage is all yours." In this way, watching is a two-way street—there's watching to learn, and being watched to see what you've learned or what you can do.

Whole-group sessions, given the attention by everyone else at the park, become prime opportunities for "performative moments" (Urciuoli, 1995) whereby participants display themselves as texts to be observed and analyzed. Jones (2011), in research on the role of digital media in learning among a group of urban skateboarders in Hong Kong, explains how recording their skateboarding similarly functioned among them. He explains that the integration of the camera into participation helps to create such performative moments that "call attention to the power of public performance in generating especially intense moments of self-enactment and create solidarity among a group of people and decrease an individual's sense of self as autonomous or isolated" (p. 602). This sense of performance and watching/being watched is amplified beyond the physical park. Often these whole-group performances are prime opportunities for videoing efforts and posting on social media whereby participants watch and are watched digitally.

FROM PRACTICES TO PRINCIPLES

Theoretically, this chapter illuminates many of the "means of learning" in this cultural community. Through the practices of doing it, skating with others, and observation, we can see the importance of "wide, keen attention" to events, "guidance from community-wide expectations and sometimes people," assessments and communication that support learning, and opportunities to "pitch in" to support the participation and learning of other participants (Rogoff et al., 2015). In addition to examining these myriad practices, and similar to the previous chapter, this chapter demonstrates the *relationships* between the means of learning (observation, talk) and other aspects of participation and learning—including the goals of learning and types and delivery of assessments, as well as, as discussed in the previous two chapters, the social and community organizational structures, the physical geography of the park, and the spatial production of that place. In other words, this chapter, perhaps more than any other in this book, reveals the *interrelated* and *interconnected* nature of learning within this cultural community.

More specifically, this chapter demonstrates how examining particular practices helps illuminate broader underlying principles of learning. In this case, this chapter reveals how learning at Franklin Skatepark is situated and contextualized—all learning that occurs there is part of the cultural practice, not removed from it. From this, participants have access to the full range of activities and multiple entry points into these activities. Thus, for anyone walking into the park, at any time, with any skill level, there are always multiple opportunities for them to participate. Furthermore, learning, teaching, and assessment have an exigent temporality, which is important given how idiosyncratic and individualized learning is and how critical it is for participants to develop their own curriculum. However, while the learning is self-selected, it is also quite social and communal, whereby cognition, resources, and problem solving are distributed. This reliance on a distribution of resources, including individuals' knowledge, means participants themselves become relational resources and valuable members, which helps inform an anticompetitive, aspirational ethos within the cultural community.

In considering the interrelated nature of participation and learning in this cultural community, which is one of the key takeaways of this chapter, I encourage examination of the means of learning in schools—both to better understand them and to explore the connections between them and other aspects of participation and learning, including assessments, discourse, and broader social and community organizational structures. For instance, in what ways are learning practices students are ushered into in schools situated within actual practice? How is discourse in classrooms congruent with the aims of learning? What opportunities are there for students to see how all the aspects of learning fit together and work toward a goal that is meaningful and purposive for them? How are students given opportunities to link their doing with their observing/listening with their connections with others?

I pose these questions, in large part, because these are the types of questions, albeit in their own words, the participants of this study would often ask me during our conversations. For them, schools felt like such a fragmented and detached experience that had neither much congruence nor much purpose for their lives beyond school. For them, the means of learning—often decontextualized lessons, tests, patterned discussions—did little to inspire them, as was the case, too, for their connections to the seeming goals of schools, which, for them, often felt contradictory to their goals for their lives.

My hope, then, with these questions—as reformulations of their questions—might push us to consider both how the organizing of learning, particularly in contrast with Franklin Skatepark, might feel and actually be a disjointed experience for many youth, particularly those whose own aims may not align with those of schooling, and might inspire possibilities for imagining new configurations of learning. I also raise these questions, in part, because of how, within the context of the skatepark, we see the young men there as quite proficient as learners. They are highly self-directed, skilled at improvisation, and supportive. In this sense, we know that their so-called failures in schools are not because they do not know how or do not care to learn.

CHAPTER SEVEN

"Whatta Ya Gotta Be a 'Scene Kid'?"
EXAMINING DISCURSIVE PRACTICES TO EXPLORE POWER
AND LEARNING AT FRANKLIN SKATEPARK

Constraint comes from the way participation is regulated within a community. Learning and identity formation are embedded in social relations with others; shifts in participation (i.e., learning) require legitimation from social others within the community. Moreover, communities commonly place constraints on who is allowed to participate, and in which ways. These constraints often reflect social systems and categories like race, gender, and language use. (Esmonde, 2017, p. 21)

Discursive practices are both means and medium. They mediate experiences, relationships, and interactions, and offer possibilities for, and impose limitations on, the construction of meaning across social spaces. They imply participation frameworks, ways of engaging in discursive and social practices, and available identity positions within sets of relationships. (Hirst & Vadeboncoeur 2006, p. 206)

THE PURPOSE OF this chapter is to examine how power—particularly manifested through performances of class, gender, sexuality, race, and age[1]—interplays with participation and learning at Franklin Skatepark. Specifically, this chapter focuses on how discursive practices—namely "heckling" (explained below)—illuminate some of the ideological underpinnings and tensions within the cultural community and how

---

1 It is important to note that I conceptualize these various identity markers from the perspective of "performance" rather than the standpoint of intrinsic qualities or materiality (Bettie, 2000; Butler, 1990; Goffman, 1959). In this sense, I recognize identity as dynamic, relational, and social(ly constructed)—and, ultimately, something continually developed, produced, and performed within socio-spatial contexts. For this study, then, I understand the participants' myriad performances of identity at Franklin Skatepark—communicated via language, clothes, mannerisms, tattoos, etc.—as constitutive with the place, the other participants, and the various social and spatial practices coproduced therein, particularly as these interplay with broader sociopolitical discourses and practices related to categories of social representation (e.g., age, gender, race).

these enable and/or constrain participation. In this way, my discussion of language as a key tool of mediation in this chapter differs from my discussion of talk in the previous chapter, where I explored how language was used to discuss particular facets of learning (e.g., talking about equipment, riding conditions). Here, I use discursive practices as entry points to examine the ways power relations shape how learning occurs and who even gets to learn, or not, in this cultural community.

Though my central focus is on heckling as a discursive practice, I supplement this discussion with other discursive practices that contribute to understandings of class, gender, sexuality, race, and age at the park (e.g., monikers such as "Mexican" Matt), as well as instances of literacy activities (e.g., tattooing) and social practices (e.g., age structuring of the annual skate contest) that also bolster understandings of power relations within this cultural community. By examining how these discursive and social practices shape participation, I illuminate how inextricable learning and identity are—that for the participants at Franklin Skatepark, learning *how* to skateboard is linked with learning how to *be* a particular kind of person and participant in this cultural community.

This examination of discursive practices also reveals how learning is inherently wrought with symbolic, social, and ideological tensions, and how, at once, learning is agentive *and* constrained (Esmonde, 2017). This exploration moves from micro-level conflicts to a broader sense of how macro-level factors (i.e., race, class, gender, sexuality, and age) inform learning at Franklin Skatepark (mezzo-level). In this sense, this chapter demonstrates how participation within a particular cultural community is shaped, in part, by participation and membership in other, overlapping cultural communities. As Gutiérrez and Rogoff (2003) explain, "These categories [race, class, ethnicity] have long-standing influences on the cultural practices in which people have the opportunity to participate, often yielding shared circumstances, practices, and beliefs that play important and varied roles for group members. People do not just *choose* to move in and out of different practices, taking on new and equal participation in cultural communities" (p. 21).

Theoretically, this chapter complicates understanding how people learn within a cultural community by revealing how instances of transgressive behavior and/or patterns of discontinuity constitute key aspects of learning and teaching within cultural communities—for better and for worse. As mentioned, it also reveals the inextricable link between learning how to do something and becoming a certain somebody, and the various ways conflicts both enable and constrain these joint process-es—to the point, even where being or (not) becoming "a different kind of person" (Lave & Wenger, 1991, p. 53) potentially excludes one from being a participant at all. Furthermore, this chapter demonstrates that cultural communities are not necessarily "welcoming" places (Fuller et al., 2005, p. 53) where "people are working together in an ideologically neutral manner toward some agreed-upon goal" (Rogers & Fuller, 2007, p. 80) but rather are full of "ideologically laden sets of beliefs, actions, and assumptions" (p. 79).

In looking at ways ideology operates at Franklin Skatepark, this chapter has implications for understanding how this cultural community func-tions simultaneously as a space in which dominant social relations and power dynamics are reinscribed and/or are transformed. For instance, at Franklin Skatepark dominant societal ideas of age are, in many ways, cri-tiqued and new possibilities regarding them are made available, whereas dominant social relations of masculinity and race are simultaneously reconfigured *and* reinforced. In this way, this chapter offers a window onto how forms and sites of youth purposive learning may help imagine new possibilities for social relations and/or better understand limitations and constraints on advancement of such progressive reconfigurations. From this examination, those of us in education might be better poised to think of the ways other contexts for learning and teaching (e.g., class-rooms, schools) might also be simultaneously functioning as sites of transformation and reification of dominant social ordering, as well as how conflicts might provide important portals to examining possibilities and barriers to social transformation.

Before moving on, I pause here to signal that throughout the chapter, there is a certain modicum of problematic language discussed—most notably related to sexuality, gender, and race. I note this to be sensitive to readers, since much of this language has connections to oppression and discrimination, and can be emotionally charged. Throughout this study, hearing this language use and not intervening was one of my big-gest ethical challenges as a researcher. This was also the one facet of the study that really pushed against my own prejudices and judgements of the participants; as a way, in part, to work with these judgments, I insert some of my own socialization, limitations, and developing understandings of these categories of representation at different places in this chapter.

I also note that these terms and analyses are specific to this particular cultural community and informed by many factors, and are not meant to speak about other skateboarders or skateparks. In fact, in recent years, there have been many entities within skateboarding that are more avowedly inclusive, including, for example, *Skateism*, a magazine focused on, among other topics, diversity and activism in skateboarding. Even *Thrasher Magazine*, a long-time industry staple, has made moves away from its intensely heteronormative male aggressive ethos (Borden, personal communication).

In this spirit of transparency, I also note that I do not give the same attention in this chapter to notions of dis/ability and ableism as I do race, class, gender, sexuality, and age. There are certainly places where ability is touched on, but my own unconscious ableist biases prevented me from emphasizing this in my data generation and analysis, and I became cognizant of as it as an area pertinent to this work only through the process of completing this book. This miss of mine feels quite ironic, given how, as discussed in Chapter 3, I trace my entry into criticality to my father's lost ability to use his body, as well as how so much of this research emphasizes bodies, physicality, and mobility. Having said that, it is important to point out that the way normalized participation in skateboarding has been constructed is often based on its physical and cognitive demands, which often systematically excludes individuals with dis/abilities (Le Clair, 2011; Ranniko et al., 2016). While some research exists at the intersections of peer inclusion and lifestyle sports (see Liikanen, 2014), as well as the role of adaptive sports' programs for individuals with dis/abilities (see Gossett & Tingstrom, 2017; Ryan et al., 2014), attention to both the social and physical complexity of skateboarding and its impact on the inclusion (and exclusion) of those with dis/ability labels is an underexplored area of research.

HECKLING AS A DISCURSIVE PRACTICE AND (INDIRECT) FORM OF SOCIAL CONTROL

Heckling, also known by the participants as "harassing," is a linguistic practice—almost a form of verbal play—whereby participants condemn, ridicule, make fun of, or "give someone shit" regarding their actions, behaviors, language, attitudes, and/or dress. Though not named as such, instances of heckling are strewn throughout the previous chapters as skaters interact with one another. For example, in the previous chapter, Derrick and Ricardo, while skating a session together, are constantly saying things to one another like, "That's gay!" or "You're a fag!"

At Franklin Skatepark, heckling serves several functions. In many instances, heckling serves to push participants to try new or more challenging tricks. In these instances, heckling, according to Luis, is "not done with any aggression or anything. It's more of a friendly kind of, you know, *razzing* each other up a little bit." TS further explains:

> RP: So, okay I've heard these phrases up at the park: "That's so gay,"
> "You're a fag," and "You're a punk." What do those things mean?
> TS: Ah, dude, most of the time it's just antagonizing, like trying to
> get somebody to do better stuff. Like dude, that's just more or
> less like when somebody goes up and says, well, "I don't want
> to do that because I don't like the fact that I might fall," "You're
> gay." You know, you just kind of, it's more or less just picking on
> them trying to progress them. It's more like daring somebody.
> Like you just sitting there like, "I dare you dude," like "Dude, do
> it." Peer pressure.

Related, another purpose of heckling is (ironically) a way of congratulating someone on an accomplishment, offering praise, or expressing some type of acceptance of them. For instance, as mentioned in Chapter 3, one of the first times I skateboarded at the park, Luis snaked me and said, "Who's the skater fag?," which he later explained was a way of accepting my participation at the park.

Another function of heckling—and the one focused on in this chapter—is to learn, teach, and police ideological normativity and expectations of the cultural community—in this case, to draw attention to something a skater is doing (or not doing), saying, or wearing, often, though not always, because of how it conflicts with the dominant norms of the community. For instance, during the explicit instructional session from the previous chapter, a younger, less experienced skater, while learning to drop into the bowl, fell (but was not seriously hurt) and stayed lying on the bottom of the bowl while others waited for him. Looking at him, an older skater said, "Get up and stop whining." While seemingly insensitive, in this instance, heckling was used to teach the less experienced skater the appropriate cultural responses—psychologically, emotionally, and physically—to handling failure and pain. This is echoed, too, in TS's explanation of helping when one gets hurt. He explains how unlike when someone falls and gets hurt, if someone falls and "just scrapes their hand, it's like, 'You pansy, get the fuck up.'"

Similarly, heckling functions to "correct" or police behavior by implicitly calling attention to "misbehavior" or behavior not deemed "appropriate." For example, Archie's clothing choices often contrast with that of many of the other participants at the park, and on occasion people will heckle him. One evening, for instance, Archie was wearing sweatpants and a bandana rolled into a headband. TS, on seeing him, said aloud, "You look like you're ready for an aerobics class," to which others within earshot laughed. Though he donned a headband thereafter, I never saw Archie wearing sweatpants again.

In many regards, these uses of heckling serve similar roles that teasing and shaming serve in other cultural communities. Rogoff (2003) explains how teasing and shaming function as indirect forms of social control by "inform[ing] people indirectly that their behavior is out of bounds or to indicate the appropriate way to act" (p. 217). Rogoff explains that teasing and shaming are especially important forms of social control in "small interrelated communities," since "people avoid intrusive or hostile interactions for expressing everyday criticisms or complaints, to avoid jeopardizing long-term relationships. In such settings, teasing provides an indirect means to express criticism, carried in discourse that is softened by humor and that does not call for a serious response" (p. 217). She explains, "Teasing and shaming, like discipline by parents and teachers, involve cultural variations in ways of compelling, persuading, or guiding children to behave in accepted ways" (p. 220).

Because so many of these instances of heckling are laden with gendered, homophobic, racialized, and classed terms, I honed in on this particular discursive practice to examine how these broader social categories of representation factored into participation at Franklin Skatepark. In the remainder of this chapter, I discuss how heckling both reveals and polices norms related to class, gender (specifically masculinity), sexuality, race, and age among the skaters at Franklin Skatepark, and ways these power dynamics inform participation and learning.

"Whatta Ya Gotta Be a 'Scene Kid'?": Transgressing and Reinforcing
Middle-Class Ideologies

As discussed thus far in this book, the majority of the participants of Franklin Skatepark, particularly the "diehard locals," identify as working-class, or, as most of them say, "blue-collar." For these participants, the park functions as an almost working-class refuge, and in some ways, the mobilization of the park as predominantly, and at times exclusively, working-class could be understood as a demonstration of collective power through the claiming of a particular place within a broader community (and schooling) context in which the participants of Franklin Skatepark do not hold or are able to exert as much power, have as much say, or feel as if they rightly belong. Here, I am reminded of many of the working-class characters in Springsteen songs who seek opportunities to find their place and exert power "in a world that somebody else owns," including fixing up muscle cars to go "racing in the street" (Springsteen, 1978).

Various mechanisms, including heckling, were used by the participants to make visible dominant middle-class cultural norms, particularly as they align with skateboarding, and reconfigure normativity and acceptability within this cultural community to align with working-class values and practices. The clothing the young men of Franklin Skatepark wore and did not wear, in particular, proved to be signifying practices that served an important locus of ideological conflict regarding class, and clothing became something people were heckled over.

Unlike most parks I visited during my research, the norms at Franklin Skatepark about clothing inverted the more popular forms of dress in skateboarding writ large, many of which reflected corporate interests and signaled vast consumption practices. Specifically, while skater-specific, designer, and/or "skinny" jeans; skating belt buckles; particular brands of shoes; brand names skateboard decks (as opposed to "blanks"); and even particular "skater" hairstyles dominated other skateparks I visited, typical attire for the locals of Franklin Skatepark included heavily worn skater shoes, blank decks, "regular" blue jeans, white T-shirts, and done-at-home crew cuts or shaggy, unkempt hairstyles. Of course, the fashion of the young men varied, but in general, when compared to the attire of other skateboard parks in the region, the participants of Franklin Skatepark revealed a style that mostly lacked the dominant aesthetic found throughout mainstream skateboarding culture—an aesthetic that was often associated with being part of "the scene," which signifies skateboarding well beyond the local context.

For the locals of Franklin Skatepark, these elements of fashion also typically correlated to broader class ideological affiliations. Specifically, more mainstream clothing and aesthetics were typically linked with middle- and upper-class—or, as most of the locals said, "white-collar"—sensibilities and associations. In contrast, the general aesthetic of the locals was typically linked with "blue-collar" lifestyles and affiliations. This tension between the working-class ethos of the local community and the corporatized, more mainstream nature of skateboarding more generally often indexed locals from "outsiders" and those who do and do not fit in at Franklin Skatepark. TS explains, "You can tell the white-collared kids right away. They're the ones who have brand new boards, they got brand new T-shirts, you know, stuff like that."

These affiliations often demarcated who did and did not participate at all at the park. TS explains how over time these "white-collared kids" typically stop skating at Franklin Skatepark:

> Honestly, I hate to say it, but they really don't fit in too well when they do come up. Like, remember that kid who used to come up in a Mercedes? That kid, like, he didn't last too long. No one really liked him.

Conversely, another participant, Adam, explains that even though he lives closer to a different, larger skatepark, he prefers Franklin Skatepark because of it is not full of "snobby rich kids":

> Well, I hate going to City Skatepark because all the little kids are little pricks, snobby rich kids. . . . They're amazing at skating and know they are and they're jerks about it. I hate . . . That's why I don't go there, just because of it. It's a good park, but I don't like going there because of the attitude.

In general, for the locals of Franklin Skatepark, being in *the* scene (meaning the broader skateboarding industry scene) was valued less and, in fact, disparaged at times, over being in the *local* scene—each of which had respective social class associations. Heckling, then, served as a way these tensions were revealed and norms regarding social class enforced.

As mentioned, clothing often served as a space for this ideological work—and heckling—to occur. For instance, Hollywood, one of the few skaters at Franklin Skatepark who wore designer jeans specifically made for skateboarding as well as other expensive mainstream, corporate-produced clothing and accessories (the exception being skateboard industry T-shirts, which virtually all participants adorned on occasion), got consistently heckled about his clothing and fashion by the other locals. One evening while skating with several others, Hollywood ripped his designer jeans. As he made his way over to the picnic table, he began to complain about his ripped jeans by pulling at them and cursing them.

An older, more experienced participant heard Hollywood complaining and asked him, "How much did you pay for them?" to which Hollywood replied, "Forty bucks! They're supposed to be reinforced for rough skateboarding. Yeah right." The older participant responded to this statement by saying, "Whatta ya gotta be a *scene* kid? Gotta have the clothing?" He paused, making eye contact with another participant who smiled and chuckled in agreement, and then he continued, "You can go to Major [a grocery superstore] and get four pairs of jeans for the same price!"

Although a brief encounter, this instance illustrates how heckling reveals conflicts between an individual's performances of class and performances of class valued by the cultural community. In this case, Hollywood's designer skateboarding jeans, which mark class affiliations, opened him up to ridicule, and, for better or worse, functioned as a moment of learning and teaching about the ways of being valued in the cultural community. Similar to how the incident previously explained whereby Archie was heckled for wearing sweatpants, Hollywood here is given the opportunity to rethink his fashion choices to align more with the cultural community, which would likely diminish the ridicule. In this instance, there is an inverse of sorts of dominant class relations: aligning with mainstream norms is stigmatized whereas promoting a working-class persona is a valued practice. While Hollywood seemingly has more economic capital than the other participants, he actually misses in this instance as he performs class in a way that demonstrates his economic capital that is valued *outside* the park but not *at* the park. In this way, his display of broader capital actually costs him *sub*cultural capital (Thornton, 1996).

Throughout my time researching Franklin Skatepark, Hollywood, as well as others who similarly aligned themselves with middle-class styles and sensibilities, never became true insiders in the cultural community—either by their own assessment or those of other participants—regardless of regular participation. In Hollywood's case, he was tolerated at best, though heckled quite regularly. Hollywood's opportunities for participation and acceptance into the cultural community were limited for various reasons, including his behaviors (others described him as an "asshole"), some of which, as in this case, were ascribed to his performances of middle-class ideologies.

From this example, we see how, within this cultural community, performances of class function as an important way to demonstrate how macro-level aspects of power operate to open up and/or shut down learning opportunities, including who can participate comfortably and who will be given access to resources, including other participants. In this way, participation is contingent, to some extent, on conformity and assimilation to the values of the cultural community—in this case, a working-class ethos. In short, this cultural community is not truly available for skateboarders who perform middle-class and more affluent ideologies and affiliations. This is not to say that middle-class performing participants cannot or do not show up to the park. They do. But their participation is limited, including their access to other participants as relational resources for learning. In other words, it would be difficult, if not impossible, for middle-class performing youth living in Finley or frequenting Franklin Skatepark to either become integral members of the cultural community or advance their skills beyond a certain level—that is, unless, potentially, they were able to perform a working-classness deemed acceptable and authentic to the core group of skaters at Franklin Skatepark.

In this way, power related to class functioned to simultaneously exclude middle-class folks and cultivate solidarity among working-class people. I note this, in particular, given the way in which power related to class here functions as the reverse of how power regarding class often operates in schools. It has been well documented that, in schools, working-class kids, even if they "show up" (like the middle-class skaters at Franklin Skatepark), have their participation systematically limited, whereas middle-class participants are afforded more opportunities and resources (Bourdieu & Passeron, 1990; Cookson, 2013; Eckert, 1989).

For this reason, it is worth considering how the participants of Franklin Skatepark covet the cultural community in the ways they do as they get to exercise control in/of some place. To return to Kevin from the book's introduction, this particular circulation of power may attend to his question, "What else would we have?" At the same time, though, I wonder how these class politics within this cultural community potentially constrain possibilities for participants' lives and aspirations regarding class and socioeconomics; for instance, might participation in Franklin Skatepark delimit participants' aspirations for class mobility? Among the core skateboarders of Franklin Skatepark there is clearly an awareness of the existing social order and a reversal of class-based values at the park, but the broader societal class hierarchy remains intact. In other words, is their class "critique," which, in some ways, is really an inversion of social hierarchies, really a form of critique or actually a reinscription of dominant class relations?

In these ways, I note a tension in the identity work and circulation of power and participation at Franklin Skatepark, particularly when it comes to opportunities for social transformation. By being exclusionary toward middle-class ideologies, the participants create a space imbued with a seeming sense of power, control, and freedom; in this way, the identity politics involving class is transgressive or at least demonstrating an awareness of and offering a critique of dominant social class ordering. At the same time, however, these exclusionary practices may also be reproducing the broader social divisions between classes and maintaining the hierarchy. Or, at least this critique does little to disrupt the broader hierarchy beyond the cultural community, and likely, similar to Willis's (1977) seminal study, may even lock participants into their position as "working-class" or "blue-collar." In other words, from the perspective of class, we can see the participants of Franklin Skatepark transgressing dominant social relations and structures in ways that may actually be reproducing them.

"You're a Fag!": Critiquing and (Re-)Enforcing Dominant Gender and Sexual Norms

As mentioned in Chapter 4, the vast majority of participants at Franklin Skatepark were heteronormative, cisgender young men, and very few female skaters participated at all—and none did on a regular basis. The non-skating female participants at the park typically fell into one of two categories: "invisible girls," who were supportive of skaters, and "ramp tramps," who were understood as being interested in sexual relations with the skaters. Moreover, I did not, throughout the research or there-after, know of any participants who identified as queer; this is not to say, of course, that there were no queer participants but rather that I was not aware of any, which may speak to some combination of the intensely het-eronormative and cisgender norms at the park and my own unconscious biases at the time.

Heckling functioned as a major way to construct and enforce gender and sexual norms among the skaters at Franklin Skatepark, particularly through terms such as "gay" and "fag." While gendered and homophobic terms are a topic worthy of an entire book-length discussion on its own, I limit my discussion here to how the terms used in heckling function as a way for the participants to safeguard certain heterosexual norms of masculinity within a predominately homosocial environment, especially one in which some dominant norms of masculinity are implicitly and explicitly challenged and critiqued.

As Beal (1996) has noted in her research on skateboarding, male skaters enact "nonhegemonic" or "alternative" forms of masculinity by devaluing and explicitly critiquing elite competition, oftentimes working together, and valuing cooperation and encouragement. However, Beal also reveals that at the same time, these same skaters often contradict themselves by adhering to and reproducing heteropatriarchal relations with the subculture, particularly through their insistence that skateboard-ing is a "naturally" male enterprise. This tension or these "incongruities," she argues, arise when "people negotiate new social relations" (p. 10) and function as a way for skaters who are cisgendered men to have some of their non-traditional gender "needs" met while at the same time creating a space apart from the feminine. In this way, as Dupont (2014) argues, "the skater's performance masculinity is a resistive action against various aspects and values embedded within these idealized and powerful forms of middle-class masculinity" but not a wholesale rejection of hegemonic masculinity (p. 561).

Similarly, while it is acceptable and even encouraged for the partic-ipants of Franklin Skatepark to enact an alternative version of mascu-linity in certain ways, it is equally important for them to be careful not to do so *too much*. In this way, participants are afforded opportunities to explore "different" experiences of masculinity within this space, and they are constrained as to how and to what extent they can fully embrace and enact these. The use of gendered and homophobic terms within the practice of heckling served as one of the ways these boundaries were established and policed.

Similar to how ridiculing someone for wanting to be a "scene kid" functioned as a way to draw attention to class norms, terms such as "gay" and "fag" drew attention to norms and acceptable performances of sexuality, masculinity, and appropriate gendered behavior. For example, in some instances in which a participant was unwilling to take a risk for fear of getting hurt or failing, he was oftentimes called "a fag" or "gay." Returning to TS's explanation of heckling earlier in this chapter, we see how he mobilized the phrase "you're gay" as a way to showcase what heckling is and how it is used to motivate: "Like dude, that's just more or less like when somebody goes up and says well, 'I don't want to do that because I don't like the fact that I might fall.' You're *gay*."

While any number of phrases or words could be used to motivate, push, or "antagonize" each other, the use of gendered, homophobic terms such as "gay" and "fag" illustrates one way in which gender and heteronormativity within this community was constructed in relation to broader discourses of masculinity and many man-dominated group interactions that often use the fear of being seen as weak or feminine as a way to keep each other acting like "real men." In other words, within many dominant constructions of masculinity, these gendered terms often cut to the core of potential humiliation for many people who are biologically sexed as male and gendered as men and socialized into dominant forms of masculinity, a phenomenon that extends well beyond the subculture of skateboarding more generally (e.g., Kimmel & Messner, 2018; Pascoe, 2012). Disparaging these aspects of masculine identity, then, functions for many men as the crux of emasculation, humiliation, and ways to one-up each other; and gendered, homophobic terms, such as "gay" and "fag," function as a central way for this disparagement to occur.

On a personal note, growing up and being socialized, particularly through school-sponsored athletics (e.g., lacrosse, basketball), within similar dominant renderings of masculinity, I learned that the most damaging way to attack or be attacked *as a man* was by being called a "pussy." I learned this from my dad, whose own sense of masculinity that he learned in a different era was shifting under his unsteady feet, and I had it corroborated from media, coaches, and teammates. For instance, during one junior varsity lacrosse game, our team was playing against a team coached by a woman, and I remember our coach, a cisgender, heteronormative man, called a timeout because our team was trailing in score. He yelled at us, exclaiming there was no way he was getting back on the bus having lost to a woman. My socialization was so solid at that time that not only did I get back onto the field with the charge of bolstering and safeguarding my coach's—and by extension, my team's—masculinity by not losing to a woman but it wasn't until years after that I recognized this for the fear of heteropatriarchy being threatened that it was.

The terms used in heckling, which are rooted in sexuality, are appropriated from larger discourses of masculinity and used as the means by which these young men measure themselves and each other as gendered people. In a predominantly homosocial environment such as Franklin Skatepark, especially one in which the participants regularly expose their vulnerabilities and inadequacies by skating—and failing and falling—in front of others, these gendered terms may enable some ways to restore or safeguard many dominant heterosexual norms of masculinity, such as competitiveness, risk-taking behavior, and athletic aptitude.

Ironically, another form of gendered and homophobic language within heckling was a way for participants to acknowledge another's accomplishments at the same time they attempt to conceal their own feelings of jealousy and inferiority. Several of the skaters explain how this dual purpose operates:

RP: So, I know you've heard phrases like, "That's gay" and "You're a fag." So, what do these things mean?

TERRY: [*Laughter.*] Yeah, we hear that.

JAMES: What they sound like.

TERRY: Yeah, pretty much like someone lands a trick before you and you're like, "You're gay; I hate you man." Like just jokin' around but—

JAMES: You feel inferior.

TERRY: Yeah.

JAMES: Like, what was my quote the other day? "That's bullshit you son of a bitch." [*Laughing.*] Just 'cuz he landed something that I didn't even think about tryin'.

Other skaters, in a different conversation, offer a similar explanation:

> RP: When someone does something, and someone else says some-
> thing like, "You're gay," or "That's gay," or "You're a fag," or some-
> thing. What does that mean, or can you give me an example—
> HOUSTON: Like, if he's doing a trick that I can't do, I'll probably call
> him "gay" or something because I can't do it.
> KEVIN: In all honesty, what it is, is like a way to express a form of
> *slight* jealousy, but at the same time, you're like, "Wow, my friend
> just did that—that's awesome!" It's almost like saying, "Man, I
> can't believe you just did that. I wish I could do that." In all hon-
> esty, it's not portrayed as negativity in most scenarios up here.

The irony or tension that this use of gendered and sexualized, pejorative language reveals helps illuminate one of the ways the participants grapple with differing, if not competing, versions of masculinity—how on the one hand they are celebrating others' accomplishments and on the other they are feeling one-upped. In these ways, heckling functions as an indirect form of communication whereby participants are able to express their emotional and relational experiences without having to explicitly do so.

In a subculture that often devalues—at least ostensibly and outwardly—competition between participants (Beal, 1996; Borden, 2019) as a means of producing nonhegemonic version of masculinity, participants may use gendered terms as a way to exist within this alternative masculinity at the same time that they undercut it and resist it through their reverting to dominant ways of acting like "men." What is especially provocative about this particular use of gendered terms is how it is used outwardly at the same time that it is used "inwardly" by participants—for when a participant is congratulating another participant by calling him a "fag" or saying that what they just did is "gay," what they are also saying is that they themselves feel inadequate, insecure, one-down—not how a "man" is supposed to feel.

Theoretically, the use of heckling to construct gender norms in this community illustrates how gender is simultaneously performed (com-municated) and produced (created) (Butler, 1990). Furthermore, the norms of masculinity circulating in this cultural community, much like those linked to class, are formed in large part through their relationships to broader social norms, or overlapping cultural communities, which sometimes come into conflict with one another. At Franklin Skatepark, these broader, dominant ideas of masculinity are, in some ways, as mentioned, critiqued to engender new social relations, but are also reinscribed as normative, thus limiting the potential for transformation of social relations regarding gender and sexuality. In many respects, this tension connects to what Borden (2019) refers to as the "great contradiction" in skateboarding regarding masculinities: that performances of masculinity in skateboarding "can be at once loud *and* contemplative, violent *and* considerate, intolerant *and* respectful" (p. 33; emphases added).

From a learning perspective, this facet of power raises questions, similar to class, about the interplay between specific socio-spatial contexts, broader societal discourses, and practices of exclusion and solidarity. In this case, how does this manifestation of heckling delimit who, from a gender and sexuality perspective, even gets to participate in this cultural community? In what ways do the norms at the park create barriers for women, and queer, non-binary, and trans men (Carr, 2017)? Would an openly queer person be given access to resources and be welcomed into the cultural community? Would someone who does not identify as a cisgender man have the opportunity to be a full participant in this cultural community? Would they even want to, given the heckling they'd likely have to endure? In what ways do the ideological tensions regarding gender evidenced in heckling reveal not only barriers but also potential openings for reconfiguring potential performances of masculinity at the park?

"Don't Mexican My Drink!": Ideologies of Race at Franklin Skatepark

As a working-class, heteronormative, and cisgendered identity functioned as dominant at Franklin Skatepark, so, too, did whiteness. From a linguistic perspective, perhaps the clearest way in which whiteness operated as normative was through the nickname Matt was given by a white skateboarder shortly after he began to become a known entity at the park: "Mexican" Matt. As Matt explains it, a friend of his who was a fellow skateboarder "said it one day and it kind of stuck," which it did, as I only ever heard Matt referred to by participants at the park—regardless of their racial affiliations—as "Mexican Matt." This qualifier of Matt being "Mexican" is a clear way in which non-dominant categories of representation get marked linguistically whereas dominant categories (in this case, whiteness) go as unmarked and maintain their normalcy and invisibility by not being signaled (Brekhus, 1998; Hill, 1998). In other words, the "Mexican" nickname functions as a way to indicate Matt is *not* white. Related, the white participants were never signaled racially, for example, by "White TS" or "Do you know Crazy K, the white guy?"

Beyond being a moniker for Matt, the term "Mexican" was also mobilized in other ways, including, on occasion, as a part of heckling. In some exchanges, "Mexican" was used as a verb—to "Mexican" something signified stealing it. For instance, if a white participant got up from the picnic table to skate and took off his shirt or left a drink half finished, he might turn to the others sitting there and say, "Hey, don't Mexican my drink!" In other instances, "Mexican" was used as an adjective—if one participant said to another, "don't be Mexican," they meant to indicate that that person was being lazy. For example, if several participants were skating in a session together, and one of them decided to stop from fatigue, another might say, "C'mon, man, keep going. Don't be Mexican!"

Similar to how participants previously explained their use of terms such *gay* and *fag* to heckle each other, they also explained that using "Mexican" in these ways was not meant to be and was not offensive or racist. For instance, one white participant explained that, though he uses the term "Mexican" at the park, he's not racist, and that using the term is "like a nickname, like, 'Mexican Matt.' We just call him Mexican Matt 'cause he's Mexican, and his name is Matt. You know, it's not being racist." When I asked why the term gets used in other ways, he explained that it's building on the stereotype that Mexican people "steal shit" and are "lazy." He went on to explain, "It's kind of like a joke thing. It's not really hate for anybody." In this way, this white participant, along with most of the other white participants, expressed awareness that their use of these terms drew upon broader cultural discourses but that they did so without intending the offensiveness of these terms that existed beyond the cultural community.

While I understand that language use in cultural communities is complex and takes on myriad meanings unique to that context (Eckert & Wenger, 2005), I also recognize these language practices interplay with broader sociopolitical discourses that are quite damaging. In this instance, I note that the type of colorblind ideology (Bonilla-Silva, 2003) espoused and the insistence that the use of these terms does not have malicious intent enables these words and their uses to continue to circulate as their offense and the ways they reify whiteness as norma-tive are rendered invisible or insignificant. Like the use of homophobic terms, which may have functioned to restore heteronormative mascu-linity within a homosocial context, the use of "Mexican" and the insis-tence that it is not offensive may maintain white equilibrium and racial comfort for the white participants. Throughout the research, I wondered, too, to what extent the use of "Mexican" by the white participants drew specifically on broader discourses that blame Latinx people for the eco-nomic challenges of white, working-class people (McDermott, Knowles, & Richeson, 2019).

Throughout my research, I only ever observed these uses of "Mexi-can" as part of heckling between white participants. I never observed a Latino participant using these terms in these ways or observed a white participant using them in relation to a Latino participant. The one excep-tion was the phrase "Mexican Matt," which was universally adopted by all participants. Even Matt used it, reporting both at the time and years afterward that the nickname "did not really bother me too much," that he was "used to it," and at times even found it "actually kind of funny." Matt does, though, qualify this by explaining how, in response to my inquiry if he thought of the nickname as derogatory or racist, it depended on the context of its use and who was saying it: "It's different when your friends are sayin' it. Like if someone's sayin' it and actually meaning it as a racist thing, then it's different. But if your friends are just messin' around and it's your nickname or something like that, then it's just like if someone else has a nickname, it's different." In this sense, the Latino participants also made delineations in the use of these terms between how they circu-lated within and beyond the cultural community.

At the same time the term "Mexican" was used by white skaters to refer to negative stereotypes, the Latino participants—namely Luis, Derrick, Santana, Matt, and Ricardo—drew on their racial identities as a point of pride and to establish individual and a collective identity. In fact, Luis, Derrick, Santana, and Matt were sometimes referred to as the "4Gs" since each of their Spanish-based actual names (either first or last) began with a G (e.g., González). Each of these young men identified themselves as "Hispanic" with family roots from Mexico, and often as "Mexican" and/or "Mexican American." As Luis explains, his father, whose family is from Mexico, was "a big part of growing up and instilled a lot of core

Hispanic teachings, and those are a lot of the things that have stuck with me and make me who I am today." Specifically, he explains that "family is a big big part of any Hispanic person. Family, and respect of women, and respect of elders. Those are the three basic values."

At times, these participants used the term "Mexican" to refer to aspects of their lives and cultural practices and were visible in their performance of racial identities. For instance, each of these young men either had or planned on getting a tattoo of what they referred to as "Mexican prayer hands," which as discussed in Chapter 4, entails a pair of hands, palms pressed together in a prayer position, wrapped in a ribbon with their family name on it. These tattoos were significant for each of these participants, as they brought together "familia," Catholicism, and their being "Hispanic" or "Mexican."

In addition to bolstering their Mexican heritage through collective identification, nomenclature ("4 Gs"), and literacy practices like tattooing, each of these participants actively critiqued racism within schools and broader society. For instance, Matt, during an interview, explained how, overhearing Derrick tell a story of getting in trouble at school, said "racism" under his breath. When I asked him about it, he explained that "it seems to be that all of my Mexican friends get in trouble [at school]." He went on to explain, "Like, there'll be a fight and they'll blame it on us or something like that." He also talked about how at school there seemed to be differential treatments and unfair punishments doled out between Hispanic and white students, and noted, for instance, that there was an incident he was involved in where the other kid, who is white, was only suspended for one day whereas he was suspended for four days. Luis, as will be explored further in the next chapter, is quite an ardent supporter of antiracism movements, including his affiliation with SHARP, which stands for Skinheads Against Racial Prejudice, something he was exposed to through his participation in skateboarding and hardcore music. In fact, Luis has several antiracist tattoos as a way to demonstrate, as he says, "the long hard stance" he takes on racism.

It is important, too, to note that the broader community of Finley is 97 percent white, and so, like gender, sexuality, and class, the ways race functions at the skatepark is nestled in broader, overlapping systems of power and ideology. Throughout this research, I often wondered if the Latino young men found, in Franklin Skatepark, a space within the broader white-dominated community whereby they had a greater sense of agency, power, and authority than they normally do in the town where they lived and the schools they attended. Related, one question I had throughout this project was the extent to which these young men's performances of race may have, in fact, been heightened because of the higher concentration of Latino young men at the park than in the town. Conversely, how might their performances of race in this cultural community have been altered if there had been fewer Latino participants?

From the perspective of participation and learning, this facet of power raises additional questions, similar to those of class, gender, and sexuality, about exclusion, solidarity, identity, and opportunity. Unlike these other domains, which were fairly exclusionary, this one does not seem to be as much so, and in some ways, a racialized solidarity is developed and performed by the Latino participants. Even still, this cultural community largely operates from a dominant racialized sense of whiteness that may extol a cost for racially minoritized participants, including, for example, exposure to the normalized racial microaggressions (Sue et al., 2007) discussed. This exposure is the case even for those Latino participants who exist as part of the core group and as leaders in the cultural community, such as Luis, who is one of the most respected members of the community, and Derrick, who is often touted as the best skater at the park. In some sense, even if these skaters do exist at this level of participation and status within the cultural community, they still are indexed as "different" or "other" due to the ways this cultural community reifies broader racialized ideologies regarding whiteness as normative.

In thinking of these dynamics, I wonder, too, how things would operate if there were participants from other and multiple racially minoritized demographics. For instance, what if there was a contingency of Black skateboarders in addition to this cohort of Latino participants? In thinking of Hollywood, who identifies as Filipino and Native Hawaiian, to what extent is his racialized identity a factor is his not being wholly accepted in the cultural community? What if there were fewer racially minoritized skateboarders in the community? What if they were not as skilled or as dedicated as Luis, Derrick, Matt, and Santana? Would they be entirely excluded? Would they even want to be a participant in that community? To what extent does inclusion within a cultural community delimit one's resistance to or overt objections to racialized language use and heckling? For instance, to what extent would any of the Latino young men's participation be affected if they most explicitly pushed back against the use of "Mexican" at the park? What potential costs (e.g., accommodating racialized microaggressions) might there be for racially minoritized participants to participate? What would it take to disrupt and transform racialized power dynamics within such a cultural community, particularly given the broader community context?

Clearly, this research has left me with more questions than answers regarding performances of race, power, and learning within this cultural community. My hope in laying out these inquiries is to stimulate possibilities for subsequent research that explores skateboarding specifically and learning in youth purposive cultural communities more generally and attends to these complex issues of racial identities and learning.

"Is This Just a Kid Thing?": Critiquing Age-Based Segregation and Social Ordering

Rooted in developmental psychological and biological systems of reasoning, most of the social ordering of young people in schools and beyond in the United States is stratified by age (Lesko, 2012; Rogoff, 2003). In this sense, U.S. culture operates very much as an age-based and age-normed culture (Chudacoff, 1989). Within schools, this is exemplified by the fact that students are segregated by age—all students of a particular age are in the same "grade" and mostly removed from participation with other students of other ages or grades. Linguistically, age-based and normative temporal ideas of development are evident in language of "readiness," "falling behind," scoring or reading "below" or "above" (grade level), and/ or "being advanced" or "delayed" (for one's age/grade).

This mechanism of social ordering is also congruent with many white middle-class norms whereby there are entire institutions and practices designed to maintain distance between adults and youth. Within education, for instance, schools and teachers often operate from understandings, rooted in notions of "adolescence/ts," that secondary students "naturally" want distance from teachers and other adults in their lives and to be among their peers (Finders, 1997; Lewis & Petrone, 2010; Petrone & Lewis, 2012; Sarigianides, Petrone, & Lewis, 2017). Other scholarship has noted how ideas of youth being "rebellious" function as coded ways to naturalize white middle-class values and experiences that do not attend to youth from immigrant, working-class, poor, or other marginalized backgrounds (Lesko, 2012; Patel, 2012). This type of social ordering and segregation is in stark contrast to other cultural communities whereby such practices are not normative. This is perhaps most clearly exemplified in the violent and destructive ways in which Indigenous communities and their educational systems dependent on intergenerational relationships have been disrupted by colonial apparatuses of schooling and social ordering (Brayboy & Lomawaima, 2018). Even many working-class communities in the United States operate from more heterogeneous arrangements of age that engender greater "fluidity" socially and economically (Eckert, 1989).

In many respects, the cultural community of Franklin Skatepark similarly critiques and disrupts normative, dominant social relations based on age in the United States. While language within the cultural community is used to organize people by age (i.e., "little ones," "old guys"), and there are definitely social arrangements that rely on more normative groupings by age (often many of the same-aged participants would hang out with each other), the park operated from a basic social arrangement of age *heterogeneity* whereby participants skated alongside other participants from a wide range of ages. At any one time, it was not uncommon, for instance, for there to be participants engaging each other who were 8, 11, 15, 19, 22, and 30-plus. As discussed in Chapter 9, this age variation opens up a range of not only learning and teaching opportunities but also possibilities for identity formation, relationships, and emotional bonds to occur for and among participants that emphasize contribution to others' learning and well-being.

Beyond this normalized arrangement of age heterogeneity, the cultural community also critiqued dominant age-based social ordering and forged new possibilities for social relations through the annual skate contest. The contest was organized by skill level (e.g., intermediate), not by age, which enabled cross-age participation among these different categories. For instance, in the exploration of the skate contest in Chapter 4, Luis, who was 19 at the time, participated in the intermediate level, where other intermediate participants were several years younger than him; inversely, Derrick, who was 14 at the time, skated in the advanced category alongside TS, 19, and Crazy K, who was nearly 30. In fact, there had been controversy at that iteration of the contest since the judges were not initially going to let Crazy K compete because he was older than 25, which, for some reason, those running the contest had declared was the age cutoff. It actually took several of the skateboarders coaxing the judges by explaining that "skateboarding doesn't work like that," as Houston would later explain, to enable Crazy K to compete officially.

In fact, several years later, the age limit for the contest was lowered to 18, which was met with resistance by many of the skaters to the point where they stopped participating in it, even if they were within the acceptable age limit. Eventually, the annual skate contest stopped taking place due to lack of interest, ironically, by skateboarders. In an interview with Houston shortly after he aged out of the contest, he explained how it upset him that such age restrictions were imposed since they were antithetical to the spirit of skateboarding in general and participation at Franklin Skatepark specifically:

> Last time I tried to do it, they told me I was too old. I told them that no competition of this type of sport has an age limit. If you're 60 years old and you can do it, why can't you do it? I was like, "What is this? Is this just a kid thing?" They told me I couldn't do it, and I got real mad and thought, "I guess this is over for me."

In many respects, the age parameters imposed by the entity organizing the contest, which was not led by skateboarders or a skate shop, is an instance in which dominant norms regarding age clashed with the ways Franklin Skatepark resisted and subverted those norms. These tensions reveal how social relations, as with both class and gender, in this case regarding age, are and are not being reconfigured within this cultural community. Houston explains how this tension between reconfigured social relations at Franklin Skatepark would be made visible with broader, normative social arrangements regarding age when he sees younger participants from the park in town, particularly when the younger participants are with their parents. He says,

> It is a little weird because I think about it sometimes, like I know this little kid from the skatepark and he's a really little kid. So, if I see him in public and he's with his parents, it's weird if I say something to him because I'm a grown man, but at the skatepark it's totally fine."

To further illuminate how age functions at the park, I draw attention to an *unusual* incident regarding age for this cultural community. During one evening, Archie, who was 14 at the time, was playing a game of skate with two participants who were 17 and 19. Archie was a slightly more experienced skater than the other two and held command of the game. In the midst of the game, Archie began to boast, saying, "I'm only 14 and I'm winning." One of the older guys immediately said to him, "Why you such a faggot?" The game continued without Archie saying much more, but when it ended, Archie, victorious, said, as he was pushing his board away from the other two, "You just got beat by a 14-year-old!" One of the older boys responded, "I can still beat the shit out of you," and the other said, "Especially with that headband . . . I'll take it off you and choke you with it."

While there are many things going on in this scenario, I draw attention to the ways this encounter showcases both how a participant's (Archie) heckling is operating from socially dominant notions of age but one that is clearly misaligned with the age-based values at the park, as well as how the heckling of the other participants in response was done, in part, to enforce the age-based normativity of the cultural community. The way Archie brought age into it this encounter was atypical for participation at Franklin Skatepark. It was anomalous that a participant would give credence to the age distinctions in drawing attention to his "victory." In fact, marking the victory at all was unusual for normal practice, unless in good-spirited play between participants who knew each other well and/ or were near equivalent in terms of skill level. But to bring in age differences that marked the specialness of the younger participant "beating" the older participant was especially rare. Again, this is not to say that, as previously mentioned, age was never drawn on to note someone's abilities (in Chapter 4, for instance, Crazy K and TS remark how Derrick was especially good *for his age*) but rather to point out that to do so in a way to boast, particularly within a competition, was peculiar.

The responses by the two older participants could easily be understood as a form of heckling whereby they are drawing on gendered language, as previously discussed, to safeguard their own feelings of inferiority or humiliation—and this very well may be the case. However, I also see their responses as a way to indicate that Archie's boasting violates age-based norms and are inappropriate for the cultural community. That

these two other participants retort to physical dominance and emascu-
lating language indicates the possibility of drawing on their age—and
consequent physical differences—as a means to do this policing. In other
words, their heckling may be a way to both indicate Archie's violation
of community norms related to age and draw on similar notions of age
from broader social relations to speak back to Archie. In this way, while
Franklin Skatepark shows probably the most promise in reconfiguring
broader social relations in relation to age, this incident demonstrates
how, at times, these dominant understandings of age factor into participation, even if only on occasion.

Overall, the facet of power related to age showcases how this cultural
community is most progressive in its recalibration of dominant social
relations. Franklin Skatepark is truly an "all ages" context where people
of various ages not only participate but also serve important functions
(O'Connor, 2018). Additionally, the age heterogeneity of this cultural
community brings people together who would not otherwise be in proximity or engage one another. In this sense, Franklin Skatepark expands
learning and participation opportunities and social relations, even if
extending those social relations beyond the cultural community are met
with tensions brought on by expectations of normalized social ordering
related to age.

This recasting of age-based norms has important implications for
understanding how and why this community functions so meaningfully
for many of its members, as well as for educators to think anew about
pedagogical possibilities that circumvent the limitations on learning
imposed by the normative age-segregation policies and practices of
schools. In fact, this aspect of power within the cultural community was
one of the most exciting facets for me, as I had grown so accustomed to
thinking of learning within the narrow parameters of age stratification.
Beyond schools, this critique of power regarding the dominant social
ordering of people provokes questions not only for learning and teaching
in schools but also for notions of intergenerationality and broader community networks. Breaking down our obsession with organizing people,
especially children and youth, by age opens up access to others who share
interests but not birth years—what I refer to as "participant peers," which
is an attempt to linguistically disrupt normative thinking of peers as an
age-based category. This overall critique of age segregation is particularly

important for those people identified as "youth" or "teenagers" or "adolescents" given how ageism adversely affects their material lives.

REPRODUCING AND/OR TRANSFORMING SOCIAL RELATIONS AND IMPLICATIONS FOR EDUCATION

Theoretically, this chapter illuminates how participation in cultural communities is always mediated, in part, by intersectional identities. Who the participants are and/or how they perform particular facets of identity matter for who gets to participate at Franklin Skatepark, how readily they have access to resources, the ways they might experience discrimination or be discriminatory to others, the way they have aspects of their identity othered or upheld, and who and how they might be. Given that scholarship on LOPI has primarily focused on cultural communities linked through geography and racial/ethnic identities, this analysis offers ways of understanding how broader power structures manifested through and by social categories of representation (i.e., race, class, gender, sexuality, age) may inform learning and participation within cultural communities, especially those that draw on participants from different racial affiliations. Furthermore, this chapter reveals how cultural communities can, at once, take steps toward both transforming *and* reinforcing these dominant social arrangements and structures of power. In other words, this chapter steps directly into the messiness of being human and existing at the intersection of identity, learning, and participation within a cultural community.

The disruptions of dominant power structures that do occur within this cultural community afford participants a sense of solidarity and exclusivity (especially regarding class), a sense of agency and power they may not otherwise feel or experience beyond the park (e.g., in schools), and even, at times, new possibilities for social ordering, relationships, and networks of support (particularly linked with age). In these ways, one can understand how Franklin Skatepark, as a cultural community, functions as a refuge of sorts and offers "a place to stand" (Lindquist, 2002). However, while these disruptions of broader power structures may engender favorable outcomes in many respects for many of the participants at the level of their cultural community, the possibilities for their gains to extend beyond the park seems limited. For instance, in his recounting of how social relations at the park do not abide by normative age ordering, Houston explains how, as an adult, when he sees a younger participant outside of the park, especially if that younger participant is with his parents, it is "weird."

The reifications of dominant power structures, particularly related to gender, sexuality, and race, as I mention in the opening of this chapter, challenged me the most—as a researcher and educator. One question that has lingered with me throughout this study, including up to this point, is how this complex interplay of disruption and reinforcement of dominant social relations may be facilitating these participants "reproducing" themselves and others in the cultural community into broader oppressive relations and dynamics through their participation. In what ways might transformation and critique of these dominant power structures occur in this cultural community? What would it take to allow for the nonhegemonic performances of masculinity to exist without having to be "safeguarded" by more dominant, oppressive expressions of sexuality and masculinity? How might racism be countered in such a space? While I don't offer answers to these questions here, I posit them to stimulate possibilities for scholarly inquiry and methodological approaches that might be more dialogic and participatory whereby the research process itself is designed not only to understand such phenomena but also to raise awareness and possibly change them.

For an education and youth studies audience, I see great value in this chapter to help locate and think strategically about the ways other social spaces, especially classrooms, may be simultaneously reconfiguring new forms of social relations *and* reproducing dominant power structures. Toward this aim, I suggest increased attention to and understanding of how *conflicts* might be understood and worked *with* in learning contexts.

From my vantage, one of the most important insights from this chapter is just how central *conflict* is to learning and teaching—and, more significantly, how conflicts *reveal* ideological, social, and symbolic tensions underlying—and enabling and constraining—participation within a learning context. In other words, conflicts offer us portals to enhance our understanding of the barriers to both micro-level learning and broader social transformation.

Admittedly, as a beginning teacher, the idea of working *with* conflict in my classroom would have scared me. Conflict felt threatening to my authority in the classroom—particularly my ability to "control" or "manage" my students. Moreover, I did not interpret moments of conflict as aspects of effective teaching or learning; if anything, they suggested failure on my and my students' part—that something was not going well or not working. Through my research with the young men of Franklin Skate Park, as well as my continued work in secondary classrooms with students and teachers, I can see now just how many learning and teaching opportunities I missed as a teacher because I lacked both an understanding of the inextricable role of conflict in learning and the in-the-moment awareness and attunement to recognize and work *with* conflict.

By not paying attention, or not giving much credence to conflicts in my classroom, I missed much of what my students were attempting to communicate and reveal to me. I can see now that often what is being revealed through conflict is integral to who students are or being asked to be(come). Therefore, recognizing conflicts as potentially useful learning opportunities may help illuminate for teachers the integral nature of learning skills and content with identity formation. In this way, conflicts (and the ideological, social, and symbolic tensions undergirding them) can help educators become aware of who they—and the curriculum, the school—are asking students to become and how their students are(n't) responding to this invitation.

Getting curious about conflicts, in this way, can help educators understand student academic (under)achievement from the perspective of identity and sociocultural affiliations, rather than individualistic, cognitive conceptions of learning. Understanding what is being revealed—and inviting students to understand what is being revealed by and through conflict—will help move conflicts from being potentially divisive to being pedagogically generative. Ultimately, attuning to and working with conflicts may help teachers hear what their students are attempting to communicate and reveal to them—a necessity for helping all students, but particularly those for whom schools typically feel like one huge conflict.

CHAPTER EIGHT

Cultural Theorists on Wheels
THE ROLE OF LITERACY IN LEARNING HOW TO
SKATEBOARD AND BE A SKATEBOARDER

A first important step in this transformative process for literacy educators is learning to see all students as learners and users of language and
literacy before they enter the classroom. Too often, many students are
viewed as deficits that hold no relevant knowledge to be drawn upon by
their teachers to improve scholastic achievement. . . . Whole genres and
youth movements such as hip-hop have come into existence via the creativity and genius of young women and men attempting to find modes
of expressing their rich and complicated lives. (Morrell 2004b, pp. 6, 39)

I N ADDITION TO actually skateboarding and spending time at the park,
one of the central ways participants within this cultural community
learn how to skateboard and be a skateboarder is through their engagement with a wide array of texts. For instance, Chapter 6 discussed how
participants watch industry-produced and amateur videos (as well as
produce them) to help them imagine possibilities and learn new footing
as part of their learning, among other things. In this chapter, I expand
this exploration of textual mediation to more thoroughly examine how
literacy—selecting, accessing, consuming, evaluating, producing, and
distributing texts—factors into participation and learning in the cultural
community of Franklin Skatepark—and beyond.

In tracing the participants' literacy practices, this chapter demonstrates how the cultural community of Franklin Skatepark functions as
a powerful—and for many participants, the *most* powerful—"sponsor" of
their literacy lives. Literacy scholar Deborah Brandt (1998) explains that
sponsors of literacy are "any agent, local or distant, concrete or abstract,
who enable, support, teach, and model, as well as recruit, regulate, sup-
press, or withhold literacy" (p. 166). In recognizing the cultural community of Franklin Skatepark as one such "agent," this research reveals how

participation at Franklin Skatepark opens up opportunities for using literacy to learn (how to skateboard, about skateboarding culture), facilitates literacy learning and development (e.g., learning rhetorical strategies, design elements), and engenders a form of "critical literacy" whereby participants, through textual activities, engage in ideological critique and action related to and extending beyond the local cultural community and skateboarding. In short, this chapter illustrates how participation in this cultural community promotes various forms of literacy—and does so in ways often more powerful and even reparative for these young men in relation to school literacies.

From a LOPI theoretical framework, this chapter is significant for several reasons. First, it documents how literacy operates as an important "means of learning" within this cultural community. At the same time, literacy also serves to chart participants' learning, particularly since literacy activities often link with identity formation and index participant statuses within the cultural community. In this way, literacy is both a means of learning and a way to document learning. Exploring literacy also reveals several important underlying principles of learning in this cultural community, including the expectation for participants to become contributors to and *shapers* of the community through their literacy practices. In this way, literacy offers a particularly useful window to understand how individual participants, through their own transformed participation, can transform the cultural community.

Unlike previous chapters, where I aim to provide broad, comprehensive overviews, with this one, I briefly lay out several broad findings from my research pertinent to literacy, and then hone in on a few key literacy activities to illuminate particular facets of how this cultural community sponsored participants' literacies. In particular, I focus my attention on the literacy practices of several of the older, more experienced participants to illustrate several ways participation in this cultural community facilitated literacies linked with critical consciousness that extended beyond skateboarding. My rationale for this decision is twofold. First, the existing skateboarding scholarship that explores textual activities is quite robust and has provided generative insights to the situated and differentiated nature of literacy practices of skateboarders. Second, given that one of the aims of this book is to offer a counternarrative of a group of young men often framed as "at-risk" and "failing," I want to showcase some of the ways they are leveraging literacy for their engagement in/ with the world.

Before diving into the data in this chapter, I situate my discussion in a theoretical framing of literacy and offer a sense of the scholarship within skateboarding studies that also examines textual engagement. I offer this framing of literacy not only to ground my analysis but also to trouble dominant renderings of literacy that emphasize decontextualized notions of skills (MacPhee, Handsfield, & Paugh, 2021). Also, I draw attention to the scholarship in skateboarding studies both to provide context for my analysis and to bolster my claim that participation in skateboarding affords diverse, rich literacy experiences.

REFRAMING LITERACY BEYOND THE ABILITY TO READ AND WRITE

A common definition of literacy—"the ability to read and write"—often engenders an understanding of literacy as a cognitive phenomenon that occurs in the minds of individuals as they read and/or write texts. This perspective is interested in understanding the mental functions, processes, and/or skills individuals need, utilize, and draw on as they read and/or write texts. For instance, this perspective of literacy might stimulate the following types of questions: How are people decoding the words on the page? How are they drawing conclusions? What, cognitively, is the reader doing with the information they are reading? How is their brain comparing it with other information? In what ways are they using phonetics to read?

Given how such perspectives of literacy emphasize individual cognitive skills, they often limit areas of inquiry related to culture, identity, and context. Therefore, for purposes of this study, I draw on *sociocultural* and *critical* perspectives of literacy,[1] which posit that it is as important to understand the *functions, uses,* and *contexts* of literacy as it is to understand the mental processes and skills used to read and write. For example, Szwed (1981), extending the work of sociolinguist Hymes (1972), argues that understanding literacy "as simply a matter of the skills of

---

1 In this very short exploration of literacy, I cannot do justice to this robust scholarly field; in my explanation, I offer several foundational citations to orient toward basic concepts rather than provide an up-to-date review of the field.

reading and writing does not even begin to approach the fundamental problem: What are reading and writing for?" To do this, he suggests the need to understand "the social meaning of literacy: that is, the roles these abilities play in social life; the varieties of reading and writing available for choice; the contexts for their performance; and the manner in which they are interpreted and tested, not by experts, but by ordinary people in ordinary activities" (p. 422). Underlying his argument is the assumption that literacy is a social and cultural phenomenon and cannot be understood as simply an individual, cognitive endeavor. Therefore, when people learn and use literacy, they are always learning social and cultural "information" and ways of being, which link with broader social and cultural values (Gee, 2015; Heath, 1983; Street, 1984).

From this perspective, then, literacy does not solely reside in people's heads as they engage in reading and writing but also in the social engagement around texts; thus, literacy is not the intrinsic property of an individual but rather the participation in social and cultural activities involving texts. As Barton and Hamilton (1998) explain,

> Literacy is primarily something people do; it is an activity, located in the space between thought and text. Literacy does not just reside in people's heads as a set of skills to be learned, and it does not just reside on paper, captured as texts to be analyzed. Like all human activity, literacy is essentially social, and it is located in the interaction between people. (p. 3)

The shift from literacy residing in individual's heads to residing in people's participation in social and cultural activities corresponds with the notion of literacy as a practice. Street (2001) explains that literacy practices refer to the values and beliefs about literacy that a group of people within a context share. As a social practice, literacy is never a neutral, decontextualized, or "autonomous" act but rather always "ideological" and implicated in broader social, cultural, and political contexts and practices (Street, 1984).

From this perspective, I explore not only which texts the participants of Franklin Skatepark access, consume, and produce but also the social and cultural *functions* of their textual activities. How do they engage these texts and in these textual practices? For what purposes do they engage these texts? In what ways are these practices shaped by the cultural community? In what ways do their literacies shape the cultural community? What role does their textual engagement play in their learning how to skateboard and be(come) particular types of skateboarders?

Conceptions of *critical literacy* extend beyond a sociocultural perspective by drawing attention to the ideological and political dimensions of the contexts of literacy activities, especially issues of power, representation, normativity, and ideology (Freire, 1970a; Freire & Macedo, 1987; Janks, 2010; Morrell, 2008; Pandya et al., 2022). For literacy educator Paulo Freire, whose work has become foundational for many within critical literacy studies, literacy learning is not simply an act of learning to read and write words on a page, or, as he says, "an inconsequential matter of *ba, be, bi, bo, bu*, of memorizing an alienated word." Instead, literacy learning is a process of reading the word *and* the world, or, as he writes, "a difficult apprenticeship in naming the world" (1970b, p. 339). From a critical perspective, a person is literate "to the extent that he or she is able to use language for social and political reconstruction" (Freire & Macedo, 1987, p. 159). Therefore, critical literacy researchers focus their attention on the ways texts and people's textual activities work to promote their critical consciousness, their "naming of the world," and/or indoctrinate them into oppressive conditions. From a critical perspective, I examine the ways the participants of Franklin Skatepark use textual practices to grapple with issues of power and ideology both related to and beyond their participation in skateboarding and Franklin Skatepark.

While early scholars operating from sociocultural and critical perspectives focused exclusively on print-based texts, the proliferation of new textual forms and practices have expanded the purview of literacy studies to include examination of "new" literacies. Proponents of the new literacies argue for expanded notions of textuality and literacy, suggesting that the changing nature of the world—economically, technologically, and socially—is changing the nature of texts and textual activities (Kress, 2010; Lankshear & Knobel, 2011; New London Group, 1996; Stornaiuolo, Smith, & Phillips, 2017). Therefore, literacy can no longer be understood as solely the province of print-based reading and writing and must take into consideration the multimodal/media nature of texts and textual practices, including, for example, gaming, fan fiction, social media, texting, TikTok, tweeting, and so on. Building with this scholarship, I operate from a definition of literacy that takes into consideration multi-modal and media texts (e.g., videos, tattoos, music, blogs, social media), as well as more traditional textual forms such as books and magazines.

Skateboarding and Literacy

Skateboarding and literacy are inextricable, especially as textual activities involve multimodal and digital media texts. Since skateboarding began, media consumption and production have been instrumental to how skateboarders learn, develop subcultural identities, and grapple with issues of power, particularly in relation to corporate and mainstream ideologies. It's unsurprising, then, that some of the most exciting recent scholarship in skateboarding studies focuses on the roles and relationships media has with skateboarding and skateboarders. Though I would frame much of this scholarship as "literacy" work, within skateboarding studies, the term "literacy" is rarely, if ever, used and is instead discussed through the lens of media consumption and production. Though multifaceted, in this brief discussion, I focus on two aspects of this scholarship: the role of media/literacy in identity formation, and the role of media/literacy in learning how to skateboard.

In many regards, media and skateboarding are in an ongoing, intimate, and constitutive relationship, for better or worse. Specifically, media—whether it be photo/videography in real time with skateboarders or corporate-created texts—shapes what skateboarding is and how to do it. This is seen at the level of learning as well as identity formation. In this way, skateboarding functions as a terrain of exchange between complex relationships with markets, sponsorships, and commercialization, which ever-changing digital media and technologies have only made even more complex (Thorpe, 2017).

Some work explores, for instance, the role of (social) media in identity formation and indexing status for skateboarders. Wheaton and Beal (2003) explored how "reading" skate media was a sign of commitment to the cultural practice. In her foundational scholarship, Yochim (2010) argues that skateboarders are a "corresponding culture" in that they are "a culture that both is in constant conversation (or correspondence) with a wide array of mainstream, niche, and local media forms and finds various affinities (or corresponds) with these forms' ideologies" (p. 4). More specifically, she explores how, for a group of middle-class, young white men, skateboard media function as both a "reflection and a projection" of self, values, and aspirations (p. 2).

More recent research has increasingly given attention to social media, especially Instagram, which, as pioneering skateboarding scholar Iain Borden says, "is massive for skateboarding today" (personal communication; see also Borden, 2019, p. 93–94). Dupont (2020) demonstrates how, for a group of "core" skateboarders, their use of Instagram functioned as a means whereby they developed, maintained, and performed their "authentic" skater identities. Specifically, Dupont explains how skateboarders today use social media to "refine and display" their understandings of the subculture, as well as make "identity claims," which get negotiated in relation to other participants on Instagram. This research demonstrates some of the ways social media operates as an integral mechanism whereby boundaries of "authenticity," status, and identity are developed and policed in skateboarding.

From a learning perspective, research has explored how media—video production, in particular—opens possibilities not only for learning but also for social relationships. For instance, Hollet (2019) examines how skateboarders "vibe" with one another through the process of filming each other attempting tricks and then discussing and editing the footage. He explains how such joint literacy engagement facilitates "symbiotic learning partnerships" whereby participants engage together in "a highly collaborative, rhythmic endeavor that emerges over a constant stream of reflection, dialogue, feedback, error, and eventually triumph" (p. 755). Jones (2011), in his research with a group of skaters in Hong Kong, explores how video production was integral to learning how to skateboard as well as cultivating community. In particular, he explains how videos were "a part of every stage of learning"—from studying them to understanding how to do particular tricks to shooting videos for self-analysis and "verification" purposes. He explains how, in general, the processes of video production facilitated social relationships, subcultural status, and possibilities to imagine futures, which is a key facet of learning.

Situated within this scholarship on literacy in skateboarding, and from the theoretical framing of literacy, in the remainder of the chapter, I explore several ways the participants of Franklin Skatepark used literacy in their learning, their development and enactment of critical consciousness, and, more generally, in their identity formation, in relation to both the more proximal cultural community as well as more distal ones.

TEXT SELECTION AND THE CHANGING NATURE OF LITERACY OVER TIME

As part of their engagement with skateboarding and related cultural communities, the participants of Franklin Skatepark accessed, consumed, produced, distributed, and evaluated a variety of texts, including, but not limited to the following:

- nonfiction books about aspects of cultural communities (e.g., biographies, histories)
- "industry" magazines and catalogs (e.g., skateboarding, music)
- skateboarding and music videos—both industry and self-produced
- digital texts, including social media (e.g., Facebook, TikTok, Instagram), blogs, and web pages—industry and other-participant-produced
- tattoos
- graffiti/tagging
- music and poetry
- skateboard decks, T-shirts, and stickers

Of note is that all the texts the participants engage are *multimodal.* In addition to the more obvious multimodality found in the combinations of audio and visual in videos, audio, and lyrics in songs, and the visual imagery, iconic symbols, and words found in tattoos and graffiti, all the print-based texts, such as magazines and books, are also multimodal. In most instances, the visual aspects of these texts carry more significance than the print—not necessarily because the visual is "easier" but rather because the visual is more closely linked to the visuality and value of watching to learn of the cultural community. For example, seeing a picture or sequence of pictures of a skateboarder is often more helpful in demonstrating how to perform a trick than reading an explanation about it.

It is important to note, too, that because participation in skateboarding is so networked with other cultural communities (e.g., graffiti art, tattooing, music), participants' textual engagement necessarily extends beyond Franklin Skatepark and skateboarding in general. Early in my research, it became apparent that it would be impossible (and even undesirable) to maintain a singular focus on skateboarding when it came to literacy. For instance, participants get tattoos related to skateboarding, write and perform music about skateboarding, decorate their boards and bodies with symbols and words related to their musical influences, integrate a range of musical genres into their production of video texts, and post skateboarding videos and other content on social media. TS explains how it is virtually impossible to distinguish skateboarding as an entity or cultural group separate from other cultural communities and practices: "Like basically there's so much around skateboarding, like with the culture of it. It's influenced music, it's influenced tattoos. . . . Like most of the bands you listen to, like there's bands like Suicidal Tendencies, all they sing about has its influence in skateboarding culture. The Kick Flips [pseudonym for local band], all they sing about is skateboarding, you know?"

Over time, selection of texts to consume and produce changes in degree and kind for participants; as the skateboarders transformed their participation in the cultural community, so, too, did their textual activities. In this way, literacy often indexed or made visible participants' status in the cultural community.

In general, less experienced skaters tend to be more consumption- than production-oriented, and the texts they engage are predominately industry-related texts, such as catalogs, videos, magazines, and web pages. In addition, very early or novice skaters often read mass-produced books about skateboarding, such as Matt Christopher novels involving skateboarding, and introductions and "how to" books. These participants consume texts mainly to learn how to skateboard and to learn practical and cultural information regarding skateboarders, places to skate, and various other industry-related information (e.g., equipment). For instance, during Santana's 15th birthday party, he and three of his friends—all of whom were beginning skateboarders—discussed a current issue of CCS (a catalog of equipment) to learn about the equipment (trucks, shoes, boards) and tools (Allen key) one needs to skateboard.

As they become more experienced, participants move away from these basic, introductory texts in favor of skateboarding-related, industry-produced texts that focus on practice in action, such as magazines and videos. During this time, participants also tend to produce their own texts, mainly to document their skating, not normally within the context of a whole-group session but rather within a small group of friends either away from the park or during nonpeak times at the park. This textual production and distribution functions mainly for "verification" (Donnelly & Young, 1988) of their accomplishments, particularly through video production.

From this point, participants strategically select skateboarding texts to consume and begin to make their textual productions more public, particularly on social media. For example, Derrick, during the third summer of data generation, explained how he didn't have much time for skate videos and books and magazines anymore, especially since he was at the park skating with others a lot more than he used to. He explained, though, that he'd recently reached a point where he felt like he hit a "plateau" and watched videos to help him move past it. It is also during this time that participants increasingly select texts that extend beyond the practice of skateboarding. For example, during that same summer Derrick both designed and received his first tattoo (an illegal, underground tattoo) and began writing and producing music with some older participants.

Over time, participants begin to spend more time listening to music and paying attention to lyrics, get more serious about conceptualizing and designing tattoos and/or graffiti art, and begin reading in-depth books related to skateboarding and these other cultural communities of practice—books that offer historical perspectives on the cultural practices and biographical information about some of its key figures. For example, when I first spoke with Larry, he had just finished reading *Scar Tissue*, a biographical perspective of Anthony Kiedis, the lead singer of The Red Hot Chili Peppers.

As participants develop a certain level of comfort and status within the cultural community, their literacy activities shift quite substantially, though this is a gradual process that occurs over time. In general, more experienced participants engage texts to locate themselves historically within broader cultural communities related to and beyond skateboarding. These participants' textual consumption is much more "critique" focused as issues such as authenticity become more significant to them. In fact, this critical consumption often engenders particular types of textual *production* and *distribution*. Finally, the literacy practices of more experienced participants typically evolve well beyond skateboarding to involve related cultural communities and sometimes critique of and/or involvement in broader sociopolitical issues and topics.

In these ways, text selection not only differs and is situated for participants primarily due to their level of participation but also functions to index a participants' status within this local and other larger sociocultural-political contexts. Which texts the participants select to consume, produce, and/or distribute reveals a great deal about who they are in relation to the contexts in which they are situated.

Unsurprisingly, many of the features of literacy within the cultural community of Franklin Skatepark are in tandem with other aspects of learning. For instance, most literacy practices—even when they occur away from the park—are situated in practice. What I mean is that the participants are engaging texts to directly support their learning and participation; in this way, their choice of texts and consumption and production activities are largely guided by what they need to learn or know—or what other participants have suggested to them to support their learning.

Like previous discussions, this situatedness facilitates a "just right timing" of the literacy activities, as well as enables the development of an individualized curriculum unique to each participant based on where they are at in their learning journey. For this reason, the literacies of the participants of the same cultural community are extremely differentiated, so much so that at any one time, every participant could be engaged in some type of literacy activity meant to support their learning, and every single one of those literacy activities could be different. Thus, like participation at the park, literacy is both quite varied among participants and *always* available as means of participation regardless of level of participation or status, given how there are so many different entry points and modalities to engage in literacy related to participation. Such diversity of literacy practices also engenders a differentiated expertise and knowledge, which can benefit the community as a whole. At the same time, so much of the literacy that occurs among participants is deeply social and contingent on other participants, including, for example, the collaboration that occurs when two or more participants create a video together.

THEORIZING THROUGH LITERACY

In this section, I focus on a few specific literacy practices of several older, more experienced participants. Whereas the previous section emphasized the ways literacy practices were differentiated dependent on participants' level of participation and status, this section explores how participation in Franklin Skatepark sponsors literacies that extend well beyond the immediate cultural community and, at times, involves a form of critical literacy that opens possibilities for social critique and action. In looking across these examples, I frame the participants as theorizing, through their literacies, about cultural practices, critique, and the broader world and their place in it; for this reason, I conceptualize these young men as "cultural theorists on wheels."

Locating Oneself Historically

For some of these young men, texts helped them locate themselves and their engagement within the larger, more global landscape of a cultural practice, especially from a historical perspective. In other words, some texts help these young men gain a sense of how what they are doing relates to what has been done before their "dropping into" the cultural practices they engage in. For virtually all of the young men who skateboard at Franklin Skatepark, the documentary *Dogtown and Z-Boys* and the Hollywood film *Lords of Dogtown* establish a historical precedence for their own participation in skateboarding, and in some ways these texts function to legitimize their cultural practice by offering a documented historical record.

Additionally, the older, more experienced participants who have branched out into other forms and cultural communities engage texts that also serve to locate them historically within a cultural practice and community outside of skateboarding. For example, when I first met and interviewed Luis, who was also a drummer in a hardcore/punk rock band, he had recently reread *American Hardcore: A Tribal History* by Stephen Blush and George Petros, a book his friend and band mate gave to him after reading it himself, in order to gain a sense of the history of hardcore/punk rock.

> LUIS: It really opened my eyes to the hardcore scene in general. At first I thought fashion had a bigger part in it than it did, but, it was purely about the music. And people just dressed fucked up because they could. There wasn't really any rhyme or reason behind it, they just did it because they could. Dye my hair fucking blue, green, yellow. Why? Because I can. Shave it? Why not?

RP: Right. Hmm.

LUIS: But reading it was definitely . . . I dunno, it was more just learning . . . more of a learning experience, really. There's slow parts in the book, but I still took it all in, because I knew it was something. It's all history. Say some people are really interested in American history, or Western civilization, things like that. I like to learn all I can possibly learn about hardcore, punk, skinhead culture, things like that.

RP: Is that probably the best thing you've read on hardcore culture?

LUIS: Oh yeah. There really hasn't been anything to that extent or depth done before. Stephen Blush really took it to the next level. He just completely went balls out. On the back of it, it even lists every hardcore band from like 1980 to 1986. And this was before the digital age, before everything was recorded digitally. He has pictures of his entire collection of vinyl, all alphabetized and stuff.

In this discussion, Luis explains how reading *American Hardcore* helped him gain a different sense of historical perspective on his current participation in the punk/hardcore scene. For example, he says how exposure to these texts helped him understand how the fashion styles emerged differently than he understood. Also, Luis explains how his interest in reading and learning about the history of the punk/hardcore scene stems from his sense of connection to this cultural community. He says that while some people like to read about American history, he "like[s] to learn all I can possibly learn about hardcore, punk, skinhead culture, things like that." In this way, Luis locates himself as a participant within this cultural community.

Luis's interest in learning the history of the cultural practice he's engaged in is reflected by TS's reading of *The Art of Getting Over: Graffiti at the Millennium* by Steven Powers, which he notes on social media as his favorite book. In a discussion with him, TS explained how, while he didn't necessarily love "reading" the book, he appreciated the history he learned about graffiti art:

I don't know. I'm not going to lie but the book . . . reading it wasn't that sweet. Like it's more just looking at like all the, like, how graffiti came to be and how everything got put together and who the people who were on the forefront. Right on the front there's people like doing chalk on the side of a train and you know it's like, okay, that took some motivation or like some ideas and stuff like that.

Similar to Luis's discussion, TS explains that his interest in the book stems from the historical perspective it offers ("how graffiti came to be and how everything got put together and who the people who were on the forefront"). Also like Luis, TS discusses his wonderment of the actions of those who came before him. Interestingly, both participants discuss how the actual reading of these texts was not all that great (Luis discusses how there were "slow parts" in *American Hardcore* and TS says that reading *The Art of Getting Over* "wasn't that sweet"), but both participants were motivated to read through these boring parts, something that contrasted sharply with how they spoke of their engagement in school-based literacy tasks.

Critical Consumption of Industry Texts

More experienced participants' consumption of texts increasingly deals with ideological concerns they, as participants within the cultural community, grapple with, including a sense of authenticity and integrity related to their cultural practice locally and extended more globally. For example, TS discusses at length why he believes *Thrasher* magazine is the best of all skateboarding magazines:

> *Thrasher* I will say is probably the best skateboarding magazine 'cause all it is is raw skateboarding. It's not a bunch of industry propaganda. And like, you know, which it comes into play now [that] Nike is buying like close to everything. I'm wearing a pair of Nikes, so I can't really say anything, but you know? Well, it's kind of funny. People are buying Hurley shirts thinking, you know, I'm buying some independent California company. No. That's owned by Nike. Like a lot of brands are starting to get bought out by bigger companies because of the fact, you know, it's [skateboarding] becoming so mainstream and it's becoming such a cash crop.

The conversation moves on to discussing the cost of boards and how parents will buy stuff for kids and the overall commercialization of skateboarding. TS mentions how everything has become "corporate":

RP: So tell me more about the corporate. You were saying *Thrasher*
and then these other magazines and how *Thrasher* was all skateboarding and . . .

TS: *Thrasher* is like, it's just kind of, like, you look at the editor. The
editor has something to do with every video they put out and it's
a lot of the same skaters but most of those skaters are guys who
aren't very popular but they're just the diehards, you know?
They're the ones you see, you know, still like 20 years from now
I guarantee I'll still see Tony Hawk in magazines. You know all
those guys. The guys who all they do is just go out and skate, you
know?

And it's just kind of like, and when you see the editor, he
looks like he was a skater, and when he talks about it, he doesn't
sound like it's a foreign thing, like, he's learned about it. It
sounds like he started skating and got into it and this is what
they became . . . and also, like back then when they all started
skating, too, they did their own magazines. You know now we
have everything handed to us, but you know, they did their own
magazines, they did their own like photographing, and they got
that "do it yourself" attitude where, you know, you're just either
making it as a skateboarder or not making it as a skateboarder.
There's so many other aspects of board building, board shaping,
photography, editing. All that stuff and distribution, and they got
into all those aspects and are now they're people who we look
at nowadays who are distributing boards out of huge mail order
magazines and stuff like that.

Within his discussion of textual consumption, TS demonstrates several
ways he critically consumes texts and culture. Specifically, TS makes
distinctions between what is and is not authentic within skateboarding
culture. For example, he claims that *Thrasher* is the best skateboarding
magazine because "it is all raw skateboarding" and "not a bunch of
industry propaganda." For TS, "raw skateboarding" constitutes skating
for the fun of skating, being a "diehard," and not participating in the cultural practices to get famous or popular or to make money. For example,
he explains how the guys who skate for *Thrasher* "aren't very popular but
they're just the diehards. . . . The guys who all they do is just go out and

skate, you know?" In this way, "raw" skateboarding is the practice, about getting on a board and doing it, not getting popular or making money.

However, TS does recognize that skateboarding has undergone (and continues to undergo) major changes, especially related to its growing popularity and commercialization (Atencio et al., 2018; Borden, 2019; Thorpe, 2017). For example, he explains how "a lot of brands are starting to get bought out by bigger companies because of the fact, you know, it's [skateboarding] becoming so mainstream and it's becoming such a cash crop." He also compares skateboarding's popularity to more mainstream sports such as football, especially as manifested through the commodification of skateboarders.

Within this recognition is a sense of the inevitability of this change in the culture as well as the ways participants, including him, are implicated in it: "I'm wearing a pair of Nikes so I can't really say anything, but you know?" In this way, his critique of texts and culture is not one based solely on making money, commodification, or the commercialization of the culture; instead, his critique is based on the manner and reasons for making money and/or the "costs" to the integrity of the culture. What is important is not whether one makes money or not but more the manner in which they do it. For example, TS, at another point in our discussion, explains how he could not be happier that Tony Hawk, a skater who has greatly profited from skateboarding becoming a "cash cow," is skateboarding's "ambassador," whereas Bam Margera is a "douchebag." The critique, or resistance, is not in the not doing it but in the motivation and purpose in doing it. Whereas it is okay that Tony Hawk has made a lot of money, it is not okay that Bam Margera has, since he did so by "just being stupid." This sentiment is also demonstrated in previous chapters when discussing respect and status within the cultural community being largely about commitment and devotion, not always just your skill level.

Also, when TS discusses the various skaters in magazines, he mentions how they skateboard for the love of the sport, not to get famous. In this sense, understanding the history of the cultural practice is important, since one can see the changes that have occurred in the sport. "Selling out" in this context would not be going commercial and/or making money as much as it would be losing a sense of integrity in doing so. Also, TS mentions how, as a result of their love of and dedication to skateboarding, many older skaters, such as a former editor of *Thrasher*, became wealthy and/or famous. He says, "He started skating and got into and whatnot and this is what they became." In this way, TS seems to suggest not only the inevitability of the changing nature of the culture but also how, if one becomes wealthy or famous as a result of this, if it happens *to* them while they are in pursuit of a more lofty goal such as skateboarding for the love of it, then achieving a degree of prosperity is okay.

Related to critically consuming texts based on their adherence to "raw" skateboarding versus industry is the idea of credibility and authority. For example, when discussing *Thrasher*, TS explains how the editor of the magazine (at the time) is credible because "when you see the editor, he looks like he was a skater, and when he talks about it, he doesn't sound like it's a foreign thing, like, he's learned about it." In this sense, credibility and a sense of authority emerge from personal and practical experience with skateboarding—of being a skateboarder—not theoretical or secondhand knowledge of the culture. This sentiment is also evidenced in many of the more experienced participants' attitudes toward a skate shop in Liberty, the nearest metropolitan area, that is a growing chain and is run and operated by non-skaters. One of the participants, for example, when asked if he shopped there, said, "Fuck [name of store]" and then proceeded to explain to me how they don't know anything about skateboarding and that the owner is not even a skateboarder.

Similarly, Luis, when discussing the author of *American Hardcore*, discusses how the author's credibility and authority comes from his wide-ranging experiences within the punk/hardcore scene when it originated, even though he wasn't necessarily central to/in the scene. He says, "Oh yeah, back then this guy [the author] . . . he wasn't exactly in the scene, but this guy knows his stuff. He's been a lot of places, done a lot of things, and he's shared that with everyone else." This form of critique is also echoed in the ways more experienced participants discuss music and musicians, especially as related to whether musicians are viewed as being technically good or not at what they do. For example, one participant said about hip-hop, "Hip-hop now, it shouldn't be called hip-*hop*, it should be called, like hip-*pop*, 'cause it's pop now. The music industry, I think it's all about 90 percent of the money now is in hip-hop, and that's like . . . guys just going out there, just saying the same thing over and over again in different ways. Can't even rhyme and know it with the song, like he's just kind of talking and making millions off of you. More power to him, but it's not hip-hop, it's hip-*pop*."

Moreover, as participants become more "critical consumers" of texts, they begin to conceptualize various ways they can produce and distribute texts, oftentimes in response to these critiques. For example, Larry explains how when he reads music reviews with which he disagrees, he feels like he wants to write music reviews. He says,

> I've always thought about it [writing for a magazine]. I've always wanted to. And more so because I read all these reviews on stuff and all these critics use, you know, all that is is one person's thoughts about something, you know, and I hate it when I see an album, I got out and buy it and just love it and I look I'm reading *Rolling Stone* and someone is like, "This is crap." I'm like, "What is wrong with the world!" you know?

This desire to produce texts emerging from critical consumption or even a sense of frustration or desire to restore a perceived sense of loss of integrity is also evident in one participant's interest in making hip-hop the "art it should be." He says, "My lyrics are like poetry. My goal is to get hip-hop back into poetry, the art that it should be."

Becoming Producers of Culture beyond Skateboarding

Over time, many of the more experienced participants shift their energy and commit their resources to pursuits outside of skateboarding, especially musical and visual art endeavors. In many respects, actually skateboarding, for these participants, functions primarily as a form of recreation. They have proven themselves and now enjoy their time at the park in a more leisurely way. For example, TS explains how he does not skateboard as much, since his new "livelihood" as a tattoo artist involves using his hands. He says, "I'm starting to fall back in skating and I'm not skating as much anymore 'cause now I got my hands are my livelihood so you know you got to account for that and you gotta start just taking it easy. You can't just be going out and skating as hard as you used to."

Similarly, James explains how things over the last few years have changed a lot for him. Whereas he used only to skate, having aspirations to go "pro," he has since branched off into other things, including playing the guitar and drums with a local band. He explains,

> Um, things have changed a lot for me the last couple years. Because like all I used to do was skate. Right now, I've kind of branched out and started doin' other things. I've been in a

couple bands the last couple years. Like three years ago I was all, "I'm gunna turn pro. That's all I gotta do—just skate." And now that I've found other things—I can prolly make it in this band. So now I'm juggling skating, working, and being in a band now, so it's like—it's kinda hard. Now I definitely skate less than I used to last year.

For these participants, their decreased participation in skateboarding is complemented by their increased participation in related cultural communities. In fact, many of these participants either have jobs or are pursuing jobs related to these cultural practices. For example, as mentioned, by the end of this research, TS was nearly finished with his apprenticeship as a tattoo artist, a job several of the younger, less experienced participants have expressed interest in pursuing; James is a member of a band and works part-time at the local skate shop; Luis, when not skateboarding or working full-time as a welder, is the drummer for a local punk/hardcore band; and Larry, in between the second and third summers of data collection, moved to California to try and make it with his band.

In many respects, skateboarding seems to function as a gateway into other cultural communities and pursuits for these participants. For example, by my third summer of data collection, Derrick, who had not previously had much to say about the role of music in his life, had written, recorded, and distributed via social media several hip-hop songs with several older participants. Also during that summer, Matt had for the first time earned money drawing tattoo designs for other people. This shift in textual production and distribution practices reveals how engagement within youth purposive cultural communities is not simply pleasurable, fun, or play for these participants but deeply engaging and meaningful forms of cultural expression, so much so that they consistently seek out opportunities within the range of cultural activities to make meaning of their lives, find an occupation, and be a contributor and producer of a cultural community.

For some of these participants, their textual production and distribution is a way for them to cultivate the pleasure, fun, and/or aesthetic, spiritual, and intellectual outlets/opportunities that drew them into the practice in the first place. For others, their textual and cultural production and distribution is a way to do/have a job that makes sense to them, one in which they can maintain a sense of dignity and feel good about, and make money.

For example, TS explains how working as a tattoo artist apprentice differs from any other type of work or school experience he had, and how for his job as a tattoo apprentice he is motivated and invested:

> It's something where I could still skateboard, I could still do most of the stuff I still liked doing, and it was also a lifestyle that I really liked living. You know it's a blue-collar job, which I've never been about white-collar stuff. I've never really liked you know doing paperwork and stuff like that. And, you know, you got to work every day for all the money you're getting. You know nothing is just handed to you. You've got to earn your reputation through your work. You know you've got to really apply yourself to make a name for yourself and actually be one of the well-paid artists.

He contrasts this with his experience of school: "Most jobs, you know, when I was still in school I used to I got up every morning, and I fucking hated it. Like I'd come in in shorts and ratty T-shirts just 'cause I didn't care. Like I didn't want to be there, I didn't care about being there."

TS's perspectives on his participation in work, school, and purposive cultural communities resonate with those of several other participants. For example, Larry discusses how while he was in school, he was not progressing in either skateboarding or music production. He explains,

> Then I dropped out of school my senior year of all years. The beginning of senior year and said screw this, you know? I just want to learn how to play guitar and skateboard, and to date I've learned probably 30 really awesome tricks on my skateboard, I've learned an endless amount of music, and I'm so happy that I did that.

He goes on to explain how he wants to go back to school (i.e., community college) to take writing classes (to help him develop screenplay ideas, write songs, and write music reviews), graphic design courses, and music theory courses (to facilitate his own musical abilities). For TS, Larry, and many other participants, these cultural communities facilitate a type of identity formation in which the participants are, or have the opportunity to become, producers of and contributors to the community's cultural practices.

Moreover, for many of these participants, textual and cultural production and distribution is an opportunity for them to "give back" to and leave a legacy within a cultural community and other participants within it that they feel have given them so much. This will be addressed in more detail in the next chapter, which focuses on the notion of contribution within learning at Franklin Skatepark.

Textual Production and Distribution for Social, Cultural, and Political Purposes

For some participants, textual production and distribution facilitates their identity formation and indexes their affiliations in relation to larger socio-cultural-political contexts, including race and ethnicity. Perhaps the most obvious—and visible—function of this type of textual production and distribution is through tattooing. Using their bodies as canvases, participants see tattoos as ways to demarcate sociocultural and political affiliations (Kirkland, 2009). For example, as mentioned in the previous chapter, all the Latino participants (Derrick, Matt, Luis, Santana) either have or plan to get tattoos related to their racial/ethnic heritage. Derrick explains how he wants to get a tattoo of "Mexican Prayer Hands"; Santana plans on getting various tattoos representing his family and religious affiliations; and Luis's tattoo of "Mi Familia" and "Mom" are ways for him to inscribe publicly familial and ethnic/racial affiliations.

Additionally, participants typically use tattoos as a memorial of family members and/or friends who have passed away. For example, Adam explains why he has a tattoo of an angel for a woman whose sons he grew up with; he says that "she was like a second mom, and she passed away like four years ago of cancer, so I got that [a tattoo of an angel]." Also, for some, tattoos are used to espouse religious and/or philosophical beliefs. Most of the participants had religious symbols integrated into their tattoos (i.e., crosses, praying hands, imagery of Jesus Christ), and some had sayings or other symbols that denoted a philosophical belief or a remembrance of some type of life lesson learned.

Participants also use textual production and distribution as a means to engage in sociopolitical critique. For example, Luis has two tattoos he designed related to his critiques of racism. One of them is a tattoo with a swastika on fire inside of a "no" symbol. Near that tattoo, Luis has a tattoo of the word "SHARP," an acronym for Skinheads Against Racial Prejudice, a sociopolitical organization that is, as its name implies, an antiracist skinhead organization.

RP: Tell me about SHARP.

LUIS: I don't stand for racial bigotry at all. That's one of the things I will take a long hard stand on, not hesitate to punch somebody in the face for it 'cuz it's just not good.

RP: How did you get hooked up with SHARP? How'd you hear about it?

LUIS: It's appealed to me ever since I was in high school. Especially growing up in Finley and being a minority and hearing racial slurs. It's just ridiculous. Even some of my friends: Nigger this, Spick that. I was just like, "Come on; this is just pointless." I wanted to join something that would take a stand against that. There's no sense to say something's not right if you don't take action against it. That's just how I feel about it.

RP: So how did you hear about it?

LUIS: Um, just being a part of the punk/hardcore scene. Ever since high school or junior high, the skinhead lifestyle appealed to me because it was just your standard blue-collar worker guy: they didn't bitch about coming from a broken home. They're just people standing up for what they believe in . . . and all the other skinheads that they hang out with are like brothers. There's a certain brotherhood within that scene. Everybody just hangs together real tight.

RP: Are there meetings you go to? Or, are you just a representative?

LUIS: It's not really like that. I don't know, it's tough to explain. It'd be like calling myself a punk. Those are different kinds of punk rockers. It's not really an organization, it's a subset of the skin- head movement. It's just somethin' that you can choose to be.

RP: That tattoo you have—have you seen that on other people?

LUIS: That's actually something I came up with. But the idea behind it; there's a lot of people that have it. I've seen that numerous places on numerous people.

Here, Luis explains how his textual production, as manifested through several tattoos, functions not only to index particular sociocultural affiliations (i.e., SHARP) but also critique racism. The two tattoos Luis discusses are both highly visible, as they are placed on his forearms; additionally, the swastika on fire draws on a well-known, emotionally charged symbol to be provocative and state Luis's case boldly, as if this symbol is imbued with the frustration he feels about this issue. Finally, it is important to note how Luis was drawn to this particular sociopolitical organization and critique through his engagement with purposive cultural communities like the punk/hardcore scene and skateboarding. In this sense, these cultural communities "sponsored" and facilitated his critical consciousness and spurred his tattooing.

CONCLUSION

One of the most apparent things related to literacy in this research is just how text-rich this cultural community is. For a group of youth who are barely making it through school, and in many instances, taking English classes multiple times to move through the schooling system, they are quite steeped in literacy practices. This, in and of itself, is significant for educators to attune to, for it helps shift notions of deficit regarding labels such as "at-risk." As evidenced throughout the chapter, these young men were highly motivated to read, view, design, create, and distribute texts. Overall, this engagement with texts is purposive, situated within practice, and connected to goals they often set for themselves. These literacies were multimodal and intensely social, including many opportunities for co-creation of texts and meaning making. Related, recontextualizing literacies from other cultural communities and practices beyond Franklin Skatepark were nurtured and useful in establishing a more robust (literacy) environment. In this sense, there was a certain openness, fluidity, and almost interdisciplinary nature to literacy within this cultural community, one that also embraced textual diversity.

Another key aspect of literacy was how this cultural community had an expectation for participants, that as they become more central participants, through their textual activities they would critique, contribute to, and produce the cultural community. In this way, there was an encouragement of innovation and a sense that participants were meant to contribute in ways other than their actual skateboarding. Therefore, participation within the cultural community of Franklin Skatepark seems to help offset some of the harm or damage done related to literacy brought on by the "readicide" often inflicted by schools (Gallagher, 2009), which certainly speaks to these guys' experiences. Thus, this cultural community operated as a profound "sponsor" of literacy for these participants—one of, if not the most, powerful one in their lives.

For the participants, there was a massive disconnect between literacy as it existed in their lives, especially as part of this cultural community, and their experiences of schooled literacies. In fact, throughout many discussions, participants emphasized how they enjoyed literacy activities (several sharing that they loved to write) and in the same conversation explained how they had such a radically different experience with literacy in schools. Larry, for example, shared how he absolutely loved writing and had developed a reputation for himself with the broader community for his poetry, which he often read on a local radio station; at the same time, he had dropped out of school because he did not feel as if it really facilitated his goals and dreams of writing (and playing) music, music reviews, screenplays, and being involved in skateboarding.

This disparity is echoed by several other participants, who would discuss their textual activities reading books related to music, shooting and editing video, writing and performing music, and making a career of "putting art on people's bodies," as one of them said, and yet, sometimes within the same sentence, explain how these practices felt completely separate from their textual experiences in schools. For example, Brett, after explaining to me his process of writing songs, explained how, when I suggested that he must do well in his high school English class, said, "Eh, in our English class we don't write a lot—like we don't do a lot of stuff like that. We learn like hyperboles and similes and synonyms and all that; we learn the parts of words, and that doesn't interest me." Luis, an avid reader, said when I asked him to explain why he graduated from high school after five years with a 1.4 GPA, that "traditional studies just didn't appeal to me."

Theoretically, this chapter illuminates how intertwined literacy is with identity and relations with others, even those who are not physically present or even alive or personally known. It also illustrates how, from a sociocultural perspective, literacy practices are differentiated, even within a cultural community, which counters a monolithic rendering of literacy. From a critical literacy framework, this chapter reveals how the participants, particularly as they advance in their transformed participation within the cultural community, develop a critical consciousness and set of consequent literacy practices. Thus, through the lens of literacy, we see how participants have varied opportunities and entry points to engage literacy at all levels—and how these change as participants (roles) change. In this sense, literacy happens in and on time and happens differently for different participants at different points of their participation. From a learning perspective, we see how texts function in myriad ways as a means of learning and participation—from learning practical information to learning new tricks to critiquing and transforming the cultural community to engaging in sociopolitical critique.

In considering the literacies of the guys of Franklin Skatepark, I urge educators and others who work with youth to consider how you and the contexts you work in are functioning as a "sponsor" of literacy. In what ways is your work with youth inquisitive, curious, and honoring of the literacies that matter to them? In what ways is your context designed so that all participants, no matter where they are at in terms of their level of participation, have an entry point with literacy to engage? Are the literacies you are asking youth to engage multimodal? Do they link textual consumption, production, and distribution together? At the core, I ask, Is the literacy youth are being asked to engage purposive? How might youth be brought in to the development of pedagogical practices whereby they can share (about) their literacies?

CHAPTER NINE

Learning to Contribute, Contributing
to Learn(ing)

WHY LEARNING HAPPENS AT FRANKLIN SKATEPARK

I think the common denominator between us was we all came from kind
of fucked up household situations or we felt outcast or ostracized in
some way. And the skatepark and skateboarding was a way for all of us
outcasts to kind of . . . we knew we were all alike in the sense that we
didn't fit in anywhere else. And it gave us a sense of community that I
think we didn't feel otherwise. Coming from a small, supposed-to-be-
tight-knit town, it felt pretty distant. And to have what we had at the
skatepark at that time was—I think it was something really special.
       —Luis, during member-checking session before finalization of this book

An essential characteristic of children's learning in family and community settings is their collaboration and contribution to shared collective
efforts. Even when practicing particular skills independently, the activity
itself is part of an endeavor recognized by all to be important for the
family or community as a whole. . . . This recognition of the shared value
and worth of what is being learned best explains the intrinsic motivation
and desire to learn on which the effectiveness of this kind of learning in
great part depends. (Paradise & Rogoff, 2009, p. 124)

O
VER THE COURSE of my research, I discovered that learning to skateboard is a difficult, painful, fun, progressive, and satisfying process
whereby participants invest a great deal of resources, including their
money, time, and effort. In addition, they make themselves vulnerable
to a process of learning that includes, as discussed, many more "failures"
than "successes"; they push themselves mentally, physically, and emotionally beyond the limits of what they thought possible; they take risks,
and they sustain short- and long-term injuries. For them, these costs
are outweighed by the benefits of their commitment and hard work, as
they show up day after day, year after year. As a researcher—particularly

one keen on understanding the means and motivations of this particular group of young men who were so abysmally disengaged in schools—I wanted to understand *why* they were so intensely motivated to learn within this cultural community.

Therefore, whereas previous chapters explored how Franklin Skatepark functions as a cultural community and serves as a context for *where, when, with whom,* and *how* learning happens, as well as *what* gets learned, the purpose of this chapter is to explore *why* the participants learn to skateboard and become members of this cultural community. From a LOPI framework, the central aim of learning within a cultural community is for participants "to transform their participation in order to enhance their contributions and role in the community" (Rogoff et al., 2016, p. 372). From this perspective, contribution—or "pitching in"—is inextricably linked with participation and learning, and this interconnectedness between learning and contribution necessarily connects to motivation.

Thus, to explore why learning happens within the cultural community, this chapter explores the notion of *contribution* as a foundational principle of learning, social organization, and motivation of/at Franklin Skatepark. Specifically, this chapter looks across three dimensions of contribution: (1) the idea of *style*, which refers to how an individual skateboarder renders himself and his way of skateboarding; (2) the way in which the park is available to participants at varied levels of participation creates opportunities to *simultaneously mentor and be mentored* by other participants; and (3) how participants contribute to the welfare of others through their *textual and cultural production and distribution,* including this book.

In considering these iterations of contribution, this final data chapter circles back to the book's introduction, where I shared how Franklin Skatepark functions as a space for the young men highlighted to "open up," as Derrick says, because they've got something to say—and that what they have to say matters, that *they* matter. In other words, the participants of Franklin Skatepark don't just go there to learn because it's fun or to have a good time. They participate in the cultural community because, over time, they develop emotional investments in—and a deep sense of belonging to—the cultural community, including the relationships they form there.

A Desire to Learn

While it may seem so obvious as to not warrant mention, the sine qua non, or absolute prerequisite, to learning how to skateboard is the desire to do so. Without this desire, simply put, learning to skateboard will not happen. I point to this obvious facet of learning, in part, to draw attention to how this is so often *not* the case within schooling contexts where students are mandated to learn and to learn content and skills they have no say in. To try to teach someone, for example, how to skateboard if they were not interested or invested in this learning, would be not only unsuccessful but also absurd.

Through getting to know the participants in this study, I discovered that many factors contributed to these young men's desire to learn to skateboard and be a participant in this cultural community. In broad terms, their motivation exists in the delicately balanced, dynamic interplay between a strong sense of *individual* initiation, direction, and control, and *group* facilitation, responsibility, and connection. In other words, on the one hand, the desire to learn is about the idiosyncratic nature of individuality and participant control, and, on the other hand, it is not only about a sense of belonging to a community but also being valued and having value *as a contributor* to others' and the cultural community's well-being.

On the individual levels, participants spoke about how their continuous self-selected participation connects with experiencing pleasure. "It is fun" is the most common response the skateboarders gave to my inquiry into why they skateboarded. They talked about the pleasure they got out of the feeling of riding on their boards (one called it "heaven on wheels"), the sense of satisfaction they would get when landing a trick they had been practicing for a long time (one compared it to "climbing a mountain"), and the "high" they get from progressing with their skills. Another key factor discussed by participants regarding the individual aspects of their participation is the level of control they had over their own learning, particularly compared to adult-coached, team sports. For example, TS contrasts learning how to skateboard with his experiences playing football before he quit:

> When I was a kid, I remember when I started playing football I used to be excited to get up and go play a game or go to practice. As it got more and more serious, though, I stopped liking it as much. It became more about, "We will do this, we will do that!"

That's not about having fun. It's more about you have to be out there playing your hardest otherwise you know you're letting the team down and stuff like that. That just kind of killed it. It was more fun to say, "I woke up this morning, and I, you know, I did something for myself. It wasn't for anybody else."

In addition to these individualized motivations for learning, participants discussed how their motivation to learn connected them to other people and allowed them to be a part of something—as Luis says to open this chapter, "It gave us a sense of community that I think we didn't feel otherwise." This desire for social connection stems from an interest in locating others who shared similar social, cultural, and ideological beliefs, identities, and sensibilities. For example, one participant mentioned he was drawn to skateboarding because of its "subversive attitude." In other instances, participants discussed the ways learning to skateboard and being a part of the cultural community created an outlet for them to explore their creativity (whether it be through their kinesthetic design, their writing music, or graffiti artwork, much of which was done collaboratively), provided a communal space for them to get away from other pressures of their lives (e.g., school), and/or get physical, intellectual, and emotional engagement and stimulation.

In these ways, this research aligns well with other scholarship that has explored motivation among skateboarders and other lifestyle sports participants (e.g., Sagor, 2002; Seifert & Hedderson, 2010), especially how, "although lifestyle sports are about idiosyncratic creative expression through performance of lifestyle activities and self-judgment of progression, there is also a motivation to participate because of the belonging and community it affords participants" (Harris & Dacin, 2019, p. 1). In fact, sports psychologists often discuss "self-determined motivation," whereby "youth are motivated to play sports when they have fun and feel valued by their peers and because they have the ability to demonstrate competency and learn new skills" (Atencio et al., 2018, p. 259).

However, from a learning and schooling perspective, particularly considering motivation, perhaps the most significant aspect of the cultural community of Franklin Skatepark is that participants there have the opportunity (and in most cases are expected to) to make legitimate *contributions* to the cultural community. This possibility and expectation of being a contributor is, in my estimation, the single most important factor in how and why Franklin Skatepark works as well as it does for so many of its participants. Of course, as all humans, the participants of this cultural community like being part of something bigger than themselves. However, there is something beyond having a place and a group to simply belong to. These young men were able to be *producers* of culture, to be *contributors* to other people's lives, and *shapers* of the course of the cultural community—and, in the cases of some of these young men, to be integral in the establishment of the park in the first place. In these ways, these young men deeply mattered at the park, to the cultural community, and in the lives of other participants. The remainder of this chapter explores three ways in which this sense of contribution informed motivation and engagement for the participants.

"THAT'S WHAT *MAKES* SKATEBOARDING": STYLE AS A PATHWAY TO BE(COM)ING A CONTRIBUTOR AT FRANKLIN SKATEPARK

Although there is no finish line, final exam, or graduation ceremony in skateboarding, there does exist something akin to an external goal in learning how to skateboard—the development of one's unique "style." Style in skateboarding does not necessarily have an easily agreed-on definition, and, as Borden (2019) explains "is notoriously difficult to specify"—ranging anywhere from an "economy of motion" to "more an attitude than a technique" to "the way you move and carry yourself on a skateboard" (p. 188). In some sense, style is less about *what* you do and more about *how* you do it. For this study, based on how the participants explain it, style is signified by having a unique approach to skating the park, a particular aesthetic in movement and appearance, and being able to land particular tricks, especially ones that no else in the community can. I understand the notion of style in this cultural community to be like a skater's signature or thumbprint, so to speak; in this way, my conceptualization of style is akin to how Vivien Fell explains it, "It's what makes a skateboarder obviously unique and immediately recognisable" (cited in Borden, 2019, p. 188).

Although every skater looks different in the way they skate, even those on a skateboard for the very first time, one's style develops over time and takes shape as one develops kinesthetic knowing (Bäckström, 2014), or, as Alex says, gets "comfortable" on a board. Matt explains what getting to that level feels like: "Well, when you get used to riding and it feels like you're walking . . . you just get used to it. You get a lot more confident with what you can and can't do." Related, TS explains how the development of style is a type of culmination point skaters get to; specifically, he explains how, after you progress enough to start getting comfortable on your board and doing basic moves (e.g., ollie), you start to "add your own little tweaks to stuff. You just start seeing ways easier for you to do it and then you start just getting used to doing it that way. And that's how you develop into your own style. You know sometimes it doesn't look that great but either way it just becomes your style of doing it."

As participants start to develop their style, they are taken more seriously as a participant of the community and no longer have to prove themselves, or at least not as much or as regularly. Using a comparison to the mafia, Luis explains about reaching the point of being, as he says, "accepted":

> You start fitting in. People become more accepting of you. And then it just progresses from there, really. With the stages of progression in skateboarding, once you finally become accepted, it's almost like . . . I want to compare it to being in the mafia, even though I never have been in it, obviously [laughs]. You start off as being a grunt, then you start wearing a suit. You do enough "right" things and you become one of the guys. You become a "made man." You're finally accepted by everyone, you just come in and try and skate, not looking for acceptance from anyone. It's kind of like being made. You don't have to worry about anyone. You just come in and think about your board.

In this sense, development of style serves to produce an enduring status for participants—one that moves them from a less experienced, next-generation skater to one who is more central to the core group of the cultural community. In this way, style becomes a concrete indicator of learning having been accomplished, as it transforms one's participation within the cultural community, which, as explained, is the central aim and marker of learning from a LOPI perspective.

However, achieving the goal of developing and having recognized one's style does not suggest that there is nothing more to learn or achieve—or, for that matter, that one's status in the park is not continuously fluid. In fact, one of the main appeals of the process of learning how to skateboard is the seemingly endless possibility for growth and development it offers. While learning how to skateboard can be a lifelong, never-ending process that promises continued growth, one of the features is that within that process, one has various levels of competency. In this way, learning to skateboard is a recursive process in which one moves between a degree of felt competency and a progression to a new level of competency. Thus, as skateboarders continue to develop, they can do so without the feeling of deficit; in other words, the never-ending progression of learning to skateboard is met with a constant sense of competency. Derrick explains, "You practice more of your tricks and get 'em better, and then all of sudden out of nowhere, you get the balance for it to where every time it's perfect. And then you, like, put a revert into it or something. Or try something out of it." In this cultural community, no matter how advanced you are, there is always more that can be learned.

Importantly, in addition to functioning as an indicator of status within the community and providing a sense of personal satisfaction, developing one's own style also functions as a crucial *communal resource* for learning, for once someone has his own style, he has something unique and specific to contribute to the community. Individual skaters and their accomplishments become important resources, in large part, as discussed in Chapter 6, because of the community's integral learning practices of observing, imitation, soliciting assistance, and providing unsolicited feedback. Therefore, just by virtue of being at the park and skateboarding, participants are contributing to others' learning. In this sense, a skater's learning is a communal *investment* and their style becomes a communal resource for learning.

In fact, the understanding of style as a communal learning resource significantly shifts notions of better/worse to *valued differences* and *differentiated expertise*. Because everyone has a unique style and therefore differing areas of mastery, participants, regardless of who might be considered "better" than another, still offer others learning opportunities. For example, Derrick explains how, though, he might be considered a better skateboarder than Matt, he can still learn from Matt because Matt's style of skateboarding is "different" and he knows different tricks:

DERRICK: Like, let's say Matt teaches me new stuff, and then I teach him new stuff. Then he's about as good as I am now, but yet I'm still that notch better because I just learned his stuff.

RP: So then even if you're the one who is more advanced, you still learn from the guy who's not as advanced?

DERRICK: Yeah, because every guy is *different*, he's got different stuff you want to learn. If everyone skateboarded the same, you know how boring skateboarding would be? That's what *makes* skateboarding—doing your own thing, creating your own style.

Similarly, Santana explains how he and Derrick learn from and teach each other not necessarily because one is better or worse than the other but because they each bring different areas of expertise:

> You see, Derrick still can't do kickflips to save his life. Like, he keeps doing it, and he messes up. That's not an embarrassment. He just can't do it. There's people who can't do it. Like, he can double heel flip, but he can't kick flip. See, like, I can double kickflip but I can't double heel flip. *It's just different. See, like if we were all the same, it wouldn't be any good.* Like, we all have different things we can do and stuff like that. But like if you keep practicing and practicing, you'll be sure to get it.

In addition to accentuating the significance of differing styles as a key communal resource for learning, Santana also reminds us of the cultural community's attitude toward failure ("not an embarrassment") and repetition ("if you keep practicing and practicing, you'll be sure to get it"). Moreover, he highlights how just because one fails or doesn't know how to do one trick does not mean one doesn't have something to offer.

This highlights, too, how learning within this cultural community is not a prescriptive, lockstep, or uniform process or experience but rather is governed by an individualized pathway for each participant whereby each seeks out particular aspects to develop and resources to assist them. For instance, Matt explains how he looks to different participants to help him learn different things: "If you want to know about how to do a boneless kickflip, I'd go to TS. But if you wanted to do a backflip, I wouldn't go to him. I'd go to Luis or someone else." Overall, this valuing of diversity and difference as assets, and styles as communal resources for learning, largely rejects normative categories of comparison within athletics and devalues competition in general, which also helps explain why something like trophies and awards at the annual skate contest, as described in Chapter 4, proved to be the lackluster experience it was.

"IT'S A GREAT FEELING TO KNOW SOMEONE IS LOOKING UP TO YOU": THE EMOTIONALITY OF RECIPROCAL LEARNING RELATIONSHIPS

In addition to how an individual's style becomes a communal resource for learning, and therefore enables opportunities for participants to be contributors to the cultural community, another social arrangement that offers opportunities for participants to be contributors are "reciprocal learning relationships." Examples of such relationships have been peppered throughout this book, including in the section above, and, as discussed in Chapter 6, they demonstrate how an individual's learning in this cultural community is, in many ways, constitutive with other participants' learning. In other words, so much of the learning that happens for the participants of Franklin Skatepark is done alongside, with, from, and, ultimately, in *relation* to other participants: they watch each other, teach each other, talk to each other, jeer at and heckle each other (for better or worse), snake each other, and fall down and get back up in front of each other.

Whereas in Chapter 6 I discussed how these reciprocal relationships work logistically to support learning, in this section, I explore the emotional impact and affective dimensions this form of participation has for the guys at Franklin Skatepark. I situate this discussion in this chapter focused on understanding why these participants invest so deeply in this cultural community because, for them, this aspect of their participation at the park was one of the most socially and emotionally powerful. They spoke of how this feature engendered a sense of value, purpose, intimacy, connection, and self-efficacy, as well as a simultaneous sense of caring for others and being cared for by others. Moreover, the emotional bonds they developed engender a sense of (and/or a desire for) belonging, which necessarily increases motivation for learning. As Paradise and Rogoff (2009) state, "A learner's emotional involvement and the accompanying self-generated motivation are not only based on being present and socially oriented toward participation. They are also the result of a deep-seated 'bond of interest and commitment' and a sharing of values and goals, as well as ongoing participation in a shared community existence" (p. 130).

Theoretically, this exploration is significant, particularly within sociocultural perspectives that recognize learning as part of a broad web of social relations. The social relations among the participants of Franklin

Skatepark include emotional connections and investments not just with the park and skateboarding but also with each other—and it is this emotionality that, in part, motivated them to learn and participate. I selected this particular social arrangement to explore emotion for three reasons. First, the consistency and depth with which the participants spoke of this feature of participation's emotional impact was unsurpassed. Second, these emotional connections further illuminate how the social arrangement of age heterogeneity functions within this cultural community. Finally, this aspect of learning highlights the centrality of *relationships* in and for participation at Franklin Skatepark.

One of the most significant aspects of reciprocal learning relationships is that participants are simultaneously given opportunities to be mentored and to mentor. In Chapter 6, I similarly explained how participants always co-existed as "learners" and "teachers." Here, I shift my language to "mentee" and "mentor" to broaden the scope of my exploration from strictly learning and teaching to more relational and social emotional understandings of joint participation. In fact, most of the participants use the language of "brother" to describe these relationships, often referring to those doing the assisting as "big brothers" and those being assisted as "little brothers." For instance, Houston, says, in relation to one of the younger participants he sees and assists regularly, "He'll come up to me and ask me if I have something to drink for him or something. It's like a buddy system, like a little brother."

Taking on the "big brother" role whereby they are the one providing assistance is a particularly powerful experience for many—and one of the most significant ways participants felt a sense of themselves as *contributors* to the cultural community. It made them feel "good" about themselves, and some even refer to it as a "high." For many, it feels like they are being "looked up to" and "idolized," sometimes in similar ways they look(ed) up to professional skateboarders or others from magazines or videos. TS explains, "You kind of went from that kid who *reads* the magazines to that kid *in* the magazines. And somebody is picking up stuff about you and seeing something in your style that they want to adapt to or adopt. It's a great feeling to know people look up to you." Related, taking on this type of big brother role also confers status, respect, and subcultural capital for participants. As Crazy K says, "Part of it is taking the younger guys, and putting them under your wing, so to speak. You look out for them, and take care of them. And in return, you get respect for that."

Participants spoke, too, about how helping others was fun and meaningful to see how the other skaters progressed and built on what they taught them. They spoke of these instances as having influence on both individual people at the park and the cultural community writ large, almost in terms of having a legacy. TS explains that, several years before, he taught a group of younger participants some moves and that it has been fun to watch them progress, but more so how he imagines they will, in turn, teach the next generation of participants:

> It's fun to see kids progress. When you teach them those little things. Like Archie, I taught him when he was younger how to ollie and stuff like that, and look where he's taken it, you know? Like, you may have taught this kid how to rock to fakey, but like when he starts to do rock and rolls and disasters and stuff like that, it's like, "Okay, now it's all you, dude." Like, we've given you this little bit [brings his thumb and index finger to nearly touching]. It's like, we gave them a foot and they've built a mile off it.
>
> There's two kids down there [at the park] that I started skating with when I was in 10th grade and they were about 10 or 11 years old. And now to see them progress and find their own style is amazing. When we started skating with them it was like whatever we were doing that was what they wanted to try and learn how to do. And now it's like they're doing stuff that I can't even think about doing 'cause they've just taken what we've done and made it that much better.
>
> It's like what I was talking about: they take something and they made it just that much better, and it will continue going like that. Like there's kids down there who are now like 9 or 10 skating with those guys, and I guarantee you the same thing will happen. They'll just keep on finding new ways to improve it and, you know, that's the good news about skateboarding, it's constantly progressing.

In addition to sharing his personal feelings about this intergenerational transmission of knowledge, TS also illuminates how individual participants can transform the cultural community of Franklin Skatepark in a way that is not beholden to, and, in fact, transcends particular participants. In this way, being able to teach younger participants enables the "big brother" to have been a contributor not only to individual partici- pants but also to the broader cultural community, which adds an extra layer of esteem about helping out.

A key aspect of the big brother–little brother dynamic is that these identity positionings are available *simultaneously*. In other words, with rare exceptions (namely, participants on the extreme end of the contin- uum of older age and/or advanced level of participation), all participants have opportunities to be both mentor and mentee—a social arrangement I refer to as the "flip side." For participants, being in the "little brother" role feels good because you get to learn from others to advance your participation and because of the ways it feels to have someone taking an interest in you. In talking about an older participant, Dominic, a biker who proved pivotal for TS's participation in skateboarding even before the park opened, TS explains how he felt attended to by him:

> Everybody looks up to him at the skatepark—biker, skater, no matter what, you look up to him because he's such a good guy. I remember times I would have no one to skate with, and I'd see him biking. Most bikers don't want to go out with skaters, and he'd be ready to head out, and he'd see me. And he'd say, "Hey, dude, I'm about ready to head over to this spot, you want to come? I guarantee there's some stuff you can do there." You know, he'd say that 'cause, of course, bikers and skaters, we look for different things and spots we'd skate. But he was just kind of that [pauses] he was kind of like that *big brother* that would always invite you along and never really leave you sitting there thinking, "Oh now I'm going to be bored."

One of the interesting aspects of TS's connection with Dominic is that it doesn't cohere around skateboarding specifically. It is the fact that Dominic was looking out for TS, keeping him in mind. TS mattered to someone, and that mattering had nothing to do with his abilities.

Related, other participants talked about how being recognized by older, more accomplished participants made them feel special and good about themselves. For example, Houston explains, "When I am being helped out by the older dudes, it's almost like a confidence booster, like, 'Oh, he thinks I'm cool—at least cool enough to give me some pointers.'" In this way, being a "little brother" can also confer status in a positive way, similar to how it does those in the big brother role—it made Houston feel like he was, to some extent, "cool." For TS, while Dominic continues to be a significant "big brother" at the park, he also has regular access to Crazy K (who TS affectionately referred to as a "geezer" in Chapter 4) and Thurman (who TS turns to often to help think through interfacing with the city regarding park issues). I point to these relationships to draw attention to the fact that, though a core member of the cultural community—and a "big brother" to many at the park—TS still benefits from and enjoys having the opportunity to be a "little brother" too.

In general, reciprocal learning relationships are made available by several broader participation frameworks and social arrangements. For instance, the fact that this cultural community values inclusion of participants of differentiated levels of participation is key to there being a range of participants who learn form and teach each other. Also, as discussed in the previous section, the valuing of diverse areas of expertise facilitates learning from and teaching one another, which, in some instances, does not necessitate participants being at different levels of participation. Another important social arrangement that makes these reciprocal relationships available is *age heterogeneity*.

Because this discussion emphasizes the social and emotional aspects of these relationships, I draw particular attention to the significance of age variation as a social arrangement within this cultural community. Though virtually all participants said that it felt good to help out others, it was this feature of being in relation to people of different ages that facilitated the deeper emotionality of the experience. This is likely the case because cross-age groupings of children actually engender an increased sense of cooperation, as well as opportunities for caretaking, learning, and teaching, whereas same-age groupings tend to produce more competition among participants (Rogoff, 2003)—not to mention that cross-age networks are particularly significant within working-class families and communities in comparison to middle-class settings (Eckert, 1989).

To highlight how significant age heterogeneity is to the emotional experience of the cultural community, I offer an extended excerpt from an interview with TS. (Here, I deliberately highlight TS's experiences again to illuminate how these dual roles of "big" and "little" brother are simultaneously available for most participants.) In the interview, TS explains how one day at the park, he helped out a "little one" who was struggling. It turns out that the younger participants' mother was in a car in the parking lot observing, and after the kid left the park, the mom came back to tell TS how much the exchange meant to the boy. In his retelling, TS explains, too, what the exchange meant to him. To frame this excerpt, particularly regarding tone, it is important to note that of the many times I had spoken to TS, there were only two times he visibly (with tears in his eyes) or audibly (with cracking voice) welled with emotion. The first was the previous excerpted discussion in which he spoke about Dominic, and the second was the retelling of the following story about the little kid he helped.

> One time I was up there [the park] and this kid was just, he was having a hard time, and I could tell. I didn't even know he had parents up there. They were in the car or something like that. And he was trying to roll into that little part of the park, and I was like, "Alright dude, just bend your knees," because no one is up there, and it just frustrates you to see somebody struggle that much. Like you know when you see them fall that many times it's almost like you're tossing up the option of either telling them to give up or to help them out—and you always go with helping them out.
>
> But I just gave him a few little pointers, like, "Bend your knees," like, "It doesn't come easy," and "We've done this for how many years—that's why we make it look so easy doing it."
>
> After a while the kid leaves, and not five minutes after the kid takes off to the car, the mom came up to me and said, "Thanks" and told me the kid isn't really that popular in school, and gets a lot of crap from kids. And I guess his only main thing is he *really* likes coming out to the skatepark. And I guess he was really psyched about what he just did and what just happened.
>
> I'm a big fan of helping a kid think he can do anything, to make some kid think he's got somewhat of a chance, or that he can be accepted. You know, to have fun.
>
> That's worth the—
>
> [pauses and then slows down his speech and his voice softens]
>
> The fact that that kid now knows.
>
> Every time he's come up there since, like *every* time, he'll just walk up and knuckle with me and stuff like that. I'll ask him how he's been and whatnot.
>
> You know, and, of course, it's just shooting the shit with a little kid so he doesn't really say much back, but just knowing the fact that he's coming there, that he's *trusting*. You know that's *a lot* when a little kid will trust you with something. And I know he'll

probably be back to the park and keep coming and keep coming
and probably get better and someday maybe even better than me.
[pauses]
It's that . . . getting a high when you're teaching somebody.
It almost feels good to be needed in something, you know?
Almost like you're a parent, but you don't have to deal with all
the bullshit.

Evidenced by the ways TS talks about Dominic looking out for him and
about the young boy's mom thanking TS for helping her son, it's clear
that the age differentials open up an opportunity for those being helped
to be more than just a learner in that context—they are "little brothers."
As a literal "little brother" myself with a "big brother" eight years my
senior, I can personally attest to the power of having an older man in
my life who I knew cared about me—something that many of these participants may not quite have experienced much elsewhere. For those in
the "big brother" roles, there is a sense of fulfillment in being able to be
of assistance, to pass on what they know and can do, to see their legacy
of sorts continuing beyond them. For better or worse, these cross-age
dynamics have the potential to be quite influential and meaningful in
these participants' lives, as they provide role models, mentors, and a
deep sense of caring and being cared for. Moreover, the social emotional
aspects of these relationships are important reasons that these young
men continue showing up to the park to learn and participate, and for
many, are some of the most prevailing aspects of their participation even
after they stop showing up to the park.

"I HOPE SOMEDAY MY MUSIC WILL DO THAT TO SOMEONE LIKE THEIR MUSIC HAS DONE TO ME": PAYING HOMAGE AND GIVING BACK TO CONTRIBUTE TO THE WELFARE OF OTHERS

Throughout the interviews in this study, I was continuously struck by how
the participants spoke of their deep investment not only for the learning
and participation of others in their immediate sphere but also in *future* participants they may never know. In most cases, they expressed their desire
to contribute as a way to "give back" or to "pay forward" what they had
been given. In this way, I'm reminded of how Citizen Potawatomi Nation

botanist and memorist Robin Wall Kimmerer (2013) explains why she writes, "For me, writing is an act of reciprocity with the world; it is what I can give back in return for everything that has been given to me" (p. 152). I am also reminded of 12-step recovery circles whereby the 12th step of the recovery program is about taking what you've received through working the first 11 steps and "carrying the message" to others in need. In doing so, one not only helps others but also the group, as well as oneself.

In their own "acts of reciprocity" and "carrying the message," the participants of Franklin Skatepark often paid homage to past participants and noted their audience of future participants—both of whom are often people they never met. In this sense, the participants of Franklin Skatepark see themselves as part of an intergenerational lineage whereby their contributions function as both expressions of gratitude for what they have been given and as ways they can provide something similar to others. As Paradise and Rogoff (2009) explain, "The social experience of the individual when learning in such family and community settings appears to be an experience of involvement, of belonging in a specific community, with personal and emotional commitment *grounded in a socially and culturally defined past, present, and future* (p. 104; emphasis added). Thus, these young men's expressions of deep reverence and gratitude for being helped engender a care and concern for others' well-being—something that often carried with it a tenderness and a deep sense of *responsibility* and *reciprocity*.

For some participants, textual and cultural production and distribution provided them with a tangible way to give back to and leave a legacy for a cultural community and other participants. For example, Larry speaks of his aspirations as a musician in relation to the inspiration he received from previous musicians and what hopes to give to other people:

> When I get so hell bent, when I get so frustrated with all these thoughts about that kind of shit [large existential questions, such as what is the meaning of life], I listen to music. And it just kind of soothes me. And *I hope someday my music will do that to someone like their music has done to me, you know? Like I want to be able to do that, but I mean, before I pass the torch you got to receive it, you know?* And I mean, you know, like AC/DC says, it's a long way to the top, you know, and if you want to rock and roll all you can do is try.

Here, Larry orients himself in the past, present, and future as one of many, doing his part. Of significance is that Larry's participation moves from consumption to production and ultimately contribution. As discussed in the previous chapter, this shift over time demonstrates transformed participation within a cultural community, which in turn transforms the cultural community. In other words, as participants learn, the cultural community shifts and changes. For Larry and the other participants, they don't just see themselves as simply people who skateboard, play music, or draw, but rather they see themselves as skateboarders, musicians, artists, promoters, and producers of culture.

In some ways, this desire to give back connects with how participants create venues and outlets for themselves and others. For example, James coordinated an all-day music festival a summer before I started my data collection in order to bring together a range of local bands and people. In response to my inquiry as to how he learns all that he knows about skateboarding and/or music, he explains how he spends time with many other people interested in the same things he is as a way to learn from them. He then goes on to explain the music festival he coordinated: "I had a show out at my house when I lived in Columbia with like 20 bands. I advertised for like two months and I had like 240 somethin' people at my house. I called it 'The show out at Hicktown' 'cuz it was in the middle of nowhere. And it was sweet. It lasted from like noon til midnight and so many people went to it—even people from way out of town." In this sense, James is actually moving beyond *transforming* a cultural community, and in some ways is potentially *establishing* a new one, or at least significantly expanding one.

Perhaps the quintessential example of this phenomenon is the initial development of Franklin Skatepark, which was made possible due to the efforts of many of the participants, especially TS (as discussed in Chapter 4). For TS, his role in the development of the park, particularly now that it is established and he is fading out of participating as much as he used to, is something that is quite meaningful for him. He explains:

> It's kind of rewarding for me because I worked three years for it and to know that many—like I haven't seen it one day where people haven't been there besides in the winter or really bad weather. But, like, it's good to know you put something, like even if I can say that all I've really done through skateboarding is put

that park there. Like, I did something that not many people get to say they've done, not many people get to be responsible for something like that.

And I'm really psyched about the fact that these kids now have somewhere to go. Like when we started skating, we used to get kicked out of the post office every frickin' day, every day. Kicked out of the high school every day. And the worst part was we didn't have cars back then so you had to skate all through town to get to these places and you were there for maybe 20 minutes before you got kicked out.

It offers kids a place to go. To learn.

I mean, it ain't exactly the most healthy environment to learn because of the way we talk up there, but at the same time you find you're almost a family there. Like, people up there I trust more than I trust some family members with, you know?

Later in the same interview, TS mentioned that he looks forward to the day where he can take his kids (if he has any) there to teach them how to skateboard. He even explains how now that he skates only on occasion, he is still contributing to the welfare of the more regular participants by showing them that it's possible for them, too, to get good jobs and continue to skateboard once in a while to strike a good work-life balance. He says, "The thing is we [older other guys who also work full time] keep going up there, and the good news is we're hopefully putting a good impression on another generation. That we're showing them a good work ethic with the fact that we're at our jobs every day but we still find time to go out there and skate and have fun." In this way, even as he slows down his participation, TS is still oriented toward making contributions to the community.

I also draw attention to how for several participants assisting me with the production of this book became a literacy practice whereby they were able to help create a counternarrative around the "stereotypes" of skateboarders, people with tattoos, punk rockers, and youth—what they hoped would contribute not only to other participants in the cultural community but also to outsiders' conceptions of skateboarders. In other words, some participants saw my study and their collaboration as an opportunity to voice their critiques and concerns related to the ways they believed dominant society perceived them. For example, Kevin, who was interested in helping me out because he believed I was "trying to build something," spoke about how he is concerned that he and the other participants get labeled as "juvenile delinquents," "skater punks," or "stoner skaters" simply because they skateboard:

KEVIN: People look at the skatepark and think that this is a haven for juvenile delinquents, and it honestly isn't. I've met some of the best people up here that I've ever met in my life.

RP: Why do you think people would think that this is a haven for juvenile delinquents?

KEVIN: Because of generalization of skateboarders—skateboarder punks, things like that. I've been skateboarding since I was 14, and the thing is, is that everybody that knows me thinks of me as a very respectful person. I don't do any drugs, drink; I'm completely sober with everything. I don't like my mind being altered, and yet, it's sad that if I come up here, I can be labeled as a skateboarder punk, as a "*stoner*" skater, something like that. It's had a lot of bad rep.

Some of the parents that stood up and said, "All those kids are bad and all that," they should honestly come up here and actually meet some of us because we're good people. And the only time you'll ever see any of us with a bad attitude is if we are shown disrespect. And that applies anywhere. This is the only place for kids, for teens to hang out, and I think it should be shown a lot more respect than it does.

Here Kevin explains how he is concerned by the ways young people, especially skateboarders in Finley and in society at large, are conceptualized and labeled (Taylor & Khan, 2011). He recognizes that just by virtue of engaging in skateboarding, he is implicated in a larger web of sociopolitical arrangements, which, in this instance, potentially index him as a deviant. He saw his participation in the research as helping to offset what felt to him as misrepresentations.

Both Kevin's understanding that engagement in a cultural community implicates him into larger sociopolitical arrangements and his interest in problematizing these is consistent with several other participants' views and motivation for helping me with this research. For example, Luis, as quoted in the beginning of this book, explains that he was interested in helping me with this book project to get word about skateboarders and punk rockers "out there," since he believes there exists erroneous ideas about participants in these cultural communities; as he says, "There's a lot of people in this world that have a common misconception about skateboarders and punk rockers, and a lot of people just think that we're just a bunch of loser, drop-out, drug users that have nothing better to do with their time than to raise hell and skateboard, and that's not the case."

CONCLUSION

More than any other, this chapter illuminates the social and emotional significance the cultural community of Franklin Skatepark has for the participants—and the ways this community was organized and structured to support these types of affective, relational, and learning opportunities. Similar to the previous four chapters, this one, too, illuminates how learning within this cultural community is deeply interconnected across the underlying structures of social and community organization, the means and motives for learning, as well as the forms of communication and assessments.

In many respects, Franklin Skatepark became the thing, the space, the community that the young men in this study didn't or couldn't find in schools or elsewhere. From my perspective, I would argue this chapter reveals the most elemental findings of the entire study—for without these opportunities to plug in, pitch in, belong, matter, and care, nothing else would really work when it comes to participation or learning. Though the next chapter will directly pick up many of the ideas from this chapter to consider the implications, I pause here to invite you to consider how notions of contribution, emotional bonds, and investment between participants and community, and the sense of mattering and belonging to a community, being linked to past and future generations, might factor into other contexts meant to serve youth. In what ways do underlying structures of schooling prevent and/or enable these types of things from being present or available? Are there ways to make them (more) available?

As a youth-focused researcher and teacher/educator, the findings in this chapter have been the most powerful and paradigm-shifting for me personally. Concretely, this set of findings and revelations led me to rethink my basic assumptions of youth (Petrone, Sarigianides, & Lewis, 2015) and revamp my entire approach to teacher education (Petrone & Rink, with Speicher, 2020; Petrone & Sarigianides, 2017)—both of which I explore in the next, final chapter, to stimulate possibilities for the applications and implications of this research.

PART THREE
BEYOND THE BOWL

CHAPTER TEN

Beyond the Bowl

REIMAGINING POSSIBILITIES FOR LEARNING,
SCHOOLING, AND YOUTH

Informal learning can provide guidance for getting beyond the factory model that has prevailed in schools in the 20th century and into the 21st century. Even if schools themselves remain a societal institution, articulating other ways of supporting children's learning can develop a deeper conceptual understanding of learning itself. In addition, articulation of alternative approaches can provide practical ideas for improving the ways that society organizes support for children's learning. What is known about learning in informal settings can be instructive for new forms of learning and their organization in a range of learning environments, including schools as well as the out-of-school settings of children's lives. (Rogoff et al., 2016, p. 357)

Despite the risks of doing so, I think we have to advocate in a way that undermines the monolithic view of adolescents as supposedly all the same and as fundamentally different from adults. We must move between and against the confident characterizations of youth, which involves including teenagers as *active* participants (not tokens) in educational and other public policy deliberations. I am not just trumpeting "one student voice," but calling for the imagining of concrete practices in which youth demand and exercise adultlike responsibilities. (Lesko, 2012, p. 199)

ALMOST UNIVERSALLY, THE two immediate questions I am asked by academics and non-academics alike when I discuss this research are: Did you skateboard? Are you a skateboarder? Though I did skateboard during the research, I did not study skateboarding due to any intrinsic interest in it. Truthfully, I didn't think much about skateboarding at all prior to this research. I could have told you who Tony Hawk was, and, returning to the recesses of my mind to some of the videos my cousin John made me watch when I was an early teenager, I could have named some of the "old school" skaters like Lance Mountain and Stacy Peralta.

I even tried, when I was younger, and only with my cousin's encourage-ment, to drop into a half-pipe, which instantly proved a truly disastrous event. Perched on the lip of a half-pipe, I pushed my foot down on the front of the board, and within a few seconds was lying flat on my back, writhing in pain. The main outcome of that experience was a strength-ened resolve to keep shooting hoops at the park and make the middle school basketball team the following season. Not until years later—and only then for the sake of research—did I dare put my foot atop a skate-board again.

While I learned much about skateboarding throughout the course of this research—and eventually learned to skateboard myself—in this chapter, I primarily focus on lessons learned from this work that have significance beyond skateboarding.[2] Throughout the book, especially in the conclusions of Chapters 4 through 9, I have made additional sug-gestions for inquiries into and implications of the findings of this proj-ect, but with this final chapter, I share several focused perspectives on what this research might mean for those interested in the betterment of young people's lives, especially those youth who are harmed by dominant systems and structures of social ordering—namely schools. In doing so, this chapter returns us to the experiences of schooling for the young men highlighted in this book, as well as the opening quote of the book in which Luis boldly claims that there's a lot to be learned from kids like him. Thus, this chapter attends to the question, What is, in fact, to be learned from these young men and this research on their participation in a particular cultural community?

To tease out these ideas—and address the "So what?" question—I trace some of the ways this research has informed my own thinking and work, theoretically and practically. I use this strategy to demonstrate how this research can have different import for different people in different contexts. In this way, I'm less interested in offering blanket, catchall sug-

---

1 Though focused on implications for education and youth studies, I do think there's quite a lot this study can do to help those interested in skateboarding, particularly related to skate-parks (especially in rural contexts). As I discuss in the first chapter, my research corroborates much related scholarship on the benefits of skateboarding and skateparks. However, I also wrestle with the tension between supporting the leveraging of skateboarding for youth devel-opment and worrying about it becoming co-opted by harmful neoliberal agendas that often operate as a discourse surrogate for ideas of "development" rooted in whiteness, coloniality, and capitalism (see pages 18–23).

gestions than I am in showcasing a *process* whereby research findings led to transformation of and for me in particular contexts. Thus, I invite each of you to imagine how the research in this book might inspire possibilities for your contexts, as well as your thinking, theorizing, relationships, scholarship, and practice.

Toward this end, I explain how this research shifted my relating, theorizing, and practice in three ways: (1) theoretically reconceptualizing secondary-aged youth, what I refer to as "a shift *from* adolescent development *to* critical youth studies" (Petrone & Rink, with Speicher, 2020)—and the development of a "Youth Lens"; (2) integrating youth labeled as "at-risk" into teacher education *as educational consultants and experts* by way of a "repositioning pedagogy"; and (3) imagining cross-age learning environments in schools to facilitate reciprocal learning relationships and youth as contributors to the learning of others.

To explore these ideas, I share my own reckoning with the findings of this research, and so before getting into these ideas, I explore how carrying out this study changed me as a scholar and as a person.

ON BEING CHANGED BY RESEARCH

If research hasn't changed you as a person, then you haven't done it right. (Wilson, 2008, p. 135)

Like the fish that is unaware of water until it has left the water, people often take their own community's ways of doing things for granted. (Rogoff, 2003, p. 13)

Even though years of going to concerts in and around New York City as a teenager and young adult harmed my hearing, I could still pick up the click-clack of wooden skateboards on cement and the rattle of "broken" ball bearings as I walked along the platform of the Long Island Railroad—even with a piercing train whistle enveloping me. I was visiting my family shortly after finishing the bulk of data generation for this book, and my sister Joann waited for me in a nearby car as I watched a group of young men skating a section of the parking lot. The group huddled as one skater pushed his way toward a ledge and attempted to tail slide it. I watched him fall to the ground—and then get back up and try it again. As I walked to my sister's awaiting vehicle, I smiled to myself, thinking of how many times I'd seen this near exact situation over the past several years.

I grew up in that town, had walked that stretch of platform hundreds, if not thousands, of times, and I never once thought about how that spot might prove an exciting challenge for boarders. And yet, after carrying out this study, I found myself not only keenly aware of the presence of these young men but also wondering about their "stories"—about their relationships with skateboarding, each other, and that place, including the broader town.

As the participants in this book explain how they see city streets and municipal spaces differently than non-skaters, I realized then that I could no longer see skateboarders and, more broadly, the demographic of "failing youth" or "youth at-risk"—whether they be on skateboards or not—without an altered consciousness of them as participants in and contributors to the world that exists well beyond the normative discourses of youth as embodiments of adult fears, anxieties, and hopes (Elman, 2014; Medovi, 2005). In fact, prior to this research, I would say I held, if not a neutral attitude, then a somewhat negative attitude toward skateboarding and skateboarders—one that connected to broader stereotypes of skateboarders as slackers, punks, and troublemakers (Bradley, 2010; Jenson, Swords, & Jeffries, 2012; Wood, Carter, & Martin, 2014). And yet, it would no longer be possible for me to see or hear about young people wearing Element T-shirts, arms full of tattoos, or even "underachieving" in school and ascribe to them the dominant narratives that position them in "crisis," as "punks," "resistant," or "oppositional." Now, behind every tattoo and atop every skateboard, I see a participant in and contributor to cultural communities.

In short, carrying out the research reported in this book changed me—personally and professionally. In fact, as a scholar and an educator, I have since marked my career in terms of "before" and "after" Franklin Skatepark. In particular, learning from the skateboarders of Franklin Skatepark broadened my thinking about learning in general, and certainly learning and teaching in schools and teacher education in particular. In many ways, this research catapulted me beyond my apprenticeship into conventional schooling—and challenged me to start noticing and wondering about the "water" I, as a teacher, educational researcher, and teacher educator, had been swimming in, unwittingly, for so long.

Specifically, the situated nature of learning at Franklin Skatepark brought into sharp focus how seriously flawed is our societal practice of removing children and youth from the doings of society so they can be "prepared" in decontextualized contexts to later be reinserted and only then contribute to the workings of our society. This social arrangement robs people of countless possibilities for authentic learning (that truly matters to them), social networks and relationships (particularly across ages), and being real contributors to the world. My biggest takeaway from this research is that how we have organized learning and teaching in the United States may actually be *interfering* with young people's authentic learning and abilities to contribute to the world. Because of this, I began to rethink the mantra I had carried with me into my earliest years of teaching and have had echoed back to me by so many other educators: this desire to help students become "lifelong learners." I now realize that students entering classrooms are already lifelong learners and that schools might actually be interrupting both their learning pursuits and their desires for learning.

Related, I also became more aware of how this segregation of youth from much of society disproportionately affects working-class and other marginalized youth, given the ways primary social systems established for youth (e.g., schools) privilege white, middle-class, heteronormative, cisgender norms and ideologies. Moreover, whereas so much of the discourse surrounding learning in schools had me previously focused on standardized assessments, classroom management, achievement data, and the like, learning from the skateboarders at Franklin Skatepark (re) stimulated my thinking and feeling related to the love of learning, the joys in connecting with others over and through learning, and the reasons why I first decided to pursue a career in education—to stoke the flames of curiosity, imagination, and joy; to find out more about myself; to engage more meaningfully in the world; and to be a part of, and maybe even inspire, other people's learning journeys as well. In these ways, carrying out and then writing about this research reminded me of Mark Twain's famous quote: "I never let my schooling interfere with my education." From my vantage, the participants of this study were seeking out an education at Franklin Skatepark.

In the end, this research has pushed me to wonder how the enterprise of schooling might better flow from notions of education and learning rather than from teaching and curricula. What would it be like if the primary question teacher education and schools cohere around was

How do people learn? And then, How might schools build on this and become places that stoke such fires for all youth? Especially for students much like the participants of Franklin Skatepark and others labeled "at-risk" or otherwise marginalized by schooling? How might schools be organized and governed by theories and perspectives of learning that consider notions of identity, intrinsic motivation, relationality, emotionality, embodiment, youth expertise, and contribution? In what ways might educational discourse and practice move further away from stressing youth out by emphasizing decontextualized demonstrations of knowledge and moving closer to youth experiences of contextualized participation? How can schools become places whereby many students do not need to "circumvent limits on learning" (Mahiri, 2000/2001) and go elsewhere to have their intellectual and learning needs met? In what ways might students themselves be invited into the process of developing and implementing pedagogies? Conversely, might we be better off to recognize that schools are largely being left behind, so to speak, by so many young people and instead make schools smaller and more limited in scope so that youth have more opportunities to create and engage in more authentic, purposive learning?

In asking these questions, I recognize that schools are institutions embedded in broader social systems, and that educators and youth workers—whether at the level of classrooms, schools, policies, or programs—are often limited in the degree to which they can affect systemic change. Furthermore, I recognize, given how schools are linked with broader systems, that school reform is challenging and takes a lot of effort and time. At the same time, based on my experiences as a teacher, as well as my experiences working with teachers over the years, I know that educators make major differences in their students' lives and in systems—and that systems can and do change, even if incrementally, at times (Kirschner & Kaplan, 2017).

REIMAGINING POSSIBILITIES FOR LEARNING, SCHOOLING, AND YOUTH

In this section, I offer several specific ways this research has stimulated shifts in my own thinking, scholarship, and practice. In sharing these, I lean toward the concrete and pragmatic, as my experiences reading some scholarship is that the recommendations seem too far-reaching and/ or vague or generalized to have any practical input in my work, which sometimes leaves me feeling even more defeated about how to mitigate inequitable social systems such as schooling. I recognize, too, that by offering these specific implications, there are many other possibilities for leveraging this research for rethinking schooling and other contexts for youth development that I leave unattended. My hope is that, by show-casing my process with having this research shift my work, you might engage in an analogous process to develop applications and implications for your own work emergent from the research reported in this book. Finally, I worry that these suggestions do not go far enough in drawing attention to, dismantling, and reimagining structures of schooling, and so I'm eager to see how these ideas might be extended by others.

Rethinking Notions of Adolescence/ts and Youth (in Education)
Prior to this research, having been apprenticed into dominant ways of thinking about and being in relation to the demographic of people typ-ically referred to as *adolescents* and *teenagers*, I very much operated from deficit-oriented renderings of such people. The normalized, ubiquitous psychologized and biologized discursive constructions of these people as being "not yet fully formed," "full of raging hormones," and "naturally rebellious" were commonsensical to me, particularly given the scientific authority these perspectives were given through discourses of "the teen-age brain." For instance, seeing the *New Yorker* cartoon that depicted a scene in which a medical doctor was telling the parent of a visibly brood-ing teen child that he was sorry because medical science had not yet come up with a "cure" for adolescence, would have likely gotten a chuckle out of me, and drawing on my former teaching experiences, brought to mind of a host of instances to "confirm" this pathological perspective of adolescence/ts.

Spending time at Franklin Skatepark changed this perspective for me in a profound way. My time with that cultural community revealed—even amid some of the enactments of the stereotypes of adolescence/ts—a much different version of adolescence/youth, adolescents/young people, and adolescent/youth development. As I mentioned in Chapter 3, I noted throughout the research my myriad surprises, and for months, most of these involved the ways participants supported each other, collaborated with one another, sought out relationships with adults and/or those older and younger than themselves, cared about their futures, recognized the ways schools constrained their options for ways of being and livelihoods to pursue, engaged in sociopolitical critique, and carried a sense of futurity and responsibility to more than just their own well-being.

This was not the vision of youth I was socialized into as I first prepared to become a teacher, or have seen many educators adopt in their preparation (Lewis & Petrone, 2010; Petrone & Lewis, 2012). For instance, I will never forget one class session during which I was teaching future teachers about the links between argumentative writing and critical thinking, and they started a debate, instigated by one of the preservice teachers, as to whether or not argumentative writing should be taught to students below 11th grade, since students at that age cannot yet think critically given their "jelly brains."

It was through this research—as the mounting data disconfirmed the "scientific" understandings of youth I'd been schooled in—that I sought out new theoretical frameworks to make sense of what I was bearing witness to. Eventually, I came on the interdisciplinary field of Critical Youth Studies (CYS), which, among other things, pushes against the totalizing developmentalist framings of adolescence/ts and illuminates how ideas of adolescence/ts, youth, and teenagers are social constructs and circulate as discourses that are contingent on and constitutive with social systems, policies, programs, and policies at any given time. Moreover, CYS opened me up to scholarship about and with youth beyond the purview of schooling—research that highlighted youth as capable and able, agentive, political, and operating in solidarity with adults—and in doing so, helped me understand the ways in which schools, as social institutions, participated in the discursive construction of youth as deficits, problems to be fixed, rebellious to adults and authority, and non-normative "others" (see more on CYS and particular citations in Chapter 1).

My foray into CYS became revelatory by making visible to me the taken-for-granted assumptions of adolescence/ts within much educational discourse, policies, and practices. From pedagogical texts to banning books to dress code policies to curricula to organizing learning by age, I recognized how steeped in developmentalist thinking schooling and adolescence were—and the negative consequences of such, particularly for youth for whom "normalized" ideas of adolescence are not available (Bettie, 2014; Eckert, 1989; Finders, 1997; Patel, 2012). Related, I began to understand how such normative and universal notions of adolescence/ts tend to render context and intersectional identities marginal or invisible; in other words, I came to recognize how adolescence, as a sociocultural construct and prevailing discourse, was constitutive with the structures of white supremacy and settler colonialism (Lesko, 2012; Petrone, González Ybarra, & Rink, 2021).

This awareness drove me to wonder what a CYS perspective might mean for education, particularly regarding literacy education. Specifically, I developed an approach to analyze and critique representations and discourses of dominant ideas of youth, adolescence/ts, and teenagers in and beyond education—what colleagues (Drs. Sophia Sarigianides and Mark A. Lewis) and I refer to as a "Youth Lens" (Petrone, Sarigianides, & Lewis, 2015; Sarigianides, Petrone, & Lewis, 2017). Drawing on CYS as an anchoring theoretical orientation, at its core, a Youth Lens invites teachers, teacher educators, preservice teachers, and secondary students to examine how texts, policies, institutions, and discourses help establish, challenge, reify, and subvert dominant renderings of adolescence/ts. In this way, a Youth Lens, and an overall CYS orientation, broadens understandings of adolescence from a universalized to a differentiated experience contingent on context, identity, and historicity. Since its development, a Youth Lens has helped shape understandings of youth engagement with videogames (e.g., Ehret, Mannard, & Curwood, 2022) and young adult literature (e.g., Silva & Savitz, 2019), as well as critiques of and interventions in secondary literacy curricula (e.g., Sarigianides, 2019), policy analysis (e.g., Sulzer, 2014), and literacy teacher education (e.g., Falter, 2016; Sulzer & Thein, 2016).

The key underlying idea of a Youth Lens is that the ways youth are named and understood has significant impact on how adults will engage and think of them; how and why curricula, programs, and policies related to youth will be developed and implemented; and even what young people might come to know and feel about themselves. In other words, the systems of reasoning used to make sense of people known as "teenagers," "adolescents," and "youth" have *material effects* on/for them as well as those people known as "adults." As Freire (1970b) notes,

"All educational practice implies a theoretical stance on the educator's part. This stance, in turn, implies—sometimes more, sometimes less explicitly—an interpretation of man and the world" (p. 205).

For this reason, a central recommendation from this research is for organizations, institutions, and educators to interrogate their own ways of knowing and naming "youth." What systems of reasoning regarding youth, adolescence/ts, and adolescent development are operating in the institution, and are reflected in policies, programs, and practices? In what ways do these systems of reasoning uphold dominant renderings of adolescence/ts as incomplete, deficit, and in opposition to adults and authority? How do or might these systems of reasoning hold youth as capable and able, caring about the welfare of others, and holders of valuable knowledge and skills?

In addition to examining and disrupting how young people are conceptualized, I also suggest that for more intentional and careful centering of youth perspectives, youth voices, and "youth epistemologies" (Watson & Petrone, 2020) we create more expansive, inclusive, and youth-focused curricula, instructional approaches, programming, and policies. A youth epistemology, as Dr. Vaughn W. M. Watson and I (2020, p. 247) have argued,

> questions and critiques power dynamics in relation to notions of adulthood as normative, and conversely, youth as non-normative, and the adultism and adult-centrism that permeates most social structures, particularly schools. Moreover, a youth epistemology engages the interplay of youth's already present knowledge and varied identities, to assert youth as critical participants and inquirers in their schools and communities.

In many ways, a youth epistemology recognizes that youth are often at the leading edges of language, literacy, and learning—of education. In fact, one need not look very far into the daily news cycles, global protests, and social media to see that "young people are not only creating and engaging myriad linguistic and literacy practices to chart, envisage and enact change but, in doing so, they are educating and *teaching*, particularly educating and teaching adults" (Watson & Petrone, 2020, p. 245).

This is not to say that there isn't a place for adults and schools in the lives of young people, even those put off by schools, but rather a push toward reconceptualizing the foundations and taken-for-granted assumptions such institutions hold toward and about youth so that more inclusive, collaborative, equitable, and less adversarial relations between youth and adults flourish—relations that carefully attend to intersectional identities of youth. As Lesko (2012), in the quote at the opening of this chapter, argues, it's essential to stop thinking of youth as "supposedly all the same and as fundamentally different from adults," and to include teens "as active participants (not tokens) in educational and other public policy deliberations" (p. 199).

Repositioning Youth in Teacher Education

One of the most powerful findings from this research is how significant the opportunities to contribute to others' lives and learning—to be a contributor—is for the participants of Franklin Skatepark. They knew they mattered at the park and that what they had to offer—who they were, what their skills and knowledge were—mattered. In this sense, they recognized that they themselves were resources. And yet, they felt a 180-degree difference in schools, where they felt they did *not* matter—that their skill sets and knowledge base were hindrances rather than assets, let alone a source of learning for others. In short, at Franklin Skatepark, they felt like they had the opportunity to, as Derrick puts in the opening chapter, "get his word out," whereas in schools they felt little such opportunity for their voice to be heard—or, as Derrick puts it, "They don't care what you've got to say."

As a teacher educator, this research helped me become more aware of how youth—especially youth labeled "at-risk" or otherwise alienated by/on schooling contexts—are often excluded not only from the development of schooling practices but also from the processes of preparing teachers to teach them. Moreover, when youth are taken into consideration in teacher education, they tend to exist as generic abstractions—often filtered through the lens of developmental notions of adolescence and adolescent development. Deeply concerned by these gaps and ironies, I began, as a teacher educator, to imagine possibilities for including youth in the process of preparing teachers.

Drawing inspiration from scholars within and beyond education who explore youth civic engagement, activism, and participatory research (e.g., Cammarota & Fine, 2008; Cook-Sather & Curl, 2014; Morrell, 2009; Tuck

& Yang, 2013), I designed and implemented a series of interventions for my teaching of future teachers whereby youth labeled "at-risk," "struggling," or otherwise existing on the fringes of schooling were integrated into teacher education as paid educational experts and consultants to teach future teachers about various aspects of learning, literacy, and schooling.

I frame this intervention as a "repositioning pedagogy" (Petrone & Rink, with Speicher, 2020; Petrone & Sarigianides, 2017), as it shifts marginalized youth from the periphery to the center of schooling:

> A repositioning pedagogy is comprised of an epistemological stance and instructional approach whereby youth are invited into the physical spaces of university-based teacher preparation as educational consultants to teach future teachers about learning, curricula, teaching, and other aspects of schooling. It centers authentic dialogue between youth and preservice teachers, emphasizing *listening to* and *learning from* youth. In this way, a repositioning pedagogy actively works to disrupt power relations and adult-centrism within teacher education by calling into question whose voices, stories, and authority matter when it comes to preparing teachers. (Petrone & Rink, with Speicher, 2020, p. 246)

From this conceptual grounding, the actual implementation of a repositioning pedagogy can be quite varied and diverse. For instance, in one manifestation, a group of Indigenous students from a reservation delivered workshops for future teachers on language revitalization, the impacts of settler colonialism on schools, and structures of support to facilitate Native youth academic success. In another iteration, a group of rural, white working-class young men who were failing out of school shared with future English teachers some of the literacy practices they engage as part of their participation in dirt biking, hunting, and welding, as well as explanations for their disconnect from school and types of pedagogical practices that would engage them more meaningfully. In another instance, a group of transgender youth worked with future educational researchers to share about their experiences as coresearchers in a participatory study, as well as to provide suggestions on carrying out ethical, caring research relationships with LGBTQ+ youth.

Overall, the purposes of a repositioning pedagogy are twofold. The first is to facilitate preservice teachers, youth workers/allies, and/or researchers in developing instructional and research practices that attune to youth cultures, literacies, and epistemologies. For instance, in one iteration of a repositioning pedagogy, students from an agrarian community in Montana taught future teachers about their knowledge and skill sets regarding ranching and farming to help the teachers develop strategic connections between these students' "funds of knowledge" and literacy-based curricula and instruction. In another example, two young women poets who were barely making it in schooling delivered a 90-minute workshop on strategies for teaching poetry. They developed a video for the session, offered their own stories of schooling, facilitated a poetry writing workshop, and then generated a set of recommendations for instructional approaches "for students like us," as they put it. During the consultancy, one of the consultants read one of her poems, which explored her resistance to being medicated to get her to be more amenable to school, which, as she described, felt itself like a type of mandated medication.

In addition to developing youth workers, researchers, and/or future teachers' skills and perspectives of youth, a second main aim of repositioning pedagogy is to provide the youth consultants opportunities for personal growth, academic development, and potentially restorative relationships to schooling. For example, in an iteration of a repositioning pedagogy whereby a group of Indigenous youth shared their stories of schooling with future teachers to teach them about the structure of settler colonialism, the consultants reported increases in standard indicators of youth development (e.g., self-esteem), academic growth (e.g., public speaking), and a deepened sense of pride in their Native identity and their reservation community. For instance, based on his experience, one consultant shared, "I felt more comfortable with myself as a person and realized I had a story to tell" (Petrone & Rink, with Speicher, 2020, p. 258).

While a repositioning pedagogy itself might be transferable to other contexts, I see it as one particular way social systems (in this case, teacher education) can become more inclusive and respectful of youth perspectives and facilitate their involvement in the processes that affect their lives (see Brown & Rodriguez [2017] and Rodriguez & Brown [2018] for considerations for implementation, especially as the work involves BIPOC youth). What is central here is how a repositioning pedagogy creates a way for youth to be *contributors* to the learning of others, and, in particular, youth for whom schools have not been hospitable places and spaces.

In other words, this is not just some vague, generalized sense of "hearing youth voices" but rather an infrastructurally supported way in which youth are integral to the learning and education of others. Because youth are repositioned as contributors, their skill sets and knowledge systems are also repositioned as desired, useful, and even needed. As one of the youth who participated in a repositioning pedagogy shared, "I felt that they [future teachers] were looking for my opinion, they *needed* my opinion, they wanted to know why we do what we do" (Petrone, González Ybarra, & Rink, 2021, p. 603).

From this foundation, I urge others who work with adults who will work with youth to explore how their practices, policies, and programs might be infrastructurally shifted so that marginalized youth can be positioned *as contributors* to the education of others. What might a repositioning of youth and their expertise look like in your context? In what ways might youth be positioned as experts? Who might be important audiences to learn from these youth? How might these audiences be prepared to be good listeners and learners in such a context, especially given how little our society typically affords opportunities for youth to be educators for others? What might be important places whereby youth have opportunities to potentially heal some of the pains institutions such as schools so often inflict on youth who don't ascribe to normalized notions of adolescence (Petrone & Stanton, 2021)?

Designing Cross-Age Learning Environments (within Schooling)
As mentioned in Chapter 2, one of my aims with this research is to offer an "implied comparative study" that asks readers to hold in their minds how learning is typically organized in schools as a point of comparison to how learning is organized at Franklin Skatepark. One of the goals of this approach is to help make more visible the taken-for-granted assumptions, practices, and social arrangements that structure participation and learning within schools—those things, in other words, that are often "invisible" to us given how familiar they are to and for us. One such instance of this for me has been the social arrangement of age heterogeneity within Franklin Skatepark. Documenting how this social arrangement factors

into participation and learning allows us to more easily see how unusual and strange it is that schools segregate children and youth by age. In what ways does age segregation inform learning and identity formation? What are other possibilities for organizing children and youth that might expand possibilities for learning?

With these questions, I've tried to imagine new ways of "doing age" in schools, particularly at the classroom level. In doing so, I have often wondered, based on what I was learning about learning at Franklin Skatepark, What type of learning environments within schools would "work" for these young men, especially when it comes to the secondary school subject "English"? Because the design of schools—as decontextualized from cultural practice—is flawed from the start and tends to marginalize working-class and BIPOC knowledge systems and skills, I can't be certain. However, based on the significance of the relationality, emotionality, and being a contributor I bore witness to at Franklin Skatepark, there is one approach to working with these particular young men and more generally youth labeled "at-risk" that has a good chance of being effective.

Specifically, I have wondered what it might mean and look like, particularly within a literacy context, if secondary-aged youth who were considered "struggling readers" or "at-risk" when it came to school performance were positioned as "reading tutors" or "literacy consultants" for younger students. In this way, these secondary-aged students, rather than being interpolated into deficit categories—labels they, by that point, will be all too familiar with, as was the case with the participants of Franklin Skatepark who regularly reported to me they were in the "stupid classes"— they were recast as having expertise, experiences, knowledge and skills that could be of value to others. In other words, how might it affect their own sense of self, as well as their literacy development and overall academic engagement—their learning—if they were repositioned as having authority and were given an opportunity to contribute to the betterment of others, especially younger children? Such a shift would view "struggling readers" in such a different light: What do struggling readers have to offer? What is their expertise? What are their knowledge systems and skill sets when it comes to literacy?

Unlike the previous implications (reconceptualization of youth, the Youth Lens, repositioning pedagogy), this is not an area I have yet developed and empirically investigated. However, to shed light on some possibilities of establishing a pedagogical intervention emergent from the social arrangement of age heterogeneity (rather than age homogeneity), I turn to a study that attempted a similar intervention. Specifically, Paterson and Elliot (2006) established a collaboration whereby ninth graders who were students in a remedial reading class tutored second and third graders who were similarly labeled "struggling readers." Specifically, the ninth graders were tutors for an elementary student to work with over the course of the school year. The ninth graders were responsible for developing the curriculum for the elementary student, and the remedial reading class functioned as a space to help the ninth graders take on the role of tutors by practicing expressive reading, comprehension strategies, phonics instruction, and so on.

Quantitative results reported that both the elementary and secondary students increased more than one year in reading scores over the course of the school year. In other words, they made significant gains, beyond typical development goals. This is particularly salient for the high school students, as their gains are often slower the later they occur in their schooling. One of the ninth graders, Zeena, sheds some light on why these gains were made: "Helping them [elementary students] reading has helped me a lot because now I am comprehending more and reading at a faster speed, and for them they are comprehending well, too" (p. 382).

Qualitatively, the secondary students experienced significant shifts in their perceptions of themselves as readers and as students in general. By the time a student enters high school with the label of "struggling reader," they often "adopt a negative stance toward reading that becomes more and more difficult to modify" (Paterson and Elliot, 2006, p. 378). In contrast, as Paterson and Elliot explain, "Because of the new roles they experienced in the tutoring program, the high school students began to see themselves differently. As Samuel [one of the ninth grade tutors] reflected, '[This program] meant that I could be a role model for somebody and help somebody out'" (p. 382). Related, another ninth grader explained how the program, in addition to helping out the younger kids, helped her out, too, because, as she says, "I'm helping somebody else. It makes me feel good to help somebody else. It makes me do better" (p. 383).

I am struck by how similar the way these ninth grade tutors talk about their experiences—and the impact it has on them—is to how the participants of Franklin Skatepark talk about their own experiences of being a resource, a mentor, and a contributor to the learning of someone else, often a younger person. It is not surprising, then, that the researchers explain that a central reason for the ninth graders' engagement and improvements in their own reading—despite entering the class with such negative attitudes toward themselves as readers—is "the fact that the high school students saw their potential to make a difference. . . . For most of them it was the first time in their academic lives that they actively worked to learn, in order to make an academic difference for others" (p. 383). Furthermore, the researchers go on to say that a "key component of the perspective shift was that students began seeing themselves as powerful change agents instead of objects of intervention" (p. 384).

Although this is but one instance of cross-age learning that has exponential effects for youth disaffected by schools and struggling to succeed within that structure, it demonstrates how stepping aside of and circumventing the constraints of how learning is organized within schooling structures might benefit students for whom the structures of schooling are alienating. In this instance, youth who have gone through nine years of a schooling system suddenly begin to find a new form of success and efficacy when they are repositioned as capable and able, as a resource, as people who have something to contribute to others. How else might age homogeneity—or any number of "invisible" social arrangements and other principles that structure learning within school—be illuminated, challenged, and redesigned so that youth for whom such normative structures of learning facilitate alienation and "failure" might find connection, empowerment, and success?

CONCLUSION

With this book, I have attempted to trace the experiences and perspectives of a group of working-class Latino and white young men in a rural context as they relate to their participation in a particular cultural community. Specifically, I have focused on the ways participation and learning occur at Franklin Skatepark, and the roles language and literacy play in these processes—and what and how this cultural community means to and for these young men.

As the central place these young men go to have their needs met for learning, literacy, intellectual stimulation, sociopolitical critique, connection, belonging, and fun, it seems important to understand the means and motivations for things that matter to this demographic, especially for those interested in developing equitable schooling and other social systems and support for youth.

By exploring "what else" these young men have, my hope is that I have not only shed light on how learning is organized and enacted at Franklin Skatepark but also, through an implied contrast, how learning is—and might be—configured within schools. In returning to Kevin's question from the opening of this book, "What else would we have?", with this book, I invite us to wonder: What else *could* we have?

References

Ali, A. I., & McCarty, T. L. (2020). *Critical youth research in education: Methodologies of praxis and care.* Routledge.

Anderson-Levitt, K. M. (1996). Behind schedule: Batch-produced children in French and U.S. classrooms. In B. Levinson, D. Foley, & D. Holland, *The cultural production of the educated person: Critical ethnographies of schooling and local practice* (pp. 57–78). SUNY Press.

Atencio, M., Beal, B., Wright, E. M., & McClain, Z. (2018). *Moving Boarders: Skateboarding and the changing landscape of urban youth sports.* University of Arkansas Press.

Austin, J., & Willard, M. N. (1998). *Generations of youth: Youth cultures and history in twentieth-century america.* NYU Press.

Azuma, H. (1994). Two modes of cognitive socialization in Japan and the United States. *Cross-cultural roots of minority child Development, 275–284.*

Bäckström, Å. (2014). Knowing and teaching kinesthetic experiences in skateboarding: An example of sensory emplacement. *Sport, Education and Society, 19*(6), 752–772.

Barton, D., & Hamilton, M. (1998). *Local literacies: Reading and Writing in One Community.* Routledge.

Beal, B. (1995). "Disqualifying the official: An exploration of social resistance through the subculture of skateboarding." *Sociology of Sport Journal, 12*(3), 252–267.

Beal, B. (1996). Alternative masculinity and its effects on gender relations in the subculture of skateboarding. *Journal of Sport Behavior, 19*(3), 204.

Beal, B. (1998). Symbolic inversion in the subculture of skateboarding. *Diversions and Divergences in Fields of Play, 1,* 209–222.

Beal, B. (2013). *Skateboarding: The ultimate guide.* Greenwood.

Beal, B., & Weidman, L. (2003). Authenticity in the skateboarding world. In R. Rinehart & S. Sydnor (Eds.), *To the extreme: Alternative sports inside and out* (pp. 337–352). SUNY Press.

Beal, B., & Wilson, C. (2004). "Chicks dig scars": Transformations in the subculture of skateboarding. In B. Wheaton (Ed.), *Understanding lifestyle sports: Consumption, identity, and difference* (pp. 31–54). Routledge.

Becker, H. (1972). School is a lousy place to learn anything in. *American Behavioral Scientist, (16)*1, 85–105.

Best, A. (2007). *Representing youth: Methodological issues in critical youth studies.* NYU Press.

Bettie, J. (2000). Women without class: Chicas, cholas, trash, and the presence/absence of class identity. *Signs, 26*(1): 1–35.

Bettie, J. (2014). *Women without class: Girls, race, and identity.* University of California Press

Billett, S. (2006). Relational interdependence between social and individual agency in work and working life. *Mind, Culture and Activity, 13*(1), 53–69.

Bonilla-Silva, E. (2003). *Racism without racists: Color-blind racism and the persistence of racial inequality in America.* Rowan & Littlefield

Borden, I. (2001). *Skateboarding the city: Architecture and the body.* Berg.

Borden, I. (2019). *Skateboarding and the city: A complete history.* Bloomsbury Publishing.

Bourdieu, P. (1984). *Distinction: A social critique of the judgment of taste.* Harvard University Press.

Bourdieu, P., & Passeron, J. C. (1990). *Reproduction in education, society, and culture* (2nd ed.) Sage Publications.

Bradley, G. L. (2010). Skateparks as context for adolescent development. *Journal of Adolescent Research, 25*(2), 288–323.

Brandt, D. (1998). Sponsors of literacy. *College Composition and Communication, 49*(2), 165–185.

Brayboy, B., & Lomawaima, K. T. (2018). Why don't more Indians do better in school? The battle between U.S. schooling and American Indian/ Alaska Native education. *Daedalus, the Journal of the American Academy of the Arts and Sciences, 147*(2), 82–94.

Brekhus, Wayne H. 1998. A sociology of the unmarked: Redirecting our focus. *Sociological Theory, 16*(1): 34–51.

Brown, T. M., & Rodriguez, L. F. (2017). Collaborating with urban youth to address gaps in teacher education. *Teacher Education Quarterly, 44*(3), 75–92.

Butler, J. (1990). *Gender Trouble: Feminism and the Subversio.* Routledge.

Callanan, M., Cervantes, C., & Loomis, M. (2011). Informal learning. *Wiley Interdisciplinary Reviews: Cognitive Science, 2*(6), 646–655.

Cammarota, J., & Fine, M. (Eds.). (2008). *Revolutionizing education: Youth participatory action research in motion.* Routledge.

Caraballo, L., & Lyiscott, J. (2020). Collaborative inquiry: Youth, social action, and critical qualitative research. *Action Research, 18*(2), 194–211.

Carr, J. (2010). Legal geographies—skating around the edges of the law: Urban skateboarding and the role of law in determining young peoples' place in the city. *Urban Geography, 31*(7), 988–1003.

Carr, J. (2017). Skateboarding in dude space: The roles of sports and space in constructing gender among adult skateboarders. *Sociology of Sport (34)*1, 1–30.

Carspecken, P. F. (1996). *Critical ethnography in educational research: A theoretical and practical guide.* Routledge.

Chudacoff, H. P. (1989). *How old are you? Age consciousness in American culture.* Princeton University Press.

Coiro, J., Knobel, M., Lankshear, C., & Leu, D. (2008). *Handbook of research on new literacies.* Routledge.

Cole, M. (1999). Cultural psychology: Some general principles and a concrete example. *Perspectives on activity theory,* 87–106.

Compton-Lilly, C., & Halverson, E. (Eds.) (2014). *Time and space in literacy research.* Routledge.

Connor, D. J., Ferri, F. B., & Annamma, S. A. (Eds.). (2016). *DisCrit: Disability studies and critical race theory in education.* Teachers College Press.

Connor, D. J., Valle, J. W., & Hale, C. (Eds.) (2015). *Practicing disability studies in education.* Peter Lang Publishing.

Cook-Gumperz, J. (2006). *The social construction of literacy* (2nd ed.). Cambridge University Press.

Cook-Sather, A., & Curl, H. (2014). "I want to listen to my students' lives": Developing anecological perspective in learning to teach. *Teacher Education Quarterly, 41*(1), 85–103.

Cookson, P. W. (2013). *Class rules: Exposing inequality in American high schools.* Teachers College Press.

Corwin, Z. B., Maruco, T., Williams, N., Reichardt, R., Romero-Morales, M., Rocha, C., & Astiazaran, C. (2020). *Beyond the board: Findings from the field* [White paper]. Pullias Center for Higher Education. https://skate.pullias.usc.edu/wp-content/uploads/2021/07/Beyond-The-Board-Findings-From-The-Field.pdf

Corwin, Z. B., Williams, N., Maruco, T., & Romero-Morales, M. (2019). *Beyond the board: Skateboarding, schools, and society* [White paper]. Pullias Center for Higher Education. https://skate.pullias.usc.edu/wp-content/uploads/2021/07/beyond-the-board-FINAL-1.pdf

Dahlquist, J., Lay, R., Bader, R., Sayers, E., & Forsyth, J. (2019). *Skate and educate: From classrooms to communities.* Pushing Boarders. Malmö, Sweden. https://www.pushingboarders.com/talks-2019-watch

Davis, L. J. (2017). Introduction: Disability, normality, and power. In L. J. Davis (Ed.), *The disability studies reader* (5th ed.) (pp. 1–14). Routledge.

de los Ríos, C. V. (2020). Translingual youth podcasts as acoustic allies: Writing and negotiating identities at the intersection of literacies, language, and racialization. *Journal of Language, Identity & Education,* September 8. https://doi.org/10.1080/15348458.2020.1795865

de los Ríos, C. V. (2021). Guitarras on the rise: Framing youth sierreño bands as translingual ingenuity. *Reading Research Quarterly.* https://doi.org/10.1002/rrq.433

de Luca, A. (2020, May 29). "It's like I'm floating": Skating New York under lockdown. *New York Times.* Retrieved September 23, 2021, from https://www.nytimes.com/interactive/2020/05/29/arts/skateboarding-nyc-lockdown.html

Derrian, A. (2019, September 2). *Skateboarding, pedagogy and motherhood.* Free Skateboard Magazine. https://www.freeskatemag.com/2019/09/02/skateboarding-pedagogy-and-motherhood/

Donnelly, P., & Young, K. (1988). The construction and confirmation of identity in sport subcultures. *Sociology of Sport, 5,* 223–240.

Dinces, S. (2011). "Flexible opposition": Skateboarding subcultures under the rubric of late capitalism. *The International Journal of the History of Sport, 28*(11). 1512–1535.

Dumas, A., & Laforest, S. (2009). Skateparks as health-resources: Are they as dangerous as they look? *Leisure Studies, 28*(1), 19–34.

Dupont, T. (2014). From core to consumer: The informal hierarchy of the skateboard scene. *Journal of Contemporary Ethnography, 43*(5), 556–581.

Dupont, T. (2020). Authentic subcultural identities and social media: American skateboarders and Instagram. *Deviant Behavior, 41*(5), 649–664.

Dyson, A. H. (2003). *The brothers and sisters learn to write: Popular literacies in childhood and school cultures.* Teachers College Press.

Eckert, P. (1989). *Jocks and burnouts: Social categories and identity in the high school.* Teachers College Press.

Eckert, P., & Wenger, E. (2005). What is the role of power in sociolinguistic variation? Journal of *Sociolinguistics, 9*(4), 582–589.

Ehret, C. Mannard, E., & Curwood, J. S. (2022). How young adult videogames materialize senses of self through ludonarrative affects: Understanding identity and embodiment through sociomaterial analysis. *Learning, Media, and Technology, 47*(3), 341–354.

Ellmer, E., & Rynne, S. (2016). Learning in action and adventure sports. *Asia-Pacific Journal of Health, Sport and Physical Education, 7*(2), 107–119.

Ellmer, E., Rynne, S., & Enright, E. (2020). Learning in action sports: A scoping review. *European Physical Education Review, 26*(1), 263–283.

Elman, J. P. (2014). *Chronic youth: Disability, sexuality, and US media cultures of rehabilitation* (Vol. 4). NYU Press.

Engeström, Y. (1999). Activity theory and individual and social transformation. *Perspectives on activity theory, 19*(38), 19–30.

Enright, E., & Gard, M. (2016). Media, digital technology and learning in sport: A critical response to Hodkinson, Biesta and James. *Physical Education and Sports Pedagogy, 21*(1), 40–54.

Erickson, F., & Shultz, J. (1981). When is a context? Some issues and methods in the analysis of social competence. In J. L. Green & C. Wallet (Eds.), *Ethnography and language in educational settings* (p. 147–160). Ablex.

Esmonde, I. (2017). Power and sociocultural theories of learning. In I. Esmonde & A. N. Booker (Eds.), *Power and privilege in the learning sciences* (pp. 6–27). Routledge.

Esmonde, I., & Booker, A. N. (Eds.). (2017). *Power and privilege in the learning sciences: Critical and sociocultural theories of learning.* Routledge.

Falter, M. M. (2016). Addressing assumptions about adolescents in a preservice YAL course. *The ALAN Review, 43*(2), 51–61.

Ferrell, J., Milovanovic, D., & Lyng, S. (2001). Edgework, media practices, and the elongation of meaning: A theoretical ethnography of the Bridge Day Event. *Theoretical Criminology, 5*(2), 177–202.

Finders, M. (1997). *Just girls: Hidden literacies and life in junior high.* Teachers College Press.

Finders, M. (1998/1999). Raging hormones: Stories of adolescence and implications for teacher preparation. *Journal of Adolescent and Adult Literacy, 42,* 2–13.

Figueroa, A. M. (2014). La carta de responsabilidad: The problem of departure. In D. Paris & M. T. Winn (Eds.), *Humanizing research: Decolonizing qualitative inquiry with youth and communities (pp. 129–146).* Sage Publications.

Fine, M. (1994). Dis-tance and other stances: Negotiations of power inside feminist research. In A. Gitlin (Ed.), *Power and methods* (p. 13–55). Routledge.

Fors, V., Bäckström, Å, & Pink, S. (2013). Multisensory emplaced learning: Resituating situated learning in a moving world. *Mind, Culture, and Activity, 20*(2), 170–183.

Foucault, M. (1975). *Discipline and punish: The birth of the prison.* Vintage Books.

Freire, P. (1970a). *Pedagogy of the oppressed.* Continuum.

Freire, P. (1970b). The adult literacy process as cultural action for freedom. *Harvard Educational Review, 40,* 205–212.

Freire, P., & Macdeo, D. (1987). *Literacy: Reading the word and the world.* Bergin & Garvey.

Fuller, A., Hodkinson, H., Hodkinson, P., & Unwin, L. (2005). Learning as peripheral participation in communities of practice: A reassessments of key concepts in workplace learning. *British Educational Review Journal, 31*(1), 49–68.

Gallagher, K. (2009). *Readicide: How schools are killing reading and what you can do about it.* Stenhouse.

Gee, J. (2015). *Social linguistics and literacies: Ideology in discourses* (5th ed.). Routledge.

Gee, J. P. (2003). Opportunity to learn: A language-based perspective on assessment. *Assessment in Education: Principles, Policy & Practice, 10*(1), 27–46.

Glenney, B., & O'Connor, P. (2019). Skateparks as hybrid elements of the city. *Journal of Urban Design, 24*(6), 840–855.

Goffman, Erving. 1959. *The Presentation of Self in Everyday Life.* Doubleday.

Golden, N. A. (2020). The Importance of narrative: Moving towards socio-cultural understandings of trauma-informed praxis. *Occasional Paper Series, 2020*(43). https://educate.bankstreet.edu /occasionalpaper-series/vol2020/iss43/7

Golden, N. A. (2017). "If you can't go through the door, there's always a window": The problem with "grit." *Urban Education, 52,* 343–369.

Golden, N. A., & Petrone, R. (2021). The social production of risk and resilience. In J. N. Lester, & M. O'Reilly (Eds.), *The Palgrave encyclopedia of critical perspectives on mental health.* Palgrave Macmillan.

Goodwin, C. (2007). Participation, stance, and affect in the organization of activities. *Discourse and Society, 18*(1), 53–73.

Gossett, K., & Tingstrom, C. A. (2017). Community-based adaptive recreation: Using an indoor water park for adapted kayaking. *Palaestra, 31*(4).

Gustavson, L. (2007). *Youth learning on their own terms: Creative practices and classroom teaching.* Routledge.

Gutiérrez, K. D., & Rogoff, B. (2003). Cultural ways of learning: Individual traits or repertoires of practice. *Educational Researcher (32)*5, 19–26.

Haines, C., Smith, T. M., & Baxter, M. F. (2010). Participation in the risk-taking occupation of skateboarding. *Journal of Occupational Science, 17*(4), 239–245.

Harris, G., & Dacin, P. A. (2019). A lifestyle sport: Idiosyncratic and dynamic belonging. *Journal of Consumer Marketing (36)*2, 328–336.

Heath, S. B. (1982). What no bedtime story means: Narrative skills at home and school. *Language in Society (11)*1, 49–76.

Heath, S. B. (1983). *Ways with words: Language, life, and work in communities and classrooms.* Cambridge University Press.

Hill, J. H. (1998). Language, race, and white public space. *American Anthropologist, 100*(3), 680–689.

Hirst, E., & Vadeboncoeur, J. A. (2006). Patrolling the borders of otherness: Displaced identity positions for teachers and students in schooled spaces. *Mind, Culture, and Activity, 13*(3), 205–227.

Hollett, T. (2019). Symbiotic learning partnerships in youth action sports: Vibing, rhythm, and analytic cycles. *Convergence: The International Journal of Research into New Media Technologies, 25*(4), 753–766.

Hollett, T., & Vivoni, F. (2021). DIY Skateparks as temporary disruptions to neoliberal cities: Informal learning through micropolitical making. *Discourse: Studies in the Cultural Politics of Education, 42*(6), 881–897.

Howe, J. (2003). Drawing lines: A report from the extreme world [*sic*]. In R. Rinehart & S. Sydnor (Eds.), *To the extreme: Alternative sports, inside and out* (pp. 353–369). SUNY Press.

Howell, O. (2005). The "creative class" and the gentrifying city: Skateboarding in Philadelphia's Love Park. *Journal of Architectural Education, 59*(2), 32–42.

Howell, O. (2008). Skatepark as neoliberal playground: Urban governance, recreation space, and the cultivation of personal responsibility. *Space and Culture, 11*(4), 475–496.

Hymes, D. (1972). Models of the interaction of language and social life. In J. Gumperz & D. Hymes (Eds.), *Directions in sociolinguistics: The ethnography of communication* (pp. 35–71). Holt, Rhinehart & Winston.

Ibrahim, A., & Steinburg, S. R. (Eds.) (2014). *Critical youth studies reader.* Peter Lang.

Ivarsson, J. (2012, November). *The turn-organization of pool-skate sessions* [Paper presentation]. American Anthropological Association 111th Annual Meeting 2012, San Francisco, CA.

Jacobson, L. (2019, September 18). *Shredding for school: Researchers study links between skateboarding and academic success.* Education Dive. https://www.educationdive.com/news/shredding-for-school -researchers-study-links-between-skateboarding-and-aca /562948/

Janks, H. (2010). *Literacy and power.* Routledge.

Jenson, A., Swords, J., Jeffries, M. (2012). The accidental youth club: Skateboarding in Newcastle-Gasteshead. *Journal of Urban Design, 17*(3), 371–388.

Jones, R. H. (2011). Sport and re/creation: What skateboarders can teach us about learning. *Sport, Education, and Society, 16*(5), 593–611.

Karsten, L., & Pel, E. (2000). Skateboarders exploring urban public space: Ollies, obstacles and conflicts. *Journal of Housing and the Built Environment, 15*(4), 327–340.

Kim, Y. T. (2011). *Can skateboarding save our schools?* [Video file]. https://www.youtube.com/watch?time_continue=2&v=lHfo1 7ikSpY&feature=emb_logo

Kimmel, M., & Messner, M. A. (2018). *Men's lives* (10th ed.). Oxford University Press.

Kimmerer, R. W. (2015). *Braiding sweetgrass: Indigenous wisdom, scientific knowledge and the teachings of plants.* Milkwood Editions.

Kinloch, V. (2009). *Harlem on our minds: Place, race, and the literacies of urban youth.* Teachers College Press.

Kinloch, V. (Ed.). (2011). *Urban literacies: Critical perspectives on language, learning, and community.* Teachers College Press.

Kirkland, D. (2008). "The rose that grew from concrete": Postmodern blackness and new English education. *English Journal, 97*(5), 69–75.

Kirkland, D. (2009). The skin we ink: Tattoos, literacy, and a new English education. *English Education, 41*(4): 375–395.

Kirkland, D. (2013). *Search past silence: The literacy of young black men.* Teachers College Press.

Kirschner, B., & Kaplan, R. G. (2017). Innovative uses of learning time: Perspectives from the learning sciences. In M. Saunders, J. R. de Velasco, & J. Oakes, *Learning time: In pursuit of educational equity,* pp. 115–130. Harvard Educational Press.

Kozol, J. (2005). *The shame of the nation: The restoration of apartheid schooling in America.* Random House.

Kress, G. (2010). *Multimodality: A social semiotic approach to contemporary communication.* Routledge.

Lankshear, C., & Knobel, M. (2011). *New literacies: Everyday practices and social learning.* Open University Press.

Lave, J., & Wenger, E. (1991). *Situated learning: Legitimate peripheral participation.* Cambridge University Press.

Leander, K. M., Phillips, N. C., & Taylor, K. H. (2010). The changing social spaces of learning: Mapping new mobilities. *Review of research in education, 34*(1), 329–394.

Le Clair, J. M. (2011). Global organizational change in sport and the shifting meaning of disability. *Sport in Society: Cultures, Commerce, Media, Politics, 14*(9), 1072–1093.

Lee, C., & Smagorinsky, P., (Eds.). (2000). *Vygotskian perspectives on literacy research.* Cambridge University Press.

Lefebvre, H. (1991). *The production of space.* Blackwell Publishing.

Lerner, S. (2021, July 22). This Apache pro skater wants kids in his Arizona town to dream big. Here's how he's helping. *Arizona Republic* [Online]. https://www.azcentral.com/story/travel/arizona/2021/07/22/doug -miles-jr-apache-passion-project-skateboard-park-arizona /7959785002/

Lesko, N. (2012). *Act your age! A cultural construction of adolescence.* Routledge.

Lesko, N., & Talburt, S. (2012). *Keywords in youth studies: Tracing affects, movements, knowledges.* Routledge.

Lewis, C., Enciso, P., & Moje, E. (2007). *Reframing sociocultural research on literacy: Identity, agency, and power.* Erlbaum.

Lewis, M. A., & Petrone, R. (2010). "Although adolescence need not be violent . . .": Preservice teachers' connections between "adolescence" and literacy curriculum. *Journal of Adolescent & Adult Literacy, 53*(5), 398–407.

Levinson, B., Foley, D., and Holland, D. (1996). *The cultural production of the educated person: Critical ethnographies of schooling and local practice.* SUNY Press.

Liikanen, V. (2014). You don't need legs to skate, you need friends! Importance of social relations in young people's alternative sports. Paper presented at the Children, Young People and Families in Changing Urban Spaces Conference, Northampton, UK, September 3–4.

Lindquist, J. (2002). *A place to stand: Politics and persuasion in a working-class bar.* Oxford University Press.

Lortie, D. (1975). A sociological study. *Journal of Teacher Education, 26,* 360–363.

Ma, J. Y., & Munter, C. (2014). The spatial production of learning opportunities in skateboard parks. *Mind, Culture, and Activity, 21*(3), 238–258.

MacLeod, J. (1995). *Ain't no makin' it: Aspirations and attainment in a low-income neighborhood.* Westview Press.

MacPhee, D., Handsfield, L. J., & Paugh, P. (2021). Conflict or conversation? Media portrayals of the Science of Reading. *Reading Research Quarterly, 56,* S145–S155.

Madison, D. S. (2012). *Critical ethnography: Methods, ethics, and performance* (2nd ed.). Sage Publications.

Mahiri, J. (2000/2001). Pop culture pedagogy and the end(s) of school. *Journal of Adolescent & Adult Literacy, 44*(4), 382–385.

Mahiri, J. (Ed.). (2004). *What they don't learn in school: Literacy in the lives of urban youth.* Peter Lang.

McDermott, M., Knowles, E. D., & Richeson, J. A. (2019). Class perceptions and attitudes toward immigration and race among working-class whites. *Analysis of Social Issues and Public Policy, 19*(1), 349–380.

McDonald, K. (2017, August 1). *What skateboarders can teach us about education.* FEE. https://fee.org/articles/what-skateboarders-can-teach-us-about-education/

MacPhee, D., Handsfield, L. J., & Paugh, P. (2021). Conflict or conversation? Media portrayals of the science of reading. *Reading Research Quarterly, 56*(1), S145–S155.

Meade, M. (1928/2001). *Coming of age in Samoa: A psychological study of primitive youth for western civilization*. Harper Collins Publishers.

Medovi, L. (2005). *Rebels: Youth and the cold war origins of identity*. Duke University Press.

Mehan, H. (1979). *Learning lessons: Social organization in the classroom*. Harvard University Press.

Michaels, S., O'Connor, C., & Resnick, L. B. (2008). Deliberative discourse idealized and realized: Accountable talk in the classroom and in civic life. *Studies in Philosophy and Education, 27*(4), 283–297.

Miller, sj, & Gilligan, J. (2014). Heteronormative harassment: Queer bullying and gender non-conforming students. In D. Carlson and E. Meyer (Eds.), *Handbook of gender and sexualities in education* (pp. 217–229.) Peter Lang.

Mirra, N., Garcia, A., & Morrell, E. (2016). *Doing youth participatory action research: Transforming inquiry with researchers, educators, and students*. Routledge.

Moje, E. B. (2000). "To be part of the story": The literacy practices of gangsta adolescents. *Teachers College Record, 102*(3), 651–690.

Moje, E. B. (2008). Youth cultures, literacies, and identities in and out of school. In *Handbook on research on teaching literacy through the communicative and visual arts* (Vol. 2, pp. 207–219). Taylor & Francis Group.

Moll, L. C., Amanti, C., Neff, D., & Gonzalez, N. (1992). Funds of knowledge for teaching: Using a qualitative approach to connect homes and classrooms. *Theory into Practice, 31*(2), 132–141.

Morrell, E. (2004a). *Becoming critical researchers: Literacy and empowerment for urban youth*. Peter Lang.

Morrell, E. (2004b). *Linking literacy and popular culture: Finding connections for lifelong learning*. Christopher-Gordon.

Morrell, E. (2008). *Critical literacy and urban youth: Pedagogies of access, dissent, and liberation*. Routledge.

Morrell, E. (2009). Critical research and the future of literacy education. *Journal of Adolescent & Adult Literacy, 53*(2), 96–104.

Nasir, N. S., Lee, C. D., Pea, R., & de Royston, M. M. (2021). Rethinking learning: What the interdisciplinary science tells us. *Educational Researcher, 50*(8), 557–565.

Nasir, N. S., & Cooks, J. (2009). Becoming a hurdler: How learning settings afford identities. *Anthropology & Education Quarterly, 40*(1), 41–61.

Németh, J. (2006). Conflict, exclusion, relocation: Skateboarding and public space. *Journal of Urban Design, 11*(3), 297–318.

New London Group. (1996). A pedagogy of multiliteracies: Designing social futures. *Harvard Educational Review, 66*(1), 60–92.

Nielsen, D. (N.d.). The world's first high school built around a skate park is in Malmö, Sweden. *Dwell* [Online]. Retrieved September 29, 2022, from https://www.dwell.com/article/bryggeriets -gymnasium-skateboard-high-school-malmo-sweden-793a3d93

Nin, A. (1961). *Seduction of the minotaur*. Swallow Press.

O'Connor, P. (2016). Skateboarding, helmets, and control: Observations from skateboard media and a Hong Kong skatepark. *Journal of Sport and Social Issues, 40*(6), 477–498.

O'Connor, P. (2018). Beyond youth culture: Understanding middle-aged skateboarders through temporal capital. *International Review for the Sociology of Sport, 53*(8), 924–943.

Pandya, J. Z., Mora, R. A., Alford, J., Golden, N. A., & deRoock, R. S. (2022). *The handbook of critical literacies*. Routledge.

Paradise, R., & Rogoff, B. (2009). Side by side: Learning by observing and pitching in. *Ethos, 37*(1), 102–138.

Paris, D. (2011). *Language across difference: Ethnicity, communication, and youth identities in changing urban schools*. Cambridge University Press.

Paris, D. (2012). Culturally sustaining pedagogy: A needed change in stance, terminology, and practice. *Educational Researcher, 41*, 93–97.

Paris, D. (2013). Listening to demographic change. In E. Tuck & K. W. Yang (Eds.), *Youth resistance research and theories of change* (pp. 134–135). Routledge.

Paris, D., & Winn, M. T. (Eds.). (2014). *Humanizing research: Decolonizing qualitative inquiry with youth and communities*. Sage Publications.

Pascoe, C. J. (2012). *Dude, you're a fag: Masculinity and sexuality in high school* (2nd ed.) University of California Press.

Patel, L. (2012). *Youth held at the border: Immigration, education, and the politics of inclusion*. Teachers College Press.

Patel, L. (2019). Fugitive practices: Learning in a settler colony. *Educational Studies, 55*(3), 253–261.

Paterson, P. O., & Elliot, L. N. (2006). Struggling reader to struggling reader: High school students' responses to a cross-age tutoring program. *Journal of Adolescent & Adult Literacy, 49*(5), 378–389.

Peralta, S. (2002). *Dogtown and Z boys: The birth of extreme* [DVD]. Sony Pictures.

Petrone, R. (2010). "You have to get hit a couple of times": The role of conflict in learning how to "be" a skateboarder. *Teaching and Teacher Education, 26*(1), 119–127.

Petrone, R. (2013). Linking contemporary research on youth, literacy, and popular culture with literacy teacher education. *Journal of Literacy Research, 45*(3), 240–266.

Petrone, R., González Ybarra, A., Rink, N. (2021). Toward an indigenizing, anti-colonial framework for adolescent developmental research. *Journal of Adolescent Research, 36*(5), 584–614.

Petrone, R., & Lewis, M. A. (2012). Deficits, therapists, and a desire to distance: Secondary English pre-service teachers' reasoning about their future students. *English Education, 44*(3), 254–287.

Petrone, R., Rink, N., with Speicher, C. (2020). From talking about to talking with: Integrating Native youth voices into teacher education via a repositioning pedagogy. *Harvard Educational Review, 90*(2), 243–268.

Petrone, R., & Sarigianides, S. T. (2017). Re-positioning youth in English teacher education. In H. Hallman, *Innovations in English language arts teacher education.* Emerald Group Publishing.

Petrone, R., Sarigianides, S. T., & Lewis, M. A. (2015). The youth lens: Analyzing adolescence/ts in literary texts. *Journal of Literacy Research, 64*(4), 506–533.

Petrone, R., & Stanton, C. (2021). From producing to reducing trauma: A call for "trauma-informed" research to interrogate how schools harm students. *Educational Researcher, 50*(8), 537–545.

Petrone, R., & Wynhoff Olsen, A. (2021). *Teaching English in rural communities: Toward a Critical Rural English Pedagogy.* Rowman & Littlefield.

Philip, T. M., & Gupta, A. (2020). Emerging perspectives on the co-construction of power and learning in the learning sciences, mathematics education, and science education. *Review of Research in Education, 44*, 195–217.

Ranniko, A., Harinen, P., Torvinen, P., & Liikanen, V. (2016). The social bordering of lifestyle sports: Inclusive principles and exclusive reality. *Journal of Youth Studies, 19*(8), 1093–1109.

Reyes, V. (2020). Ethnographic toolkit: Strategic positionality and researchers' visible and invisible tools in field research. *Ethnography, 21*(2), 220–240.

Robinson, K. (2013). Changing education paradigms: ADHD, creativity, and the education system. Retrieved from https://www.youtube.com/watch?v_dUNWW2D3BM

Rodriguez, L. F., & Brown, T. (2018). Toward transformative practices in teacher development: Lessons from research with youth of color. In E. A. Lopez & E. L. Olan (Eds.), *Transformative pedagogies for teaching education: Moving towards critical praxis in an era of change.* Information Age.

Rogoff, B. (2014). Learning by observing and pitching in to family and community endeavors: An orientation. *Human Development, 57*(2/3), 69–81.

Rogoff, B. (2003). *The cultural nature of human development*. Oxford University Press.

Rogoff, B., Callanan, M., Gutierrez, K. D., & Erickson, F. (2016). The organization of informal learning. *Review of Research in Education, 40*(1), 356–401.

Rogoff, B., & Mejía-Arauz, R. (2022). The key role of community in learning by observing and pitching in to family and community endeavors. *Journal for the Study of Education and Development, 45*(3), 494–548.

Rogoff, B., Moore, L. C., Correa-Chávez, M., & Dexter, A. L. (2015). Children develop cultural repertoires through engaging in everyday routines and practices. In J. E. Grusec & P. D. Hastings, *Handbook of socialization: Theory and research* (2nd ed.) *(pp. 472–498)*. Guilford Press.

Rogoff, B., Paradise, R., Mejía Arauz, R., Correa-Chávez, M., & Angelillo, C. (2003). Firsthand learning through intent participation. *Annual Review of Psychology, 54*, 175–203.

Rogoff, B., Turkanis, C. G., & Bartlett, L. (Eds.). (2001). *Learning together: Children and adults in a school community*. Oxford University Press.

Ryan, J. B., Katsiyannis, A., Cadorette, D., Hodge, J., & Markham, M. (2014). Establishing adaptive sports programs for youth with moderate to severe disabilities. *Preventing School Failure: Alternative Education for Children and Youth, 58*(1), 32–41.

Säfvenbom, R., Wheaton, B., & Agans, J. P. (2018). "How can you enjoy sports if you are under control by others?": Self-organized lifestyle sports and youth development. *Sport in Society, 21*(12), 1990–2009.

Sagor, R. (2002). Lessons from skateboarders. *Educational Leadership, 60*(1), 34–38.

San Pedro, T., & Kinloch, V. (2017). Toward projects in humanization: Research on co-creating and sustaining dialogic relationships. *American Educational Research Journal, 54* (1, Suppl.), 373S–394S.

Sarigianides, S. T. (2019). Performative youth: The literacy possibilities of de-essentializing adolescence. *English Education, 51*(4), 376–403.

Sarigianides, S. T., Petrone, R., Lewis, M. A. (2017). *Re-thinking the "adolescent" in adolescent literacy*. National Council for Teachers of English Press.

Sefton-Green, J. (2012). *Learning at not-school: A review of study, theory, and advocacy for education in non-formal settings*. The MIT Press.

Seifert, T., & Hedderson, C. (2010). Intrinsic motivation and flow in skateboarding: An ethnographic study. *Journal of Happiness Studies, (11)*, 277–292.

Shannon, C. S., & Werner, T. L. (2008). The opening of a municipal skatepark: Exploring the influence on youth skateboarders' experiences. *Journal of Park and Recreation Administration, 26*(3), 39–58.

Shaver, T. (2020). From the skatepark to the classroom: The literacies of skateboarding. *Literacy Learning: The Middle Years, 28*(1).

Silva, A. F., & Savitz, R. S. (2019). Defying expectations: Representations of youths in young adult literature. *Journal of Adolescent & Adult Literacy, 63*(3), 323–331.

Smith, L. T. (2012). *Decolonizing methodologies: Research and Indigenous peoples.* (2nd ed.). Zed Books.

Sorsdahl, K., Davies, T., Jensel, C., Oberholzer, D., Gelberg, L., & van der Westhuizen. (2021). Experiences and benefits of a youth skateboarding program in South Africa: From the physical to the emotional and beyond. *Journal of Adolescence Research.* Retrieved from https://journals.sagepub.com/doi/full/10.1177/07435584211052983

Springsteen, B. (1978). Racing in the street [Song]. On *Darkness on the Edge of Town* [Album]. Bruce Springsteen, Jon Landau, Steven Van Zandt (assistant).

Springsteen, B. (1982). Atlantic City [Song]. On *Nebraska* [Album]. Bruce Springsteen.

Springsteen, B. (1984). No Surrender [Song]. On *Born in the USA* [Album]. Jon Landau, Chuck Plotkin, Bruce Springsteen, Steven Van Zandt.

Springsteen, B. (1987). Walk Like a Man [Song]. On *Tunnel of Love* [Album]. Bruce Springsteen, Jon Landau, Chuck Plotkin.

Stornaiuolo, A., Smith, A., & Phillips, N. C. (2017). Developing a transliteracies framework for a connected world. *Journal of Literacy Research, (49)*1, 68–91.

Street, B. (1984). *Literacy in theory and practice.* Cambridge University Press.

Street, B. (2001). Literacy events and literacy practices: Theory and practice in the new literacy studies. In M. Martin-Jones & K. E. Jones (Eds.), *Multilingual literacies: Reading and writing different worlds* (pp. 17–31). John Benjamins Publishing Company.

Sue, D. W., Capodilupo, C. M., Torino, G. C., Buccceri, J. M., Holder, A. M. B., Nadal, K. L., & Esquilin, M. (2007). Racial microaggressions in everyday life: Implications for clinical practice. *American Psychologist, 62*(4), 271–286.

Sulzer, M. (2014). The common core state standards and the "basalization" of youth. *English Teaching: Practice & Critique, 13*(1), 134–154.

Sulzer, M. A., & Thein, A. H. (2016). Reconsidering the hypothetical adolescent in evaluating and teaching young adult literature. *Journal of Adolescent and Adult Literacy, 60*(2), 163–171.

Szwed, J. (1981). The ethnography of literacy. In M. F. Whiteman (Ed.), *Writing: The nature, development, and teaching of written communication.* Lawrence Erlbaum Associates.

Taylor, M. F., & Khan, U. (2011). Skate-park builds, teenaphobia, and the adolescent need for hang-out spaces: The social utility and functionality of urban skateparks. *Journal of Urban Design, 16*(4), 489–510.

Taylor, M., & Marais, I. (2011). Not in my back schoolyard: Schools and skate-park builds in Western Australia. *Australian Planner, 48*(2), 84–95.

Thornton, S. (1996). *Club cultures: Music, media, and subcultural capital.* Wesleyan University Press.

Thorpe, H. (2017). Action sports, social media, and new technologies: Towards a research agenda. *Communication & Sport, 5*(5), 554–578.

Tsikalas, S. G., & Jones, M. A. (2018). Creating skateboarding spaces or corralling skaters? The Rise of public skateparks in rural northeast Alabama. *The Geographic Bulletin, 59,* 55–69.

Tuck, E. (2009). Suspending damage: A letter to communities. *Harvard Educational Review, 79*(3), 409–427.

Tuck E., & Yang, K. W. (Eds.) (2013). *Youth resistance research and theories of change.* Routledge.

Urciuoli, B. (1995). Language and borders. *Annual Review of Anthropology,* 525–546.

Vadeboncoeur, J. A. (2005). Naturalized, restricted, packaged, and sold: Reifying the fictions of "adolescent" and "adolescence." In J. A. Vadeboncoeur, & L. Patel Stevens (Eds.), *Re/constructing "the adolescent": Sign, symbol, and body.* Peter Lang.

Vadeboncoeur, J. A. (2006). Chapter 7: Engaging young people: Learning in informal contexts. *Review of Research in Education, 30*(1), 239–278.

Vasudevan, L. (2008). Looking for angels: Knowing adolescents by engaging with their multimodal literacy practices. *Journal of Adolescent & Adult Literacy, 50*(4), 252–256.

Vasudevan, L., & Campano, G. (2009). The social production of adolescent risk and the promise of adolescent literacies. *Review of Research in Education, 33*(1), p. 310–353.

Vivoni, F. (2009). Spots of spatial desire: Skateparks, skateplazas, and urban politics. *Journal of Sport and Social Issues, 33*(2), 130–149.

Vossoughi, S., Davis, N. R., Jackson, A., Echevarria, R., Muñoz, A., & Escudé, M. (2021). Beyond the binary of adult versus child centered learning: pedagogies of joint activity in the context of making. *Cognition and Instruction, 39*(3), 211–241.

Vygotsky, L. S. (1978). *Mind in society: The development of higher psychological processes.* Harvard University.

Watson, V. W. M., & Beymer, A. (2019). Praisesongs of place: Youth envisioning space and place in a literacy and songwriting initiative. *Research in the Teaching of English, 53*(4), 297–319.

Watson, V. W. M., & Petrone, R. (2020). "On a day like this": How a youth epistemological approach can shape English education [Editorial]. *English Teaching: Practice & Critique, 19*(3), 245–251.

Wheaton, B., & Beal, B. (2003). "Keeping It Real": Subcultural Media and the Discourses of Authenticity in Alternative Sport. *International Review for the Sociology of Sport, 38*(2), 155–176.

Williams, W. (2018). *Listen to the poet: Writing, performance, and community in youth spoken word poetry.* University of Massachusetts Press.

Willing, I., Bennett, A., Piipsa, M., & Green, B. (2019). Skateboarding and the "tired generation": Ageing in youth cultures and lifestyle sports. *Sociology, 53*(3), 503–518.

Willis, P. (1977). Learning to labor: How working-class kids get working-class jobs. Columbia University Press.

Wilson, S. (2008). *Research is ceremony: Indigenous research methods.* Fernwood Publishing.

Winn, M. T. (2011). *Girl time: Literacy, justice, and the school-to-prison pipeline.* Teachers College Press.

Winn, M. T. (2013). Toward a restorative English education. *Research in the Teaching of English, 48*(1), 126–136.

Wolff, W. I. (Ed.) (2018). *Bruce Springsteen and popular music: Rhetoric, social consciousness, and contemporary culture.* Routledge.

Wood, L., Carter, M., & Martin, K. (2014). Dispelling stereotypes: Skateparks as a setting for pro-social behavior among young people. *Current Urban Studies, 2,* 62–73.

Yochim, E. C. (2010). *Skate life: Re-imagining white masculinity.* University of Michigan Press.

Index

able-bodiedness, 24, 50, 53–54
ableism, 157. *See also* dis/ability
activism, 19, 62, 157, 241
"activity theory/systems" (Engeström).
    See learning
adolescence/ts, 11, 15–17, 21, 26, 53–55, 59,
    174, 179, 231–33, 237–42
adultism, 58–59, 63, 240
advocacy, 17, 21, 48, 51, 62, 231
age: age-based and age-normed culture,
    174; age heterogeneity, 14, 26, 38, 59,
    65, 175, 178, 216, 219, 244, 246; age
    segregation in schools, 174–75, 177–78
    (*see also* segregation in schooling);
    cross-age learning, 12, 122, 175, 219, 221,
    233, 244, 247; doing age, 245
agency, 9, 46, 155, 173, 179, 182, 238, 247
American Hardcore (book), 76, 193–95,
    198
antiracism, 172, 202–3. *See also* racism
Apache Passion Project, 19
assembly-line instruction framework
    (ALI), 24, 36–38, 40–41, 43, 45;
    extrinsic rewards and, 40, 43, 56–57
assessment, 11–12, 31, 36, 39, 41, 43–46,
    99–100, 111, 135, 137, 139–40, 144–46,
    151–52, 163, 226, 235
at-risk discourse, 7–8, 12, 14, 64, 133, 135,
    183, 204, 233–34, 235, 241–42, 245. *See
    also* deficit-oriented discourse
authenticity, 18, 24, 47, 59, 163, 188, 191,
    195–96, 235–36, 242; "subcultural
    authenticity" (O'Connor), 83

Beal, B., xi, 18, 96, 111, 165, 168, 187
bedroom communities, 80

bicycling, 117–18. *See also* BMX
blue-collar. *See under* class
BMX, 131. *See also* bicycling
board slapping, 4, 70, 92, 137, 145
Borden, I., xi, 19, 21, 82, 88, 106–7, 157,
    168–69, 188, 197, 211
Bryggeriets Gymnasium, 19

California, 90, 118, 195, 200
capitalism, 21, 232. *See also* commercial-
    ization
CCS (skateboarding equipment catalog),
    190
cisgender. *See under* gender
class (social), 7, 8, 17, 23–25, 29, 41,
    43, 46, 48, 53–57, 61, 65, 70, 114,
    146, 154–55, 157, 159–66, 168–69, 171–
    76, 179, 188, 219, 235, 242, 245, 247;
    blue-collar, 3, 7, 10, 80, 82, 160–61,
    164, 201, 203; middle-class
    24, 54–56, 65–66, 160–65, 174, 188,
    219, 235; upper-class, 161; working-
    class, 7, 17, 23–24, 55–56, 65, 160–
    64, 169, 171, 175, 219, 235, 242, 245,
    247
classism, 57. *See also* class
classrooms, xi, 11, 15, 56, 103, 118–19, 152,
    156, 180–82, 235–36, 245; classroom
    management, 180–81, 235
cliques, 6
cognitive dissonance, 12
collaboration: in competition, 96–98,
    100, 110–11; in creating cultural
    artifacts, 76, 188, 192, 210; in
    learning practices, 16, 31, 35–36, 38, 40,
    98, 141, 207, 237, 246; in problem

collaboration (*continued*)
  solving, 100; in research, 50–51, 64,
  224; between youth and adults, 241
colonialism. *See* coloniality
coloniality, 21, 34, 175–76, 239, 242–43
commercialization (of skateboarding), 11,
  18–19, 21–22, 36, 38, 57, 107, 160–62,
  187, 195–97
commitment: to becoming part of a
  cultural community of skateboarders,
  86, 88, 91, 127, 131, 144, 187, 197, 215,
  222; to endeavors outside of skateboarding, 199; to formal schooling, 89; to
  learning and mastery of skateboarding,
  84, 88, 91, 127–28, 130–32, 144, 197,
  207; the role(s) of failure in, 127, 130
  (*see also* failure); to the well-being of the
  skatepark, 82, 91, 131
communal resources. *See under* cultural
  community
"communities of practice" (Lave &
  Wenger), xi, 44, 191
community, sense of, 207, 210
community college, 7
community development, 21
community renewal, 20, 80
conflict, 30, 32, 39, 46, 54, 80, 97, 99, 118,
  119–20, 155–56, 158, 160, 162, 169, 181;
  working with, 180–81
contribution. *See under* cultural community
coping (lip of skateboard ramp), 3–4, 78,
  92, 104, 108, 112–13, 120, 126, 131, 138,
  142, 143, 147
corporatization (of skateboarding). *See*
  commercialization
counternarratives, 12, 14, 16, 18, 20–22, 33,
  48, 133, 164, 174–75, 178–80, 183, 205,
  224, 240, 242. *See also* discourse
COVID-19, 107
critical consumption, 191, 195–96,
  198–99
critical ethnography. *See under* ethnography
Critical Youth Studies (CYS), 11, 15–17, 63,
  233, 238–39
cultural artifacts, 28, 62, 76, 107. *See also*
  collaboration
cultural community, 8–9, 22–27, 29–30,

37, 39–42, 44–48, 50–51, 54, 61–63,
  65, 67, 71, 74, 79–81, 82–84, 86–88,
  98–100, 103, 109–13, 115–16, 119–20,
  123, 127–29, 131–34, 137, 139–41, 143–46,
  148–49, 151–52, 154–60, 162–64, 168–
  71, 173–80, 182–83, 186, 189–95, 197,
  200–201, 204–6, 208–19, 222–26, 232,
  234, 237, 247; being a contributor to, 15,
  26, 91, 183, 200–202, 209–11, 215–16,
  218, 233–35, 241, 244–45, 247; being a
  shaper of, 100, 183, 211; and communal
  resources, 213–15; contribution within,
  14–15, 22, 26–27, 35–36, 39–40, 42–43,
  63, 83, 109, 131, 175, 202, 204, 207–27,
  235–36, 241, 245, 247; off-site participation and learning in, 45–46, 115–16;
  participation in, 10, 22, 25, 28, 30, 35,
  37, 40, 45, 47, 51, 64, 66, 72, 87, 83, 99,
  103–23, 134, 139, 147, 151–52, 154–55, 157,
  161, 163–64, 169, 172, 174–76, 178–79,
  183–86, 189–90, 193–94, 196, 200–201,
  206, 208, 210, 215–16, 218, 221, 223,
  232, 242, 247; respect and, 5–7, 63, 66,
  69, 86, 88, 91, 97, 112, 118–19, 128, 129,
  144, 169, 172–73, 197, 216–17, 225
cultural practices, 10–11, 15, 17, 37, 44, 50,
  55, 57, 64, 131, 152, 155, 172, 187, 191,
  193–97, 200–201, 245
curriculum, 11–12, 15, 18–19, 127, 132–34,
  146, 150, 152, 181, 192, 235, 238–40,
  242–43, 246

deficit-oriented discourse, 6–7, 9, 14–15,
  17, 26, 50, 59, 135, 182, 204, 213, 237–38,
  240, 242, 245–47
delinquency, 7
detention, 5
deviance, 225
diehard locals, x, 10, 22–23, 62, 66, 78,
  82–83, 97, 99, 116, 160, 196
difference, 178, 214, 236; differentiated
  experience, 239; differentiated expertise,
  18, 192, 213; valued difference, 213
digital media and learning, 22, 29, 149,
  151, 187, 189. *See also under* learning
dis/ability, ix, 7, 48, 52–54, 59, 61, 84, 157.
  See also ableism
discipline, 14, 15, 18, 128, 137, 144, 159,
  204, 238

discourse, 122, 154, 169–71; of adolescence, 16–17, 26, 234, 237–39; of development, 232; discursive practices, 154–81; educational, 15, 146, 152, 235–36, 238–39; of freedom, 5, 89, 164; governmental, 16; reification of hegemonic, 21, 24, 34, 114, 156, 171, 173, 180, 239; of sexuality, gender, and/or masculinity, 146, 166–67; of teasing and shaming, 159; scholarly, 7. *See also* counternarratives; deficit-oriented discourse; failure

distal learning. *See under* learning

distributed problem solving, 18, 97, 100, 115, 121, 152

DIY: ethos, 196; skateparks, 20

Dogtown and Z-Boys (documentary film), 64, 76, 193

Do Rad Things, 19

dropping in: and dropping out, 3, 7, 9–10, 85, 89, 201, 205, 226; as metaphor, 9–10, 16–17, 193; and skateboarding, 9, 92, 104, 111, 117, 118, 126–27, 142–44, 147, 158, 232

dropping out. *See under* dropping in

educational reform. *See under* school(ing)

educational sociology, 9. *See also* sociology; sociology of youth

educators, 7, 9, 11, 13–15, 31, 33, 57–59, 121–22, 178, 180–82, 186, 204, 206, 226, 234–36, 238–41, 244; preservice teachers, 238–39, 242

emasculation. *See under* masculinity

"embodied participation frameworks" (Goodwin), 148

"embodied spatial claim" (Ivarsson), 120

embodiment, 14, 18, 22, 30, 50, 100, 107–8, 120, 122, 125, 128–30, 145, 157, 190, 202, 234, 236

emotion, xi, 18–20, 23, 38, 45, 49, 54, 77, 111, 135, 143, 156, 159, 168, 203, 207–8, 210, 215–16, 219–22, 226; emotional bonds, 26, 77, 136, 175, 215, 226; emotionality, 45, 54, 76, 215–16, 219, 236, 245

emplacement. *See* place

empowerment, 19, 247

essentialism, 11, 33

ethnography, 13, 15–16, 23–24, 27, 48–49, 52, 55, 58–59, 62–63, 65, 78; critical ethnography, 24, 48, 62–63; "ethnographic toolkit" (Reyes), 48, 58, 60, 62

failure: discourse of academic failure, 7–8, 10, 12, 14, 16, 32, 54, 64, 78, 93, 129, 133, 153, 183, 234, 242, 247; as generative component of learning (in skateboarding), x, 4, 29, 42–43, 127, 129–31, 134–35, 137, 143, 159, 166–67, 181, 207, 214

family: cultural community as, 6, 45, 97, 221, 224; forms of support from, 20–21, 86, 195; heritage and culture of, 90, 171–72, 202; issues within, 7, 89–90; memorialization of, 89–90, 93, 202; and observation of youth mentorship, 219; and research practices, 12, 58, 65, 73; and role(s) in learning, 6, 27, 35–37, 44–45, 159, 207, 222; at the skatepark, 86, 114, 176, 180, 219–20; stereotyping of skateboarders by, 225

FAR Skate Foundation, 19

Finley (town), 4, 59–60, 64, 69, 77–82, 86–87, 94–95, 97–99, 137, 163, 172, 203, 225

Foucault, M., 98

freedom. *See under* discourse

Freire, P., 186, 239

"funds of knowledge" (Moll et al.), 57, 243

gender, 7, 16, 18–19, 21, 23, 25, 29, 41, 43, 46, 48–50, 52, 60–61, 65, 70, 81, 87, 98, 114, 138, 146, 154–57, 159, 164–69, 172–73, 176–77, 179–80; cisgender, 24, 50, 60, 164–65, 167, 169, 235; gender norms, 54, 164–65; invisible girls discourse, 87, 164; ramp tramp discourse, 87; transgender youth, 242

gifted and talented, 12, 133

governance, 11, 65, 18–19, 21–22, 65, 70, 83, 96–98, 107, 114, 214, 236

governmentality. *See* governance

graffiti, 60, 71, 95, 97–98, 100, 115, 138, 189, 191, 194–95, 210. *See also* textual production, consumption, and distribution

hanging out. *See* skateparks

hardcore punk: cultural community and

hardcore punk (*continued*)
"scene" of, 3, 193–94, 198, 203–4, 224–26, 234; music, 81, 172, 193–94, 198, 200
Hawk, Tony, 19, 196–97, 231
heckling, 25, 43, 46, 146, 154–55, 157–63, 165–71, 174, 177–78, 215
hegemony, ix, 44, 48, 57, 62, 165, 168, 180
heteronormativity, 24, 50, 60, 114, 157, 164–67, 169, 171, 235
heteropatriarchy, 165, 167
hip-hop, 81, 182, 198–200
homosociality/homosocial environments, 165, 167, 171
Hong Kong, 21, 151, 188

identity, xi, 16, 25, 28, 31, 35, 41, 46, 49, 55, 60, 83, 93, 154–55, 164, 166, 169, 171–75, 179, 181, 183–84, 187–89, 201–2, 205, 210, 218, 236, 239–41, 243, 245; identity politics, 164; identity work, 164
identity formation, 16, 41, 55, 154, 175, 181, 183, 187, 189, 201–2, 245. *See also* identity
ideology, 21, 23, 25–26, 28–29, 46, 54, 146, 154–56, 158, 172, 180–81, 183, 185, 186, 187, 195, 210, 235; achievement ideology, 6, 56–57; class and, 160–64, 172; gender, sexuality and, 169, 172; race and, 169–70, 172–73
immigrant youth, 16, 175
implied comparative study, 32, 244
Indigenous youth. *See* Native youth
injuries, 20, 42–43, 54, 93, 97, 114–15, 127, 129–31, 137, 207
intersectionality, 62, 179, 239, 241
in/visibility: and gendered relations, 87, 164; of social structures, arrangements, and/or relations, 11–12, 16, 28–32, 45, 49, 54, 57–58, 71, 73, 80, 87, 94, 97, 160, 164, 170–72, 176, 190, 202, 238–39, 244, 247
invisible girls. *See* gender; in/visibility
irresponsibility. *See* responsibility

jail, 4

labeling, 6–9, 14, 16, 34, 64, 133, 135, 157, 204, 225, 233, 236, 241–42, 245–46. *See also* stereotypes

language: of aggression and/or oppression, 60, 156, 170, 174, 178; communication, learning, and, 8–9, 14–15, 24, 33, 42–43, 49, 72, 91, 124–29, 145–46, 155, 182, 186, 240, 247; and context of social space, 117–18, 120, 154, 170, 175; gender, sexuality, and, 138, 154, 156, 167, 168, 177; homophobia and, 17, 67, 154, 156, 158, 167, 170; mentorship and, 216; race and, 61, 154, 156, 170, 173; settler colonialism and language revitalization, 242; as tool of mediation, 155
learning: co-learning and co-instructing, 139–40; cross-age learning, 12, 122, 175, 219, 221, 233, 244, 247; digital media and, 22, 149, 151, 187; distal, 149, 189; formal, 21–22, 24, 32–34, 54–56, 58; geographies of, 149; imitation and, 149–50, 213; and improvisation, 14, 153; informal, 17, 24, 27–28, 30–34, 231; kinesthetic, 22, 125, 128, 145, 210–11; lifelong process of, 133, 212, 235; off-site, 45–46, 115; purposive, 24, 27–47, 152, 156, 174, 200–201, 204, 206, 236; remedial, 6, 246; self-initiated and -directed, 14, 25, 41, 132–33, 153; "side-by-side," 25, 149; situated, 28, 37, 44, 108, 152, 192, 234; working with conflict in, 180–81 (*see also* conflict)
Learning by Observing and Pitching In (LOPI), vii, xi, 24, 27, 31, 35–47, 51, 62, 70, 91, 108, 116, 121, 123–24, 131, 146, 147, 179, 183, 208, 212; geography, place, space, and, 45–46, 121, 152, 179; and intrinsic motivation, 39, 207, 236 (*see also* motivation)
learning environments, 35, 38, 44, 45; cross-age, 12, 59, 233, 244; informal, 10, 17, 28, 31, 35, 59, 65, 100, 127, 231; within school(s), 12, 28, 44–45, 100, 231, 245
"legitimate peripheral participation" (Lave & Wenger), 44
LGBTQIA+: homophobia, 17, 60, 67, 70, 138, 146, 158–59, 164–68, 170–71, 177; queer identity, 87, 165, 169
Liberty (micro-urban area), 79–80, 198
lifestyle sports, 19, 22, 83, 157, 210
literacy, 7–11, 14–15, 17, 20, 26, 46, 70–71, 74, 98, 124, 155, 182–206, 239–40,

242–43, 245, 247; critical literacy, 15, 183, 186, 193, 205; critical media literacy, 14; literacy education, 56, 239; literacy practices, 14, 25, 30, 46, 52, 54, 61, 83, 172, 182–83, 185, 191–93, 204–5, 224, 240, 242; struggling reader discourse, 26, 245–46
literacy event, 71
Long Island, ix, 53, 56, 233
Lords of Dogtown (film), 193

MacKaye, I., 19
mandatory helmet rules, 21, 82
Margera, Bam, 197
masculinity: 48, 53–54, 114, 159, 165–69; and class, 53, 61, 168; emasculation, 166, 178; gender, sexuality, and, 87, 165–67, 171, 180; nonhegemonic and/ or alternative forms of, 165, 168, 180; performativity and, 169, 180; and race, 60, 156; toxic masculinity, 60, 131
mental and emotional health, 17–19, 135. *See also* emotion
mentorship, 149, 221, 247; brotherhood discourse, 203, 216, 218–19, 221; simultaneity of mentoring and being mentored, 26, 38, 208, 216, 218
metrocentrism, 59
microaggressions, 173–74
"microphysics of representability" (Ferrell et al.), 149
micro-urban. *See under* urban(ity)
middle-class. *See under* class
Midwest, 90
misogyny, 60
motivation, 7–8, 26, 36, 37–40, 42, 64, 135–37, 145, 166, 195, 197, 201, 204, 208, 211, 225, 248; for learning, 37, 39–40, 44, 133, 137, 145, 207–10, 215–16, 236. *See also* learning
Mountain, L., 231
multimodal texts, 14, 186–87, 189, 204, 206
muscle memory. *See* embodiment
music, 3, 5, 9–10, 46–47, 52–55, 60, 73, 81–82, 85–86, 98, 111, 115, 137, 172, 187, 189–91, 193, 198–201, 205, 210, 221–23. *See also* hardcore punk; hip-hop

narrative frames, 24, 78
Native youth, 3, 19, 50, 85, 173, 242–43
neoliberalism, 18, 20–21, 232
New York, 56, 59, 60
New York City, xi, 53, 59, 233
New Yorker (magazine), 237
New York Times, 107
nicknaming, 169–71
noticing: as component of observational learning process in skateboarding, 92, 120, 131–32, 144, 148; and reflexivity in research, 12, 234

"off-site" participation. *See under* cultural community

parents. *See* family
Paris, D., 9, 51–52
participant observation, 71–76. *See also* ethnography; qualitative research
participatory events, 70–71, 108
"pedagogical third spaces" (Kirkland), 15
pedagogies, 15, 31, 42, 133, 143, 178, 181, 206, 236, 238, 242, 246; critical literacy, 15, 183, 186, 193, 205; culturally sustaining, 15; direct and indirect, 139–40; repositioning, 15, 26, 233, 242–45
Peralta, S., 107, 231
"performative moments" (Jones), 110, 151
place, 4, 6, 7, 11, 21–22, 29–30, 32, 37, 39, 45, 48, 58–62, 65, 68, 70, 81, 86–87, 89, 100, 106–8, 112, 116, 118, 121–22, 149, 152, 154, 156, 160, 164, 179, 190, 211, 224–25, 234, 236, 240, 244, 247; emplacement, 22, 108, 147
poetry, x, 10, 189, 199, 205, 243
positionality, ix, 24, 48–50, 55, 57–61, 63
power, 24–25, 30, 33, 46, 49–50, 54, 62–63, 90, 139, 143, 154–81, 186–87, 240, 242
Powers, S., 194–95
prosocial behavior, 20
psychological developmental paradigms, 16, 59, 174, 238, 24
public-private partnerships, 20
public schools. *See under* school(ing)
Pushing Boarders, 18

qualitative research, 49, 76. *See also* ethnography
queer identity. *See under* LGBTQIA+

race, 8, 18, 25, 29, 41, 43, 46, 48, 52, 60–61, 65, 70, 84–85, 114, 146, 154–57, 159, 166, 169–74, 179–80, 202
racialization, 50, 61, 159, 173–74
racism: colorblind ideology, 170; racist discourse, 61, 170–72, 180, 202–3; systemic, 11, 34, 57, 203
"radical reflexivity" (Best), 63
ramp tramp. *See* gender; in/visibility
"readicide" (Gallagher), 204
reciprocal learning relationships. *See under* reciprocity
reciprocity: acts of reciprocity 145, 222; reciprocal engagement, 107; reciprocal learning relationships, 140–41, 215–16, 219, 233; in research practices, 50–51, 58, 63, 76
reflexivity, 31, 49–51, 63–64, 180
"relational resources" (Nasir & Cooks), 125, 129, 135, 141, 144, 152, 163
representation, categories and politics of, 17–18, 48–54, 63, 154, 157, 159, 169, 179, 186, 225, 239
research methodologies, 15, 24, 48–77, 94, 113, 180
responsibility: in developing ethical scholarship, 50–51, 76–77; irresponsible use of communal space, 117; in one's own learning, 35–36, 42, 133, 141, 145, 209; social and collective, 17, 30, 42, 82–83, 91, 98–100, 133, 141, 145, 209, 222, 224, 238
Rivard, Mark, 19
Rogoff, B., xi, 24–25, 27–32, 35–43, 47, 79, 99, 114, 131, 146–47, 149, 151, 155, 159, 174, 207–8, 215, 219, 222, 231, 233
rural, 21, 23, 48, 59–60, 65, 79–80, 83, 87, 223, 232, 242, 247
rurality, 59

scars, 130–31
scene kids, 3, 154–81
school(ing): alienation from, 6–7, 20, 40, 93, 133, 135, 153, 160, 163, 181, 201, 208–10, 224, 226, 234; alternative

schools (alternative high school), 6, 95; and educational reform, 8, 11, 14, 26, 31, 236; corporate structures of, 57; decoupling learning from, 11, 32; formal, 55–56, 58; inequity and/or inequality within, 8, 57, 163, 172, 175; learning structures in, 12, 32, 34–36, 45, 57, 59, 100, 119, 122, 124, 129, 133, 135, 137, 141, 145–46, 152, 156, 174, 178, 183, 195, 204–5, 226; public schools, 7, 36, 80, 94–95; resistance or opposition to normative social arrangements and participation structures of, 8, 12, 14, 31–32, 37, 40, 137, 235, 244, 246; rethinking structures of, 9, 11–17, 26, 33–34, 231–48; school-sanctioned activities, 53, 60, 132, 166, 209; underachievement in, 7
school-to-prison pipeline, 34
segregation in schooling: age-based, 12, 37, 59, 174, 178, 245; class-based, 175, 235
settler colonialism. *See* coloniality
sex (biological), 166
sexuality, 8, 25, 49, 60–61, 87, 114, 138, 146, 154–55, 157, 159, 164–69, 172–73, 179–80
shaping cultural community. *See* cultural community
"side-by-side learning" (Paradise & Rogoff). *See under* learning
"situated learning" (Lave & Wenger). *See* learning
skateboarding: collisions, 112, 117 (*see also* snaking); commodification of (*see* commercialization); equipment for, 71, 139, 155, 190; and explicit instructional sessions, 108, 110, 124, 141–44, 158; imitation, 149, 213; and kinesthetic learning, 22, 125, 128, 145, 210–11; and learning by "doing it," x, 25, 43, 110, 123–28, 130, 137–38, 142–43, 149, 151, 158, 196–97, 212, 214, 220; "pushing" and working through pain, 110, 130–31, 136, 138; session skating (group), 25, 42, 70, 74–75, 103, 106, 108–11, 118, 123, 125, 130, 135–37, 139, 144–45, 148, 150–51, 158, 170, 191; session skating (solo), 111, 123, 125, 127–29, 131–32, 134; street skating, 104, 106, 112, 126–27, 134, 139, 234; style and aesthetic in dress, 71, 84,

86, 160, 162, 194; styles of, developing unique, 26, 88, 90–91, 104, 128, 131, 149–50, 208, 211–17; transition skating, 104, 107, 127; watching others/noticing (*see* noticing)

skateboarding tricks, 3, 6, 29, 40, 42, 72, 75, 88, 91–92, 110–12, 117, 123–32, 134, 136, 138–39, 145, 147–51, 158, 188, 201, 206, 211–14, 217

Skateism (magazine), 157

Skateistan, 19

Skatepark Project, 19

skateparks: and commercial interest, 22; and counternarrative, 22; as cultural phenomena, 13, 19–20; design of, 17, 104, 116, 183; DIY skateparks, 20; etiquette within, 118; and gendered participation, 87, 164; governance and community regulation of, 20–22, 82–83, 96–98; "hanging out" at, 4, 6, 10, 25, 58, 68, 70, 86–88, 90, 103, 106, 108, 113, 175, 203, 225; as learning environments, 12, 103, 121; learning spatial relations of, 107, 113, 116, 119, 121–22, 133, 145; materiality of, 30, 96, 104, 106, 147, 154; on Native American reservations, 19; and neoliberalism, 20; in rural areas, 21, 23, 65, 83, 87, 232, 247; skateboarders' repurposing layout and spatial relations of, 29, 103–4, 106–7, 113, 147; spatial awareness of, 40; spatial production and spatial politics of, 18, 21, 25, 98, 103, 106–7, 112, 121–22, 147, 152; in urban areas, 19–20, 83, 86

"skater's eye" (Borden), 106

skate videos: distribution of, 112, 151; learning from, 25, 46, 115, 124, 132, 139, 148–50, 182, 187–91, 196, 216; and motivation, 137, 191; production of, 25, 46, 65, 67, 71, 106, 108, 110, 112, 151, 188–92, 205, 243; and research methodology, 75–76

skinhead culture, 194, 203

Skinheads Against Racial Prejudice (SHARP), 172, 202–4

"single story" (Adichie), 16

snaking, 25, 40, 103, 104, 116–21, 145, 158, 215

social arrangements, 12, 14, 31, 35, 37, 70,

74, 96, 117, 122, 135, 175–76, 179, 215–16, 218–19, 235, 244, 246–47

social control, 21, 37–38, 65, 157–59, 164, 180

socialization, 30, 33, 59–60, 157, 166–67, 238

social marking, 57, 67, 86, 154, 169–70, 177. *See also* labeling; sociology of the unmarked

social media, 25, 75–76, 110, 115, 149, 151, 186–91, 194, 200, 240

social organization, 11, 14, 26, 32, 36–39, 45, 83, 119, 121, 135, 208

social reproduction, 7, 32, 57, 146, 164–65, 179–80

social solidarity, 151, 163, 169, 173, 179

social stigma, 162

sociocultural theory, 23–29, 31, 44–46, 63, 146–47, 181, 184, 186, 205, 215, 239

sociology, 9, 11, 15–16, 18

"sociology of the unmarked" (Brekhus), 170

sociology of youth, 15–16. *See also* educational sociology; sociology

space, 8, 12, 15–16, 20, 22, 29–30, 32, 34, 45–46, 53–56, 59–60, 65, 71, 75, 83, 87, 103–22, 128, 140, 147, 149–50, 154, 156, 162, 164–65, 172, 180, 185, 208, 210, 226, 234, 242, 244, 246; liminal space, 47; spatial and temporal relations, 25, 29, 103; spatial production, 18, 103–22, 147, 152

sponsorship: of literacy, 20, 25, 52, 115, 182–83, 205–6; school-sponsored athletics, 166; in skateboarding and/or skateparks, 20–21, 81, 83, 187

Springsteen, Bruce, 5, 9, 52–54, 160

status, 47, 62, 65, 67, 82–88, 99, 109–10, 112, 115, 128–30, 134, 141, 151, 173, 183, 187–88, 190–93, 197, 212–13, 216, 218

stereotypes, 170–71, 224–26, 234, 237. *See also* labeling

storywork, 50

"subcultural authenticity" (O'Connor), 83. *See also* authenticity

"subcultural capital" (Thornton), 47, 84, 112, 162, 216

subculture, 47, 83–84, 112, 162, 165–66, 168, 187–88, 216

suburban. *See under* urban(ity)
subversiveness. *See* subculture
surveillance, 18, 97–98
suspension (from school), 172
symbolism, 20, 80, 130, 147, 155, 180–81, 189–90, 202–4
systemic inequality, 7–8, 11, 32, 157, 163, 236

tattoos, 10, 25, 46, 61, 69, 71, 74, 76, 80–82, 85, 89–91, 93, 98, 115, 130, 154–55, 172, 187, 189–91, 224, 234; cultural production and, 199–202; textual production and distribution of, 204
team sports, 132, 136, 166, 209, 232
"temporal capital" (O'Connor), 83
textual production, consumption, and distribution, 10, 25–27, 182, 189, 191, 196, 199–202, 204, 206, 208, 222
Thrasher Magazine, 76, 93, 148, 157, 195–98
"totalizing lifestyle" (Borden), 19
transgender. *See* gender
Transworld (magazine), 76

unconscious bias, 51, 57, 60, 157, 165
upper-class. *See under* class
urban(ity), 19–20, 24, 48, 59, 65, 79, 83, 86, 107, 151; micro-urban, 80; suburban, 53, 65

"verification" (Donnelly & Young), 110, 115, 131, 188, 191

Wal-Mart, 80, 150
watching. *See* noticing
whiteness, 21, 61, 169–71, 173, 232
white supremacy, 61, 239
working-class. *See under* class

youth cultures, 17, 47, 243. *See also* subculture
youth development, 8, 9, 18, 19–21, 26, 50, 232, 237, 243
"youth epistemologies" (Watson & Petrone), 240
"Youth Lens" (Petrone et al.), 17, 26, 233, 239, 245